Praise for *A Wh*

Engineers without Borders Canada belie... ...ngy ... ... bal engineer and engineering profession. A Whole New Engineer *lays out a compelling case for this engineering transformation.*

—**Sal Alajek,** Portfolio Manager, Engineers without Borders Canada

At Purdue, our College of Technology has embarked on a major transformation project, and two of our exemplars for change were Olin College and the iFoundry effort at the University of Illinois. Read A Whole New Engineer *to understand the secret sauce before trying this at home.*

—**Gary Bertoline,** Dean of Technology, Purdue University

The University of Twente has embarked on the revision of its educational model, and two approaches that inspired us were those of Olin and iFoundry. The minds behind these educational reforms have written a provocative, stimulating, and inspiring book called A Whole New Engineer, *and I urge you to read it.*

—**Ed Brinksma,** Rector Magnificus, University of Twente

If you really care about engineering education, read A Whole New Engineer *and join a growing global movement to reimagine its purpose and rethink its practice, inspired by the students' passion for innovation.*

—**Andreas Cangellaris,** Dean of Engineering, University of Illinois

A Whole New Engineer *offers refreshing insights for those who are seeking innovative ways to groom the next generation of engineers.*

—**Chan Eng Soon,** Dean of Engineering, National University of Singapore

A Whole New Engineer *illustrates how an emotional connection between the instructor and engaged learners is a must for twenty-first-century learning.*

—**Jim Cooper,** President and CEO, Maplesoft

A Whole New Engineer *provides excellent ideas about how to make engineering colleges more motivationally aware and supportive of their students, development.*

—**Edward L. Deci,** University of Rochester, author of *Why We Do What We Do*

Calling communication skills "soft skills" does them a grave disservice. Sharpening speech acts and engaging in conversation with greater intention and skill can transform leadership, strengthen team cohesion, and lead to increased individual and shared meaning. The authors of A Whole New Engineer *are to be commended for advocating more focused attention on language and communication in the education of the next generation of engineers.*

—**Fernando Flores,** author of *Conversations for Action and Collected Essays*

The book lays out the emotional and cultural skills that engineers need to succeed as designers and entrepreneurs.

> —**Peter J. Denning**, co-author of *The Innovator's Way*

A Whole New Engineer *imagines and brings to life the kind of engineering education I would have liked to have had.*

> —**Erica Lee Garcia, P.Eng.**, Founder, EngineerYourLife.net

Much debate about educational reform is cast in strictly rational terms. It's both ironic and moving that a couple of engineers have nailed the importance of love, empathy, and caring as foundational in rethinking education.

> —**Mark Goulston**, author of *Just Listen* and *Real Influence*

As people change careers or occupations later in life, it takes spirit, strength, and a thirst to find meaning in this life. A Whole New Engineer *explores a new kind of education where the courage to do so is cultivated earlier and with greater purpose.*

> —**Kerry Hannon**, author of *What's Next?*

Connecting and working closely with others is a neglected skill in engineering education, and A Whole New Engineer *shows the way to an engineering education where it is built in.*

> —**Georges Harik**, Investor and Google Employee #9

Everyone involved with educating engineers should read this book twice—once for inspiration and a second time for planning. A Whole New Engineer *provides a road map for overhauling the stale, soul-deadening, plug-into-the-equation style of engineering education. In its place will emerge a system built on creativity and collaboration and initiative.*

> —**Dan Heath**, co-author of *Made to Stick*, *Switch*, and *Decisive*

This is an intriguing book for anyone interested in a whole new kind of higher education, where innovation can flourish as students take charge of their learning.

> —**Beverly Jones**, Leadership Coach, ClearWaysConsulting.com

Goldberg and Somerville have given us a detailed road map on how we can reform higher education in general to turn out the confident risk takers and critical thinkers desperately needed to make the world better for everyone in it.

> —**Linda P. B. Katehi**, Chancellor, University of California, Davis

Luck Companies work to develop values-based leadership throughout the company and around the world. Coaching creates value for clients by shifting from knowing and telling to not knowing, asking, and listening. In an engaging and provocative fashion, A Whole New Engineer *combines the best of both of these worlds by developing a hybrid values-based and coaching approach to engineering education.*

> —**Kelly Lewis**, Sr. Director of Leadership, Luck Companies

A radical evolution in engineering education is long overdue. A Whole New Engineer is the inspiring road map we need. It's time to stop talking and start doing!
—**Janusz Kozinski,** Founding Dean of the Lassonde School of Engineering

A Whole New Engineer *overturns many of the ways that we think about engineering and engineering education in an engaging and reflective manner.*
—**Peter Kroes,** TUDelft, author of *A Philosophy of Technology*

A Whole New Engineer *describes some of the many ways that a coaching mind-set is important to reimagining engineering education in the twenty-first century.*
—**Pat Mathews,** Director, Leadership Coaching Program, Georgetown University

A Whole New Engineer *should appeal not only to engineering educators but to any educator with the courage to think beyond the idea that learning is a purely cognitive experience.*
—**Diane Michelfelder,** co-editor of *Philosophy and Engineering*

Goldberg and Somerville have vividly described the required new learning culture, which goes well beyond course content and curriculum. It requires a whole new mind-set to produce A Whole New Engineer. *If you care about America's future, you should read this book.*
—**Richard K. Miller,** President, Franklin W. Olin College of Engineering

This is a deeply felt and well-crafted volume—a pleasure to read—that will challenge not just engineers but all of us to think about the proper place of engineers and engineering in society.
—**Carl Mitcham,** Director of the Hennebach Program for the Humanities, Colorado School of Mines, and author of *Thinking through Technology*

A Whole New Engineer *is my everyday companion to both inspire me and guide me practically toward full and effective transformation of engineering education.*
—**Alessandro F. Moreira,** Dean of Engineering, Universidade Federal de Minas Gerais

A Whole New Engineer *is a provocative book that should be read by every prospective engineering student, employer, and educator.*
—**Lueny Morell,** Provost, New Engineering University

It is refreshing to engage in a stimulating and focused conversation about the future needs of engineering education.
—**Patrick J. Natale,** Executive Director, American Society of Civil Engineers

This isn't just a book about engineering. It's a book about education, entrepreneurship, and—ultimately—the future. Read it and prepare to take notes!
—**Daniel H. Pink,** author of *To Sell Is Human, Drive,* and *A Whole New Mind*

A Whole New Engineer *is an energizing new approach to engineering education and reveals how outstanding schools are enabling the development of whole engineers.*
—**Pam Rogalski**, co-founder, Engineering Leadership Council

Much organizational change is blind to culture and emotion, and as a result, much change is ineffectual. A Whole New Engineer *approaches the change of engineering education with new cultural assumptions based on the power of experiential education and the involvement of the learner in the process.*
—**Edgar H. Schein**, MIT Sloan School, author of *Humble Inquiry*

As a venture capitalist and an entrepreneur, I can confidently assert that the world needs more entrepreneurial engineers. A Whole New Engineer *shows the way toward a stable and passionate supply.*
—**Tim Schigel**, Founder and Chairman, ShareThis, and Fund Manager, Cintrifuse

The refreshing approach advocated by this book will help cultivate the necessary intellectual, emotional, and social virtues for engineers of the future to act as leaders and innovators.
—**Jon Alan Schmidt**, Burns & McDonnell

Empathy and emotional courage are essential for engineers wishing to comfortably collaborate in solving today's complex problems. A Whole New Engineer *makes a convincing argument that engineering students need not sacrifice their humanity on the altar of mathematical rigor!*
—**Jeff Shelton**, co-host, *The Engineering Commons* podcast

The world economy has shifted strongly from product to service, and we need to think differently about engineering in this context. A Whole New Engineer *thinks different, feels different, and can bring about change with both head and heart.*
—**Jim Spohrer**, Director, IBM University Programs, co-editor of *The Handbook of Service Science*

A Whole New Engineer *asks a fascinating question: What would engineering education and practice be if it were increasingly mindful? Answering this question more precisely will inspire a new kind of engineer and engineering education.*
—**Chade-Meng Tan**, Google, author of *Search inside Yourself*

Far more than an inspiring story about the transformation of engineering education, this remarkable book serves as a call to action and blueprint for reinventing all education for the twenty-first century. Everyone concerned about the preparation of the next generation for their—and our—future should read this important book.
—**Tony Wagner**, Harvard University, author of *Creating Innovators*

A
Whole
New
Engineer

A Whole New Engineer

The Coming Revolution in Engineering Education

DAVID E. GOLDBERG
and MARK SOMERVILLE
with Catherine Whitney

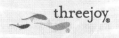

Douglas, MI

Published by
ThreeJoy Associates, Inc.
Douglas, Michigan

Publisher's Cataloging-in-Publication Data
Goldberg, David E. (David Edward), 1953–

    A whole new engineer : the coming revolution in engineering education / David E. Goldberg, Mark Somerville, with Catherine Whitney. – Douglas, Mich. : ThreeJoy Associates, Inc., 2014.

    p. ; cm.

    ISBN13 hardcover: 978-0-9860800-0-5
    ISBN13 softcover: 978-0-9860800-4-3

    1. Franklin W. Olin College of Engineering--Curricula. 2. Illinois Foundry for Innovation in Engineering Education (iFoundry) 3. University of Illinois at Urbana-Champaign. College of Engineering. 4. Engineering--Study and teaching--United States. 5. Engineering schools--United States. 6. Educational change. 7. Educational innovations. I. Title. II. Somerville, Mark, 1967- III. Whitney, Catherine.

    T171.F73 G65 2014
    620.001—dc23   2014945538

FIRST EDITION

Project coordination by Jenkins Group, Inc.
www.BookPublishing.com

Interior design by Brooke Camfield

Printed in the United States of America
23 22 21 20 19 • 7 6 5 4 3

To all engineers who embrace challenges and opportunities
with passion, courage, connection, and skill

Contents

Preface
A Few Words about This Book

As academics, we are accustomed to writing for an audience of our peers—others who speak the language of academic research. *A Whole New Engineer* is a different animal because are we addressing not only fellow academics but also a wide world of others—students, parents, educators, employers, practitioners, and policymakers—who are interested in this topic. We recognize that its joint messages of transforming *engineering* and transforming *education* are part of a world-changing conversation that is occurring in many corners of society—not just in schools but also in businesses, in government, in private and public think tanks, and across the World Wide Web.

We point this out as a way of explaining—especially for the academics reading this—why this book doesn't follow the usual conventions of academic writing (although sources are cited appropriately). More than a book of research, this is a memoir of our experiences and conversations around engineering education transformation.

In *A Whole New Engineer*, we step outside the constraints of traditional research and engage with our topic in a narrative that is compelling for anyone interested in the transformational potential of education, how we can meet the demands of the new "small-world" era of technology, what happens when a college or university decides to turn tradition on its head, and, perhaps most important, how we can find the answers beyond research data by getting inside the hearts and minds of teachers, students, and other stakeholders in the future of engineering.

Although our names are at the front of this book, the process of writing it has been widely collaborative and inclusive of a great variety of voices. We are indebted to the many people whose work, ideas, input, and reflections have helped give the book its emotional power, intellectual integrity, and progressive force. We are grateful to the Jenkins Group, who steered our efforts every step of the way, in particular, Jerry Jenkins, Leah Nicholson, and Yvonne Roehler. Catherine Whitney, our writing collaborator, was invaluable in shaping the text to be compelling and accessible. Thanks, too, to Paul Krafin. We also appreciate the marketing expertise of Peter Winick and Karen Salmansohn's work on early Big Beacon graphics and the manifesto.

We are thankful to the many individuals who agreed to interviews and otherwise contributed in direct ways to our efforts: Sal Alajek, Morgan Bakies, Carl Bass, Andrew Bell, Vince Bertram, Andreas Cangellaris, Debbie Chachra, Chan Eng Soon, Jim Cooper, Peter Denning, Lawrence Domingo, Sebastian Dziallas, Ozgur Eris, Woodie Flowers, Erica Lee Garcia, Rebecca Getto, Mark Goulston, Domenico Grasso, Kerry Hannon, Trevor Harding, Georges Harik, Dan Heath, Kylie Hensley, Geoffrey Herman, Joseph Hunter, Karen Hyman, Stefan Jaeger, Matthew Johnson, Aman Kapur, Jaime Kelleher, David Kerns, Sherra Kerns, Mark Killgore, Janusz Kozinski, Russ Korte, Karen Lamb, Jerry LeMieux, Cory Levy, Ben Linder, Bruce Litchfield, Larissa Little, Michael Loui, Rob Martello, Garrett Meyer, Rick Miller, Michael Moorhead, Alessandro Moreira, Lueny Morell, Susan Fredholm Murphy, Patrick Natale, Lawrence Neeley, Charlie Nolan, Ozgur Eris, Janaki I. Perera, Daniel Pink, Meagan Pollock, Dorothy Powers, John Prados, Gill Pratt, Ray Price, Brendan T. Quinlivan, Julia Ribeiro, Pamela Rogalski, Rebecca Schatzengel, Tim Schigel, Garrett Schwanke, Polina Segalova, Jeff Shelton, Jim Spohrer, Lynn Andrea Stein, Juliana Stockton, Jon Stolk, Liz Threlkeld, Jessica Townsend, Linda Vanasupa, Bruce Vojak, Tony Wagner, Kevin Wolz, and Yevgeniya V. Zastavker. We also recognize the contribution of the late Michael Moody to the formation of Olin College, and of Duncan Murdoch, who retired from Olin in 2006.

Our conclusions in this book owe much to the groundbreaking work of many individuals across a variety of fields. Those with whom we had direct contact are mentioned in the previous paragraph. Here, we acknowledge a debt of gratitude to a number of other innovative teachers, writers, scientists, and thought leaders mentioned in the book: Marilee Adams, Teresa Amabile, Chalmers Brothers, Brené Brown, Edward Deci, Carol Dweck, Fernando Flores, Thomas Friedman, Howard Gardner, Daniel Goleman, Chip Heath, Dean Kamen, Gary Klein, John Kotter, David Middlebrook, Sugata Mitra, Carl Rogers, Richard Ryan, Saras Sarasvathy, Edgar Schein, Daniel Siegel, and Chade-Meng Tan.

Dave Goldberg wishes to thank the many people who put their hearts, souls, and backs into getting iFoundry off the ground at the University of Illinois. Michael Loui and Andreas Cangellaris were partners in the precursor Engineering and Technology Studies at Illinois (ETSI) effort and iFoundry, respectively, and Dave thanks them both for great pairwork. Karen Hyman was an outstanding administrator and leader as iFoundry's inaugural Associate Director, and Ray Price filled the breach as iFoundry's second co-director when Andreas Cangellaris was called to serve his home department as Interim Head early in the iFoundry launch sequence. Linda Katehi, Ilesanmi Adesida, and Chuck Tucker played critical leadership roles in nurturing and supporting the activity within both the university and the college before it was clear exactly what iFoundry could do. Tracy Johnson was lead staff person and den mother to the 2009 and 2010 iFoundry cohorts. Angie Dimit was a very early supporter and sustainer of Teamwork for a Quality Education (TQE), and she later helped iFoundry run a gazillion events. Geoffrey Herman picked up the torch on the iFoundry notion of intrinsic motivation conversion, made it work, and both connected it to the literature and grounded it in solid research. Other early iFoundry staff, fellows, ETSI network members, student advisors, corporate and organizational advisors, faculty advisors, and the 2009 and 2010 cohorts of iFoundry freshmen meshed together to form a very special learning community. Bless you and thank you. Dave thanks Peter Fox for ThreeJoy's first office. Dave sends a special thanks to Dianne Fodell, an early iCOA (iFoundry corporate and organizational advisor representing IBM) for being the first person to say that iFoundry was important enough to write a book about.

Dave thanks his colleagues at Franklin W. Olin College. Working with Sherra Kerns, Mark Somerville, Rick Miller, and others at Olin has been an amazing once-in-a-lifetime experience. Dave is especially grateful for Sherra's enthusiasm and encouragement during iFoundry's early and uncertain days, and for the experience of working shoulder to shoulder with Sherra and Mark on the Engineer of the Future meetings at Olin in 2009 and Illinois in 2011. Dave also thanks Rick Miller, Vin Manno, and Michelle Davis for their support of this book project.

Dave thanks his colleagues in the growing philosophy and engineering community, an important influence on the thinking behind iFoundry and Big Beacon. Joel Moses and Taft Broome kicked off the events that led to the first Workshop on Philosophy and Engineering in 2007 (WPE-2007) at Delft, and Dave is grateful to have been included in those early conversations. It has been both a joy and a learning experience to work with philosophers and reflective practitioners such as Larry Bucciarelli, Bill Grimson, Billy Koen, Peter Kroes, Li Bocong, Natasha McCarthy, Carl Mitcham, Diane Michelfelder, Mike Murphy, Byron Newberry, Joe Pitt, Jon Schmidt, Ibo van de Poel, Pieter Vermaas, and others who have participated in WPE and who have participated in and continued the Forum on Philosophy, Engineering, and Technology (fPET). The generous collaboration of the Society for Philosophy and Technology (www.spt.org) is gratefully acknowledged. Dave especially thanks Peter Kroes for bringing him to the Philosophy Department at TUDelft for an extended and mind-clearing visit just after Dave resigned his tenure at Illinois.

Dave wishes to thank his leadership coach, Bev Jones, for her patience, insight, mind-blowing questions, and all-around coaching skill; he is also grateful to Bev's pointer and recommendation letter to the Georgetown Leadership Coaching Certificate program. Attending Georgetown was the single most transformative experience of his life to date.

Dave acknowledges all of cohort 30 at the Georgetown program for being such supportive colleagues on that life-changing journey with special shouts out to Rose Hanson, Iris Ioffreda, Nancy Lamberton, and fellow witnesses to the morning of March 18, Daryl Nardick, Sarah Happel, Graham Segroves, and Mike McGinley. Pat Mathews and Frank Ball were outstanding cohort 30 course coordinators, and all the faculty were terrific, but a special thank you goes to Learning Circle Advisor, Kelly Lewis, who was both especially helpful during the course and afterward when she and Dave entered into an engaging and extended conversation regarding educational transformation in middle school and the university. That conversation had an important effect on the Big Beacon vision decks of 2011 and 2012.

Dave acknowledges the early Big Beacon volunteers and staff. Erica Lee Garcia and Meagan Pollock signed on as volunteers with only the manifesto and a prayer to go on. Kai Zhuang has joined more recently, and his enthusiasm is both a joy and a renewable energy resource. Salma Burney is steadfast in helping the Twitter chat trains run on time. Dave is also grateful to John Bennett for starting the #BigBeacon twitter chats and for the many #BigBeacon Twitter chat participants and the lively online conversations on Wednesday evenings at 8:00 pm Eastern time during the school year. Join us!

Dave thanks Rick Miller, President of Franklin W. Olin College, Pamela Rogalski, leader of the Engineering Leadership Council and Jeff Shelton, head of the Engineering Commons podcast, for being the first individuals and organizations to sign memoranda of understanding with Big Beacon to help transform engineering education. More are in the works, and Big Beacon is especially interested in collaborating with early stage grassroots and student-led change initiatives as well as engineering and education media outlets.

ThreeJoy Associates' early clients were a source of critical learning and financial support. Dave is particularly grateful to Chan Eng Soon of the National University of Singapore for his trust and support in working with the Design Centric Curriculum (now the Design Centric Programme) at its inception. Dave thanks Alessandro Moreira and Juliane Correa (with support from Vicente Falconi) at UFMG, Hee Joh Liang and Pee Suat Hoon of Singapore Polytechnic, Shirley Williams and Kwee Siew Chai at Ngee Ann Polytechnic, Gary Bertoline and Fatma Mili at Purdue University, and Ed Brinksma and Jennifer Herek at University of Twente for important engagements and learning experiences. Dave is grateful to all his coaching clients for helping him appreciate and practice the transformative power of deep listening and presence.

Finally, Dave is grateful to his wife Mary Ann and sons Max and Zack for their love and support during this latest adventure.

Mark acknowledges the entire Olin community: faculty, staff, students, parents, and friends of Olin, past and present. Being a part of the team that helped Olin become reality was transformative for him, and he wishes to thank everyone he has worked with, laughed with, argued with, and imagined with over the last decade. Although the nature of narrative requires focusing on a the stories of a smaller number of people, the founding of Olin was very much a "we" endeavor, a collaborative effort that was not about individuals so much as about the community. While only a small fraction of them are called out in this book, many, many people all played critical roles in making Olin the creative, collaborative community it is today, and he thanks them all for the opportunity to work with them. He also thanks the Olin administration, particularly Rick Miller, Vin Manno and Michelle Davis, for their support of his work on this project.

Mark also acknowledges the many teachers who trusted him, showed him that work can be joyful, and inspired him to pursue work in education. He especially thanks Melvin Oakes, James Duban, and Christine Maziar, who played particularly critical roles in his undergraduate education; Jesús del Alamo, who advised him throughout his time at MIT; Terry Orlando, who gave him his first opportunity to engage in curricular innovation; and the Department of Physics and Astronomy at Vassar College, who were wonderfully supportive and engaging colleagues during his first years as a professor. He also thanks the entire Active Learning in Engineering

Education community; his interactions with this group early in his career were especially important to his learning.

Mark wishes to thank the Aldert Kamp and the Bachelor's Curriculum Innovation Committee at Delft University's Aerospace Engineering faculty for allowing him to join them in realizing a new, innovative undergraduate curriculum there. His time in Delft was formative, and showed him both that the challenges around changing engineering education are universal, and also that change is possible in all kinds of institutions—from small startups to large, top-ranked programs.

Mark also thanks friends and colleagues at Olin and elsewhere who asked the right questions, or listened without judgment during challenging times. He particularly thanks John Geddes, Zach First, David Kerns, Sherra Kerns, Benjamin Linder, Vin Manno, Rob Martello, Borjana Mikic, Michael Moody, Gill Pratt, Stephen Schiffman, Sarah Spence-Adams, Lynn Stein, Jon Stolk, and Jessica Townsend.

Finally, Mark thanks his wife Babette and daughters Charlotte and Josephine, who have suffered the side effects of one too many projects over the last few years. Their support and love made all the difference.

Introduction
An Improbable Journey

This book was not supposed to happen—at least, that's our conclusion as we review the improbable events that brought it into being. It emerged out of several extraordinary circumstances: the collaboration of people who ordinarily never would have been working together, the establishment of a college that never should have been built, and the creation of an incubator that didn't have permission to exist but went ahead anyway. In the wake of these unlikely occurrences, a bunch of engineers found a surprising key to engineering education transformation. And it, too, was unexpected. This book is the story of unlikely events that led to a surprising conclusion.

There have been plenty of organizations and individuals trying to change engineering education in recent decades. There have been dozens of books, research papers, and reports. The idea has great traction. The National Academies have been working on it seriously, as reflected in reports such as *Rising above the Gathering Storm*. The National Science Foundation has poured millions of dollars into efforts to change engineering. The National Academy of Engineering produced an ambitious project, the Engineer of 2020. The Duderstadt Report, *Engineering for a Changing World: The Millennium Project*, received wide interest. The President's Council on Competitiveness focused on engineering education as a key initiative. Across the United States and internationally, more and more people are taking engineering education reform seriously. And things are starting to happen. Both of us have worked with institutions around the world, and we see the energy that people are bringing to curriculum change efforts. We've also seen increasing levels of institutional support for change. Nonetheless, advances have been slow to come. Too often, exciting initiatives that looked promising have slid back into business as usual. Against that backdrop, a small group of engineering educators began doing some unconventional things and made some surprising discoveries.

Our story of the journey begins with the founding of Olin College in Needham, Massachusetts. Like any start-up, Olin was born in an atmosphere of enormous energy, with the bold and somewhat hubristic goal of reinventing engineering education. Mistakes were made, and sometimes the process was messy—even embarrassing. But despite the bumps along the way, Olin has been enormously successful. By conventional metrics (e.g., quality of incoming students, placement rates and salary levels for graduates, national rankings), Olin performs extremely well. In addition, Olin is now internationally recognized for its thriving, innovative, student-centered educational environment, which values intrinsic motivation; collaborative, project-based classroom settings; and a "whole-mind" approach to learning. Not even a decade old, Olin is widely seen as a beacon for other engineering schools.

However, the nagging concern among those at Olin, as well as those who were inspired by Olin, was that by its nature this rare start-up was unique and could not be replicated in existing schools. Olin, with its large endowment, tiny student body, and explicit focus on engineering education, didn't look anything like their institutions. We often heard the skeptical refrain from other educators, "If you gave me a $500-million endowment and kids with 1500 SAT scores, I could do that too." We wondered about the extent to which it was true.

Meanwhile, in a very different setting, at the University of Illinois, a group of faculty was starting up a small incubator called iFoundry to experiment with what seemed to be minor changes. They, too, were struck by what was occurring at Olin and even formed an institutional partnership with Olin—something that had never been done before. Still, they realized it was one thing to start a college from the ground up and quite another to change a huge bureaucratic university from within. With extremely limited curricular space, very few financial resources, and no power to compel academic departments to take part in the reform effort, we referred to iFoundry initially as a "peashooter of a program." The shock came when iFoundry's initial small-scale approach, which consisted of one course and an extracurricular program, achieved a tremendous rippling effect of student engagement and innovation.

How did that happen? How could iFoundry, working on a shoestring, get an effect similar to that of Olin? Olin had spent half a billion dollars to create a transforming vehicle for engineering education—and Olin started with a blank slate. iFoundry spent maybe a couple hundred thousand dollars, within the confines of a huge research institution. It seemed impossible, and yet it happened.

As we reflected on these experiences, we came to recognize that our initial thinking about the keys to educational reform was wrong. The key variables weren't pedagogical. They weren't financial. They weren't curricular. They weren't research. They weren't any of the usual things we've always talked about as the engines of change. The variables were deeply *emotional* and *cultural*.

In *A Whole New Engineer*, we'll tell the story of our improbable collaboration and what we, along with like-minded colleagues, discovered about the importance of these components in transforming engineering education. We'll describe how our experiences at Olin and iFoundry led us to uncover five pillars of engineering education that create both the spirit and the results we were looking for. Rather than focusing on content, curriculum, and pedagogy—which are the typical areas where these discussions start and finish—we go off the beaten path to explore the emotionally intrinsic values that enable students to accomplish great things and to experience meaning in their lives and work. Using these pillars as a guide, we highlight some of the manifestations of the educational transformation we've witnessed and describe these experiences through the voices and reflections of many faculty, students, and educational innovators.

The emotional transformation of engineering education isn't magical thinking. Nor is it a vague abstraction or a series of touchy-feely practices. It is based on a philosophy of education that is grounded in the real world and in the lives of the students we serve. It's available to everyone. It isn't expensive. It can't be accomplished in the old paradigm under the old assumptions about how education change happens, but in the right atmosphere, the change flows organically from the students themselves. That atmosphere requires systematic language change, culture change, and personal change by students, faculty, and all the stakeholders in education.

To read this book is to join us on a journey into the mind, heart, and body of engineering—illuminating the possibilities that exist when we begin to shift our thinking and feeling about our field. We'll show living examples of educational breakthroughs, provide a window into our own failures and successes, and raise the most critical questions for engineering education: How do we produce the innovators that are needed for our times? How do we inspire students to become intrinsically motivated to learn? How do teachers step down off the stage and involve themselves as coaches inside and outside the classroom? How do we renew the culture of engineering education to make it relevant, creative, and fulfilling? How do we harness the best ideas about change and make use of them in educational settings?

This is not a theoretical exercise but a lively engagement of ideas and stories demonstrating what it is like to be on the front lines of an educational revolution. We are eager for those on the journey to make their voices heard, and we hope this book gives people permission to talk about emotional variables—which many find hard to do. We open the conversation in the spirit of learning and sharing, to find the meaningful breakthroughs that will transform the field we love so much. The journey continues, and we welcome the surprises that are still in store.

David E. Goldberg
Mark Somerville

1

Engineering Happiness
The Olin Experience

M.A. Rosenoff: *"Mr. Edison, please tell me what lab rules you want me to observe."*

Thomas Edison: *"There ain't no rules around here. We're trying to accomplish something."*

The year was 1885. A new outfielder for the Detroit Wolverines, twenty-five-year-old Franklin W. Olin, had acquired a more than respectable batting average of .316 playing for Washington and Toledo in the major leagues of the day. He would only play one game for Detroit, and baseball would not become his profession. Another vision called to him. At the same time he was playing ball, Olin was a student of civil engineering at Cornell. While there he combined his love of baseball and engineering, inventing the first indoor batting cage in college baseball. Ultimately, his achievements in engineering, not sports, would put him on the charts.

Olin was an innovator and a problem solver. In 1892 he started a company to manufacture blasting powder for mining. From this start, he built his fortune by modernizing ammunitions systems and delivery, something that was in great demand during World War I and World War II, where his contributions were heralded as being decisive. By the end of the Second World War, Olin's companies employed more than sixty-two thousand people.

It is a great gift to be as distinguished and prosperous as Olin became, but he never lost sight of his humble roots as the son of a rural working-class machinist. He was drawn to the plight of young people who could not afford good educations. He often recalled his own long struggle, noting that his short-lived professional baseball career was actually a summer job to earn money for college. Seeking a higher mission, in 1938 Olin plowed a large portion of his fortune into the charitable F. W. Olin Foundation. His goal was to provide opportunity to those who were less fortunate. Among his early grants was the creation of a vocational high school in his home-town of Alton, Illinois. The superintendent recalled how the elderly Olin showed up on his doorstep one evening and to his astonishment asked whether he'd like a school. As Olin put it, "I don't want the youth of the present generation to encounter the same difficulties in obtaining a useful education that I had to overcome when I was a boy."

For sixty years, the F. W. Olin Foundation awarded grants totaling more than $300 million to construct and equip seventy-eight buildings on fifty-eight independent college campuses. The majority of the grants were for engineering and science buildings, but there were also grants for librar-ies, information technology, business, the humanities, and the arts. The foundation continued its work long after Olin died in 1951 at the age of ninety-one. However, by the 1990s problems of planning, succession, and purpose were taking hold, and the board felt beleaguered.

In particular, Lawrence Milas, the foundation president, was experiencing an identity crisis. As the problems in engineering education grew increas-ingly apparent across the nation, with a continuing decline in enrollment, he worried that the foundation's funding wasn't having a real and measur-able impact on educating engineers. Milas felt that something different was required. But what? He brooded about it so much that his wife, Marjorie, grew exasperated. "Why don't you just start your own damn college?" she asked. Milas laughed off the remark, thinking a person would have to be crazy to do that.

But the idea would not let go. It seemed a fantastic dream, to start something from the ground up instead of supporting and tweaking programs in existing schools, with all their inherent strictures. Looking for inspiration from the founder, Milas went back and began reading foundation board minutes from the 1940s. There he discovered that not long before his death, Olin had floated the idea of starting a new institution. For Milas this was a sign that creating a school would be true to Olin's ideals. In early 1993, he approached the board with a radical idea—that it take the entirety of its endowment and pour it into a visionary new entity that would change engineering education, going out of business in the process. The board viewed Milas's idea as a high-risk proposition. What if it didn't work? Did they dare to put Olin's legacy on the line with such a scheme? Despite their concerns, however, the board members voted to allow Milas to investigate the matter further.

The coming years were devoted to study and consultation with leading educators, businesses, and organizations such as the National Science Foundation and the Accreditation Board for Engineering and Technology. They kept encountering the same feedback: engineering education was desperately in need of a renovation, but no one seemed to have an answer as to how that might happen. They first considered giving the money to an excellent engineering school, then to a fine private university with everything in place except an engineering school. Both options would have had little effect on changing education. Finally, they concluded they had no option but to start over and create an entirely new entity.

In 1997 the board voted to launch a school as a laboratory to test a new direction in engineering education. Free of encumbrances from the past, it could be anything they imagined. The Franklin W. Olin College of Engineering was chartered in Needham, Massachusetts, with an initial commitment of around $200 million, one of the largest grants in the history of American higher education. Of the school that was his brainchild, Milas said, "The new school will be dedicated to developing a new paradigm for engineering education consistent with the goals established by the National Science Foundation and the greater engineering community. A totally new college will provide an exceptional opportunity to innovate."

> *The new school will be dedicated to developing a new paradigm for engineering education consistent with the goals established by the National Science Foundation and the greater engineering community. A totally new college will provide an exceptional opportunity to innovate.*
>
> **—Lawrence Milas**

With the imprimatur of the Massachusetts Board of Higher Education and a scheduled date of opening for the fall of 2001, Olin College was in the works. The foundation purchased seventy-five acres of woodland from Babson College, adjacent to the school on the Needham-Wellesley town line, and began construction. A 1997 statement of purpose for the charter to the Massachusetts Board of Higher Education defined the bold dream:

> We envision a 21st Century in which the industrial and commercial community is truly a global marketplace. . . . We believe that modern engineering education provides the optimum basic preparation for the leaders of the future we see. We believe that engineers will continue to be expected to practice their profession in the traditional technical capacities. In addition, however, we believe that engineers will be called upon and must assert their leadership as managers of technology-based commercial ventures and governmental agencies, as senior corporate leaders, entrepreneurs, political leaders, and as specialized professionals in the fields of medicine and law. We believe that engineers will be so important in this future society

because their education uniquely provides them with the essential knowledge, skills, processes and perspectives to understand the complex system that modern life has become. Many educational programs provide graduates with either the "know how," the "know why" or the "know when." The Franklin W. Olin College will enable its graduates to develop within themselves the necessary synthesis of these three ingredients to emerge as the effective leaders needed to chart our course through the future. In short, we see a future in which an undergraduate engineering education becomes the true "Liberal Education," i.e. an education which liberates one to lead a personal and professional life of full citizenship in one's local, national and global communities.

The founding precepts stated the goal more directly: "Olin is intended to be different, not for the mere sake of being different, in order to become an important and constant contributor to the advancement of engineering education in America and throughout the world. . ."

Employee number one

Richard K. (Rick) Miller, then dean of engineering at the University of Iowa, had a revelatory experience early in his career. While teaching at the University of California, Santa Barbara, and trying to raise a family on his meager salary, he took on a consulting job with Astro Research Company that lasted fifteen years and changed his life. The task was to design a space-craft for chasing Haley's comet. It was a real and important program, and it challenged everything Miller knew. "I thought I was an engineer," Miller reflects, "but I discovered I wasn't. There weren't answers in any engineering textbook about how to do what we were doing."

During his experience, Miller learned that what engineering was really about was designing—"not a body of knowledge but a process, a way

5

of thinking." As Miller thought about it, he settled on a simple starting point: an engineer is someone who says, "There has to be a better way." That visceral sense of need then led to figuring out what to do about it, which usually meant a process of trial and error, which, Miller noted, was exactly the way the Wright brothers went about it.

This experience stayed with Miller. Later, when he was teaching at the University of Southern California, he volunteered to teach the aerospace design course and asked students to come up with conceptual designs to resolve real problems in the space program. He then brought in practicing engineers from companies to review the student presentations at the end of the course. To everyone's astonishment, the reviewer from McDonnell Douglas said, "You have inadvertently stumbled onto our patent. And this patent is how we won a $200 million contract to build the Space Station."

Miller recalled, "Their eyes as big as saucers, the kids came to me. They asked, 'What's a patent?' and 'How do we make money on our ideas?' These things were not taught in engineering school." When he investigated, Miller found that the only way to learn these practical skills was to be in the business school, and due to institutional barriers, "there was no way to get there from here." (Since this experience many years ago, USC has developed an excellent engineering entrepreneurship program that addresses the concern very well.)

Increasingly, Miller was recognizing that engineering programs were focused too narrowly and weren't in the best long-term interests of most undergraduate students. So, when he became dean at the University of Iowa, he started to address the issue. Along with colleagues, he helped create a curriculum for teaching entrepreneurial principles to engineers through the newly formed Pappajohn Center for Entrepreneurship. The Technological Entrepreneurship Certificate Program for engineers was the first of its kind, bridging the College of Engineering and the College of Business.

Living in Iowa City and working on new concepts at the university—including a redesign of engineering education and the culture change in the College of Engineering—Miller was immersed in some exciting efforts. Curricular changes initiated during his leadership focused on educating engineers beyond technology. It is a mission that continues to this day, with about half of all Iowa engineering graduates leaving with double majors or minors outside engineering. He was happy in Iowa, and so was his family. In 1997, he turned down an opportunity to go elsewhere. He and his family were looking forward to staying put. Then a letter arrived from Milas, telling him that he'd been nominated by John Straus, the president of Harvey Mudd College, whom he respected deeply, to become president of a new college of engineering. Milas was eager to schedule a meeting.

Miller flew to meet Milas in Florida. Their meeting lasted over a weekend, and Miller found himself responding to the vision of a college founded on the principles of continuous improvement and innovation. "He told me he was serious about continuous improvement," Miller said. "He wanted Olin to be constantly changing, so that everything, in effect, would have an expiration date. I had never heard anybody seriously propose this continuous improvement." On the plane home Miller was inspired to write Milas a letter with a vision of what such a new college might do differently. Milas liked the "white paper" very much, and he persuaded Miller to agree to be a candidate. After a national search, the search committee unanimously selected Miller, who became the president and first employee on February 1, 1999.

Very quickly, Miller assembled a founding leadership team from the ranks of highly respected faculty across the country, including David V. Kerns, Jr., a distinguished professor and former associate dean of engineering at Vanderbilt as provost; Sherra E. Kerns, chairman of Vanderbilt's flagship department of electrical engineering and computer science, as vice president for innovation and research; Stephen P. Hannabury, former assistant dean of the School of Management at Boston University, as vice president for administration and finance; and Duncan C. Murdoch, former director of admissions at USC and former dean of admissions at Harvey Mudd College and Rose-Hulman Institute of Technology, as vice president for external relations and enrollment. They were all on board and relocated to Needham by September 1, 1999.

For husband-and-wife academics David and Sherra Kerns, the move from Tennessee represented a once in a lifetime opportunity. "We were happy at Vanderbilt," David said. "We'd had offers from several top universities in the country, and had finally decided there was no way we would move. We planted sixty trees in our yard." But Olin shook loose that resolve. "We didn't want to look back and say we could have done it and we didn't."

One of the first initiatives of the new operation was a partnership with Babson College, which boasted one of the nation's premier programs for entrepreneurs. Babson's dean of admissions, Charlie Nolan, watched the process with building interest. "When I learned of the Olin/Babson partnership and what Olin was trying to do, my jaw dropped," he recalls. "All I wanted was to be a part of building a college from scratch." When he was asked to be on a search committee for a dean of admissions, he said, "Hire me!" And they did. Nolan turned down an opportunity to join Johns Hopkins as an associate provost to work with Murdoch at Olin. Why did Nolan leave an established career for the fragile start-up? The same reason others were attracted. "I have an entrepreneurial spirit," he says, "and that was the very definition of Olin."

They set about recruiting the founding faculty. The characteristics sought in recruiting Olin faculty were carefully considered. "Inspirational teaching at the undergraduate level" and dedication to students were foremost, as well as interest and experience in integrating creativity into the classroom, a willingness to be part of a team—whether that meant partnering, leading, or following—and a willingness to take reasonable risks to make significant impact.

In a more conventional setup, the curriculum would be designed first, and then a faculty would be hired tailored to teaching that curriculum. Olin upended tradition by hiring a faculty first, then allowing it to design a curriculum from scratch. "We didn't want to do things that traditional schools do out of habit," David Kerns said. "We wanted to think everything through in a fresh way, so we didn't waste any part of the unique opportunity."

To recruit faculty, the core group needed to let the wider academic world know Olin existed. In 1999, the Kerns's hosted a reception at a Frontiers of Education meeting, where three hundred faculty from across the country were in attendance, offering free wine and cheese in exchange for listening to a brief presentation about Olin College. As word got out, applications began to flood in—over fifteen hundred in the first year. People were attracted to the idea of designing something new, and many of the original faculty left positions at leading universities around the country, such as MIT, Vanderbilt, and Berkeley, to join the new school. One was the former director of space sciences at NASA; one was a concert pianist-turned-PhD engineer; one had played a key role in the Human Genome Project. They had credentials such as Rhodes scholarships, professional awards, and patents.

Faculty members came to Olin knowing they would have to accept some unusual conditions. There would be no tenure and no department structure to divide and isolate specialties. Instead of departments, Olin would have one interdisciplinary group, with faculty mixing freely. Some classes would be cotaught by teachers of different disciplines. It was a radical departure, and it meant taking a leap of faith. Still, some of the best professors in the country went along, for the chance to take on a once-in-a-lifetime challenge.

"We felt a huge responsibility," Sherra Kerns recalled. "As an MIT colleague said, 'If you don't do something different and exceptional, no one will give money to offer a clean slate program ever again.'"

Mark Somerville: **Joining a start-up**

I remember first hearing about Olin College in 1997, about a year and a half before I finished my PhD. From the outset, it seemed like the place I wanted to be. The mission to change engineering education resonated with me, and the opportunity to invent from scratch was enormously appealing. But when I made some inquiries, I was disappointed to learn that Olin would not be hiring faculty until 2000 or so.

So I put aside thoughts of Olin and pursued positions at top liberal arts colleges, because I felt that these environments valued student development, close student-faculty interaction, and high levels of faculty intellectual vitality. I accepted a tenure-track position at Vassar College in the physics department. Vassar was a wonderful place, and I was very happy there. I got to work with very good students and colleagues. I had a lot of fun teaching. I was able to get funding from the NSF for experimental and modeling work in high-speed transistors, and I had some success in involving undergraduates in my research. But despite how great Vassar was, I found myself continuing to think about Olin. In 2000, I decided to explore the idea of joining the faculty.

I remember my interview vividly. The atmosphere was more of a *dot-com* start-up than an academic one. Everyone was very intense and very excited about what they were doing. I also remember that the faculty members I talked to were all over the map with respect to where they thought the college was going. Olin liked to talk about "starting with a blank slate," but it seemed to me that there was a different blank slate in every person's office! Perhaps naively, I interpreted this wide range of views as healthy, and I was very excited to say yes when I received an offer from Olin.

Quite a few of my friends at Vassar thought I was crazy, and there were plenty of times when I thought they were right. But as David Kerns, Olin's founding provost, put it, "The chance to start a college from scratch is not a once-in-a-lifetime opportunity: it's a *less*-than-once-in-a-lifetime opportunity." I have never worked as hard as I have during my time at Olin, nor have I ever had as much fun.

My initial expectations for Olin were, in retrospect, quite limited. Although I got good teaching evaluations at Vassar, I think I was also fairly conservative both pedagogically and intellectually. I suppose I hoped that Olin would become a liberal arts college for engineers, with a curriculum that included broad grounding in the arts and sciences and a culture that was more supportive than that at many engineering schools. But I don't think I appreciated the possibilities that a more student-centered, whole-person, collaborative, intrinsically motivated education offered. Indeed, I would say that I have spent every one of my twelve years at Olin learning more about just how powerful this different educational paradigm can be. Of course, I realize that many of the ideas that are embodied at Olin are anything but new—John Dewey, Carl Rogers, Edward Deci, and others articulated most of the concepts that matter years ago—but seeing them in action, and getting the chance to practice them, has been an amazing opportunity.

Designing from a blank slate

In the planning stages, one thing was clear: the philosophy and structure of Olin College would not be built on the foundation of traditional colleges. In order to develop a new culture of innovation and continuous improvement, the foundation itself would have to be different. To capitalize on this opportunity, the college launched its first strategic plan, Invention 2000, a two-year effort to fundamentally rethink engineering education and college operations. This effort involved sending teams of two to three faculty members to visit thirty-one college campuses and numerous corporate learning centers to assess best practices in every aspect of college life, from curricula to student life issues, to see whether there was a better way to deliver undergraduate engineering education.

From those plans emerged the "Olin Triangle," a graphical representation of the faculty's aspirations for the curriculum. At the peak of the triangle was superb engineering, supported by entrepreneurship, philanthropy, and ethics, as well as arts, humanities, and social sciences.

In February 2001, Provost Kerns arranged a retreat at the Warren Conference Center in Ashland, Massachusetts, for the founding faculty to consider the Olin curriculum and other academic matters. Kerns divided the group into three teams, each of which was to propose a curricular model. It was hoped that the teams would present thoughtful approaches, discuss them amicably, and agree on where to plant the flag. That didn't exactly happen. Instead, each team became so attached to its own model that compromise seemed impossible. The faculty retired for dinner, frustrated by a lack of progress. After dinner, faculty members began spontaneously returning to the meeting room, where stickies lined the walls with the proposed models, until everyone was gathered. They met late into the night. By the end of the evening, the group had articulated what they called the "Bold Goals," as a philosophical underpinning of the Olin curriculum. The Bold Goals were:

- Hands-on design projects included in the education plan for every year.
- An ambitious and authentic senior capstone project representative of professional practice.
- Opportunities to work independently, as team members, and as team leaders.
- Opportunities to perform before audiences comprising experts in the field of the presentation or performance.
- An international or intercultural immersion experience.

- A substantial constructive contribution to society through social responsibility and philanthropy.
- Ability to communicate logically and persuasively in written, spoken, and visual/graphic forms.
- Self-sufficiency and the ability to articulate and activate a vision and bring it to fruition.

Parallel with the Bold Goals was the long-standing idea that the college should be unusually student centered, with a heavy emphasis on student feedback. But the most dramatic contribution of the students would happen almost by accident.

The college that wasn't

With the planning and building under way, the challenge became how to attract top students to the school. Charlie Nolan recalls, "We simply wanted the very best students who were fearless, who could take on the challenges of a rigorous curriculum, but who also didn't need to be at MIT. We didn't know if they were out there or not, but we were certainly going to try to appeal to the engineering students who wanted to try something different, solve the big problem." Olin's team recognized that this would not be an easy task, because of the tremendous competition from top-tier schools. The best and brightest were relentlessly pursued by the Harvards, the MITs, the Stanfords—schools whose prestige couldn't be matched. Olin would have to create a different draw—appealing to the entrepreneurial, outlier spirit. The early mailings to high school students dared them to take a fearless leap. They featured bungee jumpers ("Fearless?") and huge growling excavators. They challenged the supremacy of the Ivy League with a tantalizing suggestion:

> "There's only one thing cooler than getting into Harvard, MIT and Stanford—TURNING THEM DOWN!"

One of the first admission pieces, "7 Reasons You Should Apply to an Engineering College That Doesn't Exist," was a card fan anchored at the corner by an aluminum rivet and mailed in a silver Mylar envelope.

There was something for parents, too. Understanding that parents might balk at sending their high-achieving children to an untested college, the recruitment effort appealed to them on the basis of clear advantages: tuition would be free; world-class professors would do the actual teaching; and the major innovative technology companies, who would hire the next generation of graduates, agreed that this was the future of engineering education. Olin had to convince students and parents alike that Olin's greatest advantage was that it *wasn't* the old Ivy League.

The recruitment efforts didn't win Olin any friends at Harvard, MIT, and Stanford, but from a marketing perspective, they succeeded brilliantly, and there was a flood of interested candidates—often students who had been accepted by the best schools in the country but wanted to be part of Olin's innovative experiment.

Smoke and mirrors

By mid-2000, it was becoming clear that there was a problem. Construction was substantially delayed, and so the college would be unable to meet its September 2001 opening date. It was a sobering moment of truth. To fail to open on time would be a potentially disastrous halt to momentum. To literally become a college that didn't exist threatened to shatter the good will and budding credibility.

The crisis required a creative solution. At an intense meeting that went on past midnight, the founding team wrestled to find an answer. Clearly, no one wanted to wait; the momentum was just too great. Late into the night, someone made a suggestion: why not admit a smaller class of students—a select group whose first year would be spent helping to create the college—collaborating with the faculty on curriculum development and helping to develop the student culture? It had never been tried before, but the faculty sensed that such an opportunity might appeal to the kind of students Olin wanted to attract.

"Let's call them partners," Nolan suggested, voicing a consensus that the students become full collaborators. The name represented a radical intention: the students would be immersed in every step of the process—equal team members whose opinions and ideas would be considered and adopted.

Once settled on, the idea began to take shape. It was decided that there would be thirty partners—fifteen men and fifteen women—a complete gender equity unheard of in engineering schools. Brochures were quickly printed, selling the educational and professional value of the Partner Year concept:

> **"When Friends Ask, 'Where Are You Going to College?' . . . Tell 'em you're building your own."**

Duncan Murdoch took Olin's pitch to the national meeting of high school guidance counselors, and this effort was instrumental in transforming the attitudes of parents and guidance counselors from automatically dismissing the school as half-baked to recognizing an exceptional opportunity. Students responded in droves.

Olin invited prospective partners to come to Needham for the first of two Candidate Weekends to learn about Olin and see whether they wanted to be part of the idea of helping to build the college that didn't exist. This couldn't be a normal admissions weekend—after all, Olin had no campus, only the most rudimentary vision for a curriculum, and no current students.

This was not a job for us; it was a cause.

—Charlie Nolan

But the weekend revealed that the lack of things that make up a "normal" college was more than compensated for by the people who were there—both the prospective students, who were enormously excited by the chance to be part of building a college, and the entire Olin community, whose energy and commitment to the enterprise were palpable.

The highlight of the weekend, which still resonates in the memories of the participants to this day, was a design and build project, which would go on to become an enduring admissions ritual at the college. Because there wasn't a campus or a curriculum to present, the founding team decided that the best thing to do would be to give the prospective partners a chance to *experience* what Olin might be like. The candidates were put on teams, and each team was given several four-foot-by-eight-foot pieces of expanded polystyrene board—blue foam—along with rudimentary cutting tools and a few pencils. They were told, "In two hours your team will be given twenty minutes to assemble a tower. Your objective: to assemble the tallest tower possible." The faculty also emphasized that the point was to play and to explore what it meant to actually do something, to build something—which is a basic way of being an engineer. It was an activity—not a competition. With two hours to prepare, the teams set off.

As anyone who has ever worked with blue foam knows, it's a very challenging material. It's difficult to cut and hard to fasten the pieces together—especially with no fastening materials except pencils. The teams struggled to figure out the challenge, forming tight identities in the process. At the end of two hours, the teams had their plans. Not unexpectedly, when they began to build, some of the towers had spectacular failures that led to loud wails but also a lot of laughter and fun. Some of the towers were actually quite impressive and tall. But rather than recognizing only the team that built the tallest tower, the organizers called out every team for its creative contributions, excellent teamwork, or catastrophic collapses.

In this simple, even silly, exercise, the founding team of faculty and staff witnessed a breakthrough. First, the students became more than just a random collection of individuals; they became part of a community. Second, they were completely involved, not because they had to produce for a grade but because they wanted to do it. They were emotionally engaged. The faculty and staff saw in action the spirit they wanted to pervade this new college. It was very much about collaboration, having fun, and not necessarily having the right answer but learning in the process.

In imagining Olin, the team had often talked about a central value of the school being that students were able to do a lot more than most educators gave them credit for, and here they witnessed that reality before their eyes. It was the first event where they and the candidates collectively recognized the power behind student engagement, leading to community and connectedness at a level that they hadn't expected. Indeed, the engagement was so strong that when the admissions team had to decide how many partners to admit, they opted to make only thirty offers of admission for the thirty available slots, on the assumption that virtually every candidate would say yes. Of the thirty offers made, twenty-seven were accepted. However, so many students were interested that it was decided to allow everyone on the waiting list to defer and enroll the following year. Fourteen of the twenty-seven accepted the offer and became "virtual partners," an effort that was so successful it was formalized into a permanent admission policy.

A culture is born

As it turned out, Olin's construction delays and subsequent decision to turn this problem into an opportunity for student involvement reaped great benefits. Over the course of the Partner Year, students, faculty, and staff worked side by side to decide virtually everything about Olin—from policies around academic dishonesty, to how student life would work, to what the curriculum would look like. And, along the way, they formed a culture of student ownership and engagement: the idea that students are not consumers but rather are partners in their education. Without these experiences—without those construction delays—Olin might have been quite a different place.

The thirty Olin partners were a dedicated and talented group of fearless, enterprising students. Recruited from around the country, they had all received offers of admission from the top universities and engineering programs, such as Harvard, MIT, and CalTech. They chose Olin, despite its lack of a track record, for the unprecedented opportunity to shape their own college experience. "Other colleges may offer credentials," said Olin partner Que Anh Nguyen. "We have the chance to make history."

Gathering under a tent on the lawn of 1735 Great Plain Ave, with the sounds of construction rumbling in the background, the Olin faculty and staff welcomed the thirty partners. In his opening remarks, President Miller presented them with a challenge. "Chances are many of you have been at or near the top of your class in high school and grade school, probably for as long as you can remember," he said. "You are used to being regarded by peers and teachers alike as among the smartest ever to attend your school. Repeated reminders that you are the smartest are very hard to ignore, and you may have even established a sense of personal identity that depends on this recognition—possibly more than you realize." He paused and regarded them seriously before cautioning, "Beware of your own ambition to excel in academics here, and avoid unnecessary competition. You should know that our philosophy is that you are all capable of success, and it is our job to help you each achieve your fullest potential. We do not intend to focus on weeding out the weakest link, because there aren't any weak links among you. Class rank should not be your primary focus at Olin College—learning all you can and building lasting relationships should."

> *Other colleges may offer credentials. We have the chance to make history.*
>
> **—Que Anh Nguyen**

Those young high school graduates could not have fully appreciated Miller's message then, but in the coming year they would learn to let go of their old ideas about achievement and discover a community of innovation, collaboration, and creativity.

It's hard to overstate what a radical departure the Partner Year was in the way of doing things. Polina Segalova, an Olin partner who went on to earn a PhD at Stanford and is now a senior design engineer for a medical device company, was, in many ways, typical of the kind of student attracted to the Olin experiment. In high school at the prestigious Illinois Math and Science Academy, she had always figured on pursuing her interest in college, but as she put it, "Until my junior year I couldn't even define engineer." That changed at a college fair when she heard Duncan Murdoch from Olin admissions make a pitch for the school that didn't exist. "I was totally blown away," Segalova recalls. "It had everything I was looking for—math and science but also humanities and a focus on entrepreneurship." She applied, and when she was invited to be a partner, she jumped at the chance.

On the very first day, she had a giant reality check—and a small meltdown. She and her mother flew into Boston and got lost several times driving to the campus. When they finally arrived, somewhat frazzled, Segalova looked around and realized the reality of the situation. Olin College consisted of two trailers and a huge mound of dirt on a hill. She thought, "Oh, my God, what have I got myself into?" and burst into tears in the car. She and her mother sat there for a while, her mother gently suggesting that she could probably still get into another school. But Segalova pulled herself together, declared that she'd be all right, and marched into the new adventure. She never looked back.

Living in trailers in very close proximity to the other partners was an intense bonding experience. Sometimes they joked about feeling like a lab experiment—perhaps one designed by a mad professor—or a reality TV show. But the motivation was high. "We knew we were experimenting for ourselves," Segalova says. "We had an enormous sense of ownership. We should have been scared, but we were so excited, knowing we could shape our education."

From the outside, choosing Olin over other schools might have seemed a risky proposition, but the partners did not see it that way at all. Susan Fredholm Murphy, now a senior consultant and service delivery director at PE International in Boston and an Olin trustee, was so "blown away" by the Candidate Weekend that she didn't even wait to hear from other colleges. She signed on. "Why say no to go to a *normal* college?" she said. "I could always transfer." She saw that top-notch faculty had already left tenure-track positions and relocated their families for Olin. To her, they were the ones that took the risk. She liked the idea of a new and innovative school, and she was also attracted by the promise of a well-rounded environment—one that would encourage her to pursue her interest in ballet and jazz dancing. She knew Olin's offer was a special opportunity that couldn't be found anywhere else.

As the partners were at home packing their bags and enjoying their last days of summer, Olin's small faculty was furiously trying to figure out what they were going to *do* with the partners. The Invention 2000 plan had proposed that the curriculum would be invented *before* the partners arrived and that the partners would help to test and refine the curriculum. The reality was different.

Mark Somerville: Curriculum? What curriculum?

When I came to Olin in July of 2001, I was really looking forward to learning about the curriculum design. The strategic plan that I'd read (Invention 2000) outlined how the 2000–2001 academic year would be used for "discovery" and "invention" of the curriculum—i.e., surveying best practices and then deciding what the curriculum would look like—and the 2001–2002 Partner Year was supposed to be "develop and test"—trying out and refining the concepts outlined in the curriculum.

On arrival at Olin, I walked into the house that we were using for office space. Every inch of vertical space was covered with poster paper and Post-it notes, each outlining some aspect of what an engineer should know. It was clear that someone had been spending a great deal of time thinking about this question. But when I asked to see the curriculum design, the response was rather sheepish. I was handed a binder of incomprehensible PowerPoint slides, each outlining a different way of thinking about what a curriculum might look like.

And when I spoke with faculty, it was clear that there were still many competing visions. Although the faculty had been able to agree on the "Bold Goals" for the curriculum and although the faculty had spent enormous time talking about what an engineer should know, they had been unable to come to consensus about what the curriculum should look like.

Since there was little consensus about the curricular structure, the faculty instead opted to prototype different kinds of learning experiences to determine what the college should be *like*. They would learn by doing.

The Partner Year was divided into six modules, and during each module, teams of faculty and students would focus on different tasks, ranging from designing and testing different curricular concepts, to writing the student government manual, to investigating approaches to grading and assessment, to devising an honor code, to investigating community service opportunities.

One memorable curricular experiment involved questioning the extent to which students have to "know the stuff" before they can design things. Gill Pratt, a roboticist who joined Olin from MIT, suggested turning this on its head. Working with David Kerns and other faculty, he challenged students to design and build a pulse oximeter (a device that measures your pulse and blood oxygenation) during the first six-week module. Rather than starting with lectures about circuits, he introduced the idea of what a pulse oximeter is and conceptually how it works and then acted as a coach as students began to wrestle with the concept. Students read patents; they built simple circuits; they blew up simple circuits—but at the end of six weeks, they had successfully constructed a working pulse oximeter. It wasn't pretty; it didn't work as well as a commercial device, but it worked, despite the fact that the students who built it had just finished high school and had never worked with circuits before.

"The big revelation to me in my career had been the profound way we underestimate what kids are able to do," says President Miller. Traditional curricula are heavy on calculus and physics in the first two years, with virtually no opportunity for project involvement until the upper grades. "Why do we do it that way? Did someone discover a stone tablet on top of a hill?"

The partners had some opportunities that were far beyond what any of them could have expected in a prefreshman class. Fredholm-Murphy was part of a team that interviewed businesspeople and professors to determine what every engineering student should know about entrepreneurship before he or she graduated from college. They wrote a paper with their findings and were asked to present it at an ACE conference in Montreal. "We were surprised when the faculty said, 'You go do it,'" she said. "We figured they would make the presentation. But we drove up to Montreal and did it. The experience hooked us on the idea of doing engineering education well."

The creation of Olin's honor code ended up being an intense and meaningful process, bringing truth to the intention of the college. The code was designed as an exercise in trust—a key value at Olin. It required all members of the community to conduct themselves according to five core personal values: integrity and personal responsibility; respect for others; passion for the welfare of the college expressed through cooperation and caring; patience and understanding in respect for others; and openness to change, innovation, and continuous improvement.

Recalling the support from faculty—with whom they were on a first-name basis—Segalova says, "They were like older, wiser siblings," making the distinction that the faculty were not authority figures but guides.

As the Partner Year wore on, though, there was still little consensus about the curriculum. Conversations about which topics should be covered yielded talk of eight-year-long programs, and tensions between more prescriptive visions and more open-ended, competency-based approaches were high. In the spring, Provost Kerns organized a group of five faculty and one partner, called the Curricular Decision Making Board. The group was sequestered in a retreat at MIT's Endicott House for several days and were told not to come out without a curriculum.

When the CDMB members returned from the retreat, they presented the curriculum to the faculty in the form of "A Play in 5 Acts," titled "Once Upon a College," or "The Olin College Curriculum." It was a detailed plan, but once again, openness was the order of the day. The group underscored this fact, writing, "First, this is a work in progress. We cannot emphasize this enough. **You must not interpret any of the ideas or procedures within this curriculum as final or binding.** Olin's faculty, students, and staff embrace the ideal of continuous improvement, and we have learned to expect change. Although we often feel that we are in the final stages of the college-building process, Winston Churchill's words offer an important perspective: 'This is not the end. It is not even the beginning of the end. But it is, perhaps, the end of the beginning.' We have reached the implementation stage of this experiment, and we will certainly learn quite a bit in the weeks and years ahead."

The epilogue to the play urged the broader faculty to continue the process of creating and innovating:

> *Make your boldest thoughts take flight*
> *And innovate with all your might. . .*
> *Olin's banner, once unfurled,*
> *Will loose new dreams upon the world.*
> *And history will soon acknowledge*
> *What happened . . . once upon a college.*

"A wonderful outcome was that every member of the faculty seemed to feel they had been listened to," said David Kerns. "This curricular plan has been revisited many times since, as we learn from the successes and failures of different approaches, but there remains remarkable similarities between that and the present curriculum. The openness to change is critical, and we put an expiration date on the curriculum, which forces periodic reexamination."

Several distinguishing characteristics stood out in the inaugural curriculum. An important feature of the curriculum was that students would immerse themselves in *being* engineers from the outset. In traditional curricula, the freshman and sophomore years are largely devoted to lectures and "learning," with projects and experiences coming in the junior and senior years. In the Olin curriculum, practice would begin in the first year, and there would be very few if any big lecture courses.

Another important feature of the curriculum was that it would be broad—devoted not just to math-science topics but also to the arts, humanities, and social sciences, which would be fully integrated into the learning processes. There would also be courses and projects in business and entrepreneurship, which would ground the learning in real-world principles and practices. And none of these subjects would stand alone; rather, it was imagined that the curriculum would be highly integrated and interdisciplinary.

At every level, the goal was to be open-ended, flexible, and fully present to the development of whole human beings in the guise of whole new engineers. The Olin partners helped pioneer an innovative, hands-on curriculum, which was built around the Olin triangle of engineering, entrepreneurship, and the arts. The aim of the curriculum was to prepare technological leaders who were well-rounded "Renaissance engineers," in the tradition of Leonardo da Vinci ... and Franklin Olin.

The aim of the curriculum was to prepare technological leaders who were well-rounded "Renaissance engineers," in the tradition of Leonardo da Vinci ... and Franklin Olin.

The first class

By the time Olin was ready to admit its first full freshman class, there were six hundred applications to fill seventy-five seats, which drew some of the best students in the country. They were among the top tier academically, but that wasn't the deciding factor. "The match was critical," Nolan says, reflecting back on the recruitment philosophy. "We were looking for students with *Olinesque* qualities, meaning they would have to have a passion for innovation, be committed to cocurricular activities, be able to overcome adversity, have social skills, and be team players." Potential candidates were invited to a Candidate Weekend, where they experienced Olin and spent time working on building projects (à la the earlier blue foam event) that measured their ability to work in teams. Since the partners were already seated, fewer than fifty of the new applicants would make the cut. The final decision would belong to the community, not the admissions office, with faculty making the selection a rigorous and painful process. Looking at the spirit and enthusiasm, some at Olin wished—as they would every year—that they could admit all of them.

Olin admitted its first full class of seventy-five students, including the partners, the virtual partners and students coming directly from high school, in the fall of 2002. They set out to continue developing not just a curriculum but also a way of being—a culture. They knew they had something special going on, and they spent a lot of time figuring out exactly what that specialness was. Every decision was made in the context of unleashing student engagement by treating the students as whole people who were there to learn and develop.

In his inaugural address, President Miller stated, "Innovation and continuous improvement require certain cultural attitudes and commitments. First, an implicit humility is required to embrace the notion that improvement is always possible, and that we can always learn from others outside our community. In addition, continuous improvement is only possible if continuous assessment is employed. We must be willing to expose ourselves to review and measurement, and to take the time to learn from mistakes. Finally, and perhaps most importantly, continuous improvement requires openness to change. At Olin, one of our five personal core values is openness to change. We have already found that it is the most challenging of our values. We have no blueprint for success in this area. But we are committed to sustain our efforts and learn from our mistakes until we develop an approach that promises to succeed."

The principle of openness to change was repeatedly tested. There were bumps along the way.

Mark Somerville: "Hey, we screwed up."

In the early days, all of us were on hyperdrive. Everyone was pumped up, ready and eager to start "for real." The atmosphere was a little bit intense, to say the least. We really went overboard. Every faculty member had great ideas, every student was committed to doing amazing things—and, as a consequence, everyone pushed harder than was healthy or even humanly possible. Two weeks into the first semester, we started to notice that the students were dragging into class, exhausted, with dark circles under their eyes. One student burst into sobs in the middle of class. Another cried, "I can't do this; I can't handle it."

It was a wake-up call that our original plans had been perhaps more grandiose than realistic. And immediately upon reaching that realization, a halt was called.

We canceled classes and told the students to go outside, where we'd set up a giant bouncy castle on the lawn. Games were laid out, music was amped up, and a day of fun was announced. Everyone let off quite a bit of steam—for example, the egg toss game turned into a "throw eggs at each other" game—with students and faculty participating. It was a cooling-off period and a time to relax stressed-out brains and bodies to a point where something new and workable could be devised.

We all took a deep breath, and the next day the classes started up again with the questions, "How can we do this differently? What should we change to make it work better for you?" And changes were made based on student input. It was a learning experience, and it also ended up being a positive experience for students, who saw that the college was willing to say, "Hey, we screwed up. Let's change it," and mean it.

For our part, the faculty realized that rapid adaptation to what was happening on the ground was a firm characteristic of our educational approach. In the years to come, there would be many instances where we stepped back and made changes, often at the initiation of students.

Rising to the challenge

Still, the workload was heavy. Early on, a popular T-shirt on campus read on the front:

- Academic life
- Social life
- Sleep

and on the back:

- Pick two

Despite that, students thrived, demonstrating that hard work can be embraced with support and fun and collaboration and purpose. Through a process infused with openness and experimentation, faculty and students tried things, failed, tried different things, and thus found their way.

By the end of its first full year, Olin College had identified some key cultural signposts:

- **The decision to name student partners.** By choosing the name and the intention of making students partners, Olin defined a culture where everyone had a voice and the power distance between faculty and students was reduced.

- **The decision to select faculty with broad technical and humanistic capabilities, willing to participate in cross-disciplinary teams.** The faculty's willingness to forego the traditional signals of authority and prestige and work outside their comfort zone created a flexible, innovative classroom environment that was always student centered.

- **The decision to focus on collaboration over competition.** Olin's culture was established to challenge the conventional "survival of the fittest" mode of most engineering schools. Opportunity, creativity, and learning are enhanced in a collaborative setting.

- **The emphasis on openness and adaptation.** From the start, there was a strong element of reflection that allowed constant feedback, acknowledgment of mistakes, and openness to correction. This fluid, reflective environment allowed meaningful adaptation to the real-life experiences of students.

In May 2006, Olin College graduated its first class of seniors. This was a milestone not only for the students but also for everyone associated with the institution. In a very short period of time, this very talented group turned a wooded hillside into a respected educational institution whose reputation and influence continue to grow.

"The slate we were given was not just clean, it was nearly a void," said Sherra Kerns, reflecting on that time. "We were told to dream big dreams, and we tried. Now we have a school that exceeded most of our widest ideals, and a culture capable of perpetuating a student-centered learning institution amidst a world of faculty-centered colleges and universities."

"I would not trade my Olin experience for anything," says Segalova, who was a proud member of the first class. "My first quarter of graduate school was brutal, but thanks to what I learned at Olin, I didn't fall apart. Olin taught me not to panic when I have no idea what I'm doing—always remember that I know how to learn. It taught me to dive in and not hesitate."

As of this writing, Olin College has had nine graduating classes, and today Olin is at the top of many candidates' lists. It is admired for its solid education and its supportive, student-centric culture. It's notable that in a list of the "least happy students" published in a recent edition of *The Princeton Review's Best 376 Colleges*, six of the seven unhappiest colleges were schools predominantly made up of engineering students. Only one engineering school—Olin College—made the top twenty "happiest students" list.

When failure didn't matter

A dramatic example of the meaning of failure to success in learning occurred during the Olin Partner Year when the students decided to initiate a grand collaborative scheme of building the world's largest Rube Goldberg device. Rube Goldberg was an engineer, inventor, and cartoonist in the early to mid-twentieth century who distinguished himself with whimsical attempts to build incredibly complex chain-reaction contraptions that would solve simple tasks—for example, getting the cotton out of an aspirin bottle. Goldberg's contraptions inspired decades of fierce competitions for the Guinness world record. The Olin partners decided to try to beat the world record for one of these, a 113-step contraption to turn off an alarm clock. They divided into teams and began plotting the design.

In the course of the next two months, the phenomenal contraption took shape, filling a one-thousand-square-foot room with the steps. They included a guillotine that sliced bananas, a wooden sailboat, a compressed air cannon, and a wind-up car. It was a labor of love, fun and practical engineering, and students were completely engaged during long days and nights, piecing together each element of the chain until they had constructed a 121-step machine. They tested and retested the steps. If it worked—turned off the alarm clock in a long, uninterrupted series of actions—it would break the world record.

But when they unveiled the contraption and set it in motion, it stopped after only twenty steps. After an all-nighter when they reconfigured and retested, they unveiled it a second time. Again it failed. At a point in the chain reaction where a ball was supposed to drop through a thin layer of Kleenex into a bucket, the ball sat on top of the Kleenex and didn't drop. "This could have been a commercial for the strength of Kleenex," grumbled one student. But nobody was laughing. It was a catastrophe. The students gathered around and stared at the ball, willing it to drop. But it refused to budge, and the world record was lost.

There was great sadness at having failed to achieve what they had poured their hearts into. They had taken on a nearly impossible task and had believed they could do it. It was a big letdown. They could not yet see in their moment of supreme disappointment that what they would take away from the experience was not the sadness but the exhilaration of having taken on such a grand challenge. Later, as they reflected on the experience with faculty advisors, they kept coming back to how much fun it was, how much they'd learned about engineering dynamics, how bonded they'd become over a shared purpose. These lessons stuck, to the point where those students—long since graduated—still talk about the Rube Goldberg experiment as a seminal experience in their development as engineers and human beings. The failure didn't matter. The bonding, the learning, and the effect on their lives *did*.

From Olin to the world

Olin College was pioneering an innovative and transformational way of educating engineers. But looking on from other institutions, educators wondered what that meant for them. From their vantage point, Olin was not like them. They were deeply skeptical. These educators didn't have the opportunity to start from scratch. They didn't have half a billion dollars to create a whole new school. Mostly what they had were small groups of passionate faculty members who wanted to do something innovative but weren't sure quite how, working in institutions that were both financially and culturally resistant to change. Olin was interesting and even inspiring, but what did it have to do with *them*?

One place that question was being asked was among a small group of engineering faculty at the University of Illinois. What they created on a very small scale would demonstrate that the Olin effect was possible for everyone.

2

The Incubator
Helping a Big Old Dog Learn New Tricks

True teaching, then, is not that which gives knowledge, but that which stimulates pupils to gain it. One might say that he teaches best who teaches least; or that he teaches best whose pupils learn most without being taught directly.

—John Milton Gregory

When John Milton Gregory stepped down from the train onto Illinois soil, he was filled with a sense of confidence and a surety of mission belied by the muddy earth and windswept flatlands that spread out as far as he could see. He had arrived on this May day in 1867 to the small rural sister communities of Champaign and Urbana—usually referred to as one hyphenated entity, Champaign-Urbana—to open a university. His task was made possible by the Morrill Land Act of 1862, which granted each state in the United States thirty thousand acres on which to establish a public university.

Illinois had chosen this sweeping landscape in the east-central part of the state, opened for access by the advent of the great Illinois Central Railroad. The expanse of prairie lands would prove an ideal setting for the growth of what would become one of the largest and most prestigious public universities in the country.

At forty-five, Gregory was already a man of great achievement—a scholar, a preacher, a statesman, and, most of all, a teacher. When Gregory arrived, having accepted a position as president of this yet-to-be-created institution, his vision went well beyond the modest mandate he was given. Land-grant colleges were conceived as a way to bring practical learning to the industrial classes. Indeed, the name of Gregory's school was the Illinois Industrial University. (It would be changed to the University of Illinois in 1885.) The focus was to be mechanical arts and agriculture, with smatterings of other studies, but far from a multifaceted education—much less the types of studies that Gregory favored. He was an educational innovator, expanding the franchise of broad learning from the elite to the prairie population, advocating—against great resistance—a blending of liberal arts with industrial and agricultural training. He believed in a well-rounded education, utilizing the fullness of mind and body.

A year after Gregory's arrival, the university opened in a large abandoned building that had been built before the Civil War as a prospective training school for ministers. He stood at the door on the first day and welcomed seventy-seven students.

The Midwesterners who chartered the school were not looking for innovation, and they certainly weren't looking for liberal arts. Gregory's tenure would be marked by constant heated battles, but he would prevail. He was president for only thirteen years, but in that brief period, under his firm leadership, the university blossomed into a learning center where the mind and imagination were cherished tools. Not only was Gregory ahead of his times but also he might even have been ahead of *our* times. In his remarkable book, *The Seven Laws of Teaching*, published in 1884 after he left the university, he wrote as follows:

While facing your pupils, how often have you wished for the power to look into their minds, and to plant there with sure hand some truth of science or some belief of the gospel? No key will ever open to you the doors of those chambers in which live your pupils' souls; no glass will ever enable you to penetrate their mysterious gloom. But in the great laws of your common nature lie the lines of communication by which you may send the thought fresh from your mind, and awaken the other to receive and embrace it . . . The duty of the teacher is essentially not that of a driver or a taskmaster, but rather that of a counselor and guide.

Now, 130 years later, these words sound unexpectedly fresh, vibrant, and relevant to higher education today in a way that will resonate strongly with this and subsequent chapters.

Gregory's love of the school was so great and his dedication to its purpose so lasting that he asked upon his death that he be buried on the campus. His wish was granted. His grave rests in a grove next to a path he was said to have walked each day. A bronze plaque attached to an ancient boulder bears the epitaph: "If you seek his monument, look about you."

The prairie school grows

From these humble beginnings, the University of Illinois at Urbana-Champaign grew to become a sprawling campus spreading across the twin cities over fourteen hundred acres, with 286 buildings and more than forty-four thousand students, of whom thirty-two thousand are undergraduates. It has a College of Law; a College of Veterinary Medicine; a College of Agricultural, Consumer, and Environmental Sciences; a College of Liberal Arts and Science; and a College of Business, among other schools and programs. But it is perhaps best known for having a College of Engineering that is among the best in the world, with seventy-five hundred undergraduate students, three thousand graduate students, more than four hundred faculty members, and annual research expenditures nearing a quarter of a billion dollars.

The University of Illinois has been the home to many inventors and inventions. For example, the first generalized computer instruction system (PLATO), the transistor, the LED (light-emitting diode), magnetic resonance imaging, and, more recently, the graphical web browser (Mosaic) were either invented at Illinois or invented by one-time Illinois faculty or staff members. Its reputation for quality and innovation draws aspiring engineers from around the globe.

Large research universities such as the University of Illinois have become a standard for higher education both in the United States and around the world, paving a path to opportunity for hundreds of thousands of students. Yet beginning in the last decades of the twentieth century, as the entire world entered a period of rapid globalization and change brought about in part by technological and economic forces, it became increasingly clear that engineering education needed to change with the times. The same forces that brought Olin College into being were placing pressures on existing engineering programs to change. Responding to the demand, a small group of educators at the University of Illinois engaged in an unlikely effort. If the founding of Olin was the act of creating an engineering David, the story here is that of reforming an engineering Goliath.

Birth of an incubator

Andreas Cangellaris is an upbeat electrical and computer engineering (ECE) faculty member at Illinois with a twinkle in his eye and a spring in his step. A native of Greece, he came to the United States as a graduate student and earned his PhD from Berkeley in 1985. Professor Cangellaris came to the University of Illinois in 1997 after stints at General Motors Research Labs and the University of Arizona.

He served as head of ECE and was recently named dean of engineering at Illinois, but in May 2007, Andreas was doing what Illinois engineering professors do in their "spare" time: he was working on a research proposal, and it was a pretty big one. In particular, Cangellaris was preparing a grant proposal for the National Science Foundation Engineering Research Center program, and he had approached one of this book's authors (Goldberg) to discuss the educational component of the proposal.

The conversation turned to the teaching and learning of creativity and innovation, including both technical and nontechnical ways to approach these subjects, and Cangellaris jumped up and said, "Why don't we teach our current students this stuff?" Goldberg shrugged his shoulders and quietly said that he didn't know why. Cangellaris continued, "This is important for Illinois. I'm going to the dean, and we're going to do something about this." So he went to the dean, came back, and proudly reported, "Dave, good news—the dean wants to appoint a committee, and he wants us to help him write the charge."

David Goldberg: "No more committees"

When Andreas came back with this news, I shouldn't have been surprised with his words or the dean's response, but I wasn't happy. I had just served on a college committee that had met for weeks in the most animated and most productive of sessions, crafting a long and detailed report with many practical and useful steps, and it was already clear that none of the recommendations would ever be implemented by the college. I told Andreas that I was getting too old to serve on yet another committee that had great ideas with no follow-up or execution.

In an e-mail response to Andreas, I wrote the following, "I do believe you are right to champion this cause. My objection to a committee is that nothing will come of it. . . . In my view, the right way to test these ideas and get them into practice is to create a three-year pilot unit to work out the curriculum of the future." In my mind this pilot would involve the collaboration of major departments on a volunteer basis, and the departments would allow their students to receive curriculum credit on a pilot basis using the dean's signature authority to override the approved curriculum.

I continued, "Why would we spend the next year talking about this with people only to see the report end up like every other report? When MIT gets an idea, they put up a website and start doing it. When we think we've decided to do something, we appoint a committee, and then we don't do anything. So, if you're really serious, let's get permission, get some money, and start doing it."

Andreas was initially taken aback by my reaction. "For a while last Thursday I thought I was losing you," he replied in an e-mail. "However, I should have known better considering your conviction of the trans-formational impact of such an undertaking. I agree with you—why waste time?"

Forging ahead

After this initial interaction, the decision was made to move ahead. Without official sanction from above, using only their research, teaching, and service autonomy and authority as professors, Cangellaris and Goldberg started meeting regularly, and they knocked out the initial concept. Simply stated, the idea was to form a pilot program or a programmatic incubator to help improve undergraduate education. The first metaphor borrowed from industry was the forming of a *pilot plant* for a new process: build it small, work out the kinks, and then scale it up.

The second metaphor of an incubator, commonly invoked in entre-preneurial circles, was also used: scaffold a start-up with business, legal, accounting, and financial support; get the product working and launched; and then release the company into the wild when it can stand on its own two feet. By contrast with entrepreneurial incubators, however, the idea here was to start up new educational programs, courses, materials, and curricula, not new businesses.

Both metaphors seemed apt, and both were used depending on the audience and the situation. A name was chosen—the Illinois Foundry for Tech Vision and Leadership, abbreviated as iFoundry. The lowercase "i" sounded modern, looked hip, and brought the "I" of Illinois into a short, catchy moniker. The term "foundry" sounded solid, invoked the past, and gestured at the "forging" of young minds. The project was launched.

Why would we spend the next year talking about this with people only to see the report end up like every other report? If you're really serious, let's get permission, get some money, and start doing it.

—David Goldberg

These ideas weren't entirely without precedent. A 1994 whitepaper, entitled *Change in Engineering Education: One Myth, Two Scenarios, and Three Foci,* which was later published in the *Journal of Engineering Education* in April 1996, discussed the forces for change, the myths preventing change, various models of scalable change (one of which foreshadowed the coming of MOOCs) and critical loci to bring about effective change. In spring 1997, a pilot program called *Teamwork for a Quality Education* (TQE) in the Department of General Engineering at Illinois promoted the use of a community of student-led teams to help get students to take more responsibility for their own learning. Although students and participating faculty responded enthusiastically to the experience, it was never integrated into the curriculum, and subsequently was halted when the champions could no longer justify doing the course as a teaching overload. Both the whitepaper and the TQE experience directly informed the design of iFoundry.

A whitepaper outlining the concept was written proposing the immediate establishment of iFoundry. A key insight in writing the whitepaper was that innovation in universities is stymied by the very organizational structure of the faculty and the nature of academic decision making. The iFoundry team called this an academic NIMBY problem, where NIMBY stands for "not in my backyard." Under normal circumstances, faculty members claim to be open to innovation and new ideas, and then new curricula are put to faculty vote. The NIMBY response, "Curriculum reform is a lovely idea; just don't change my course," is similar to the siting of a nuclear power plant in which consumers want the power but not the plant. After the NIMBY reaction, a form of politicking called *logrolling* takes place: "You vote not to change my course, and I'll vote not to change your course." As a result, coalitions form that largely oppose change, and in the end, not much changes.

The iFoundry incubator idea overcame these difficulties in two key ways: first by creating a place where change and innovation are essential, even expected—the incubator itself—and second by making a promise to respect faculty governance. Central to the initial and sustained success of iFoundry was the promise that changes piloted in iFoundry would ultimately be put to a faculty vote after the pilot trial, but instead of facing NIMBY and logrolling, that vote would take place in a different environment, an environment with (1) a practical solution, (2) a real-world trial, (3) testimonials of engaged faculty and students, and (4) assessment data.

A second insight of the whitepaper was the need to move faster than universities usually move and to keep moving. The white paper noted, "The wrong way to launch this is to think about it over the next year, write plans, wring our hands, and worry. This will signal business as usual and a lack of urgency. The right way to launch this is to hold a fall one-day workshop and kickoff."

In the ensuing months, five departments—aerospace engineering, civil and environmental engineering, electrical and computer engineering, general engineering, and materials science and engineering—engaged in the transformation conversation, including associate heads from a number of those departments. Student leaders also joined the discussions as active participants together with a number of faculty members friendly to the idea of a reform effort. The white paper was circulated, a website was launched, and regular meetings were held. Something was starting to happen.

Engineer of the Future 1.0

On September 5, 2007, the University of Illinois held a half-day internal workshop called "The Engineer of the Future." The topic was compelling and of passionate interest to some members of the faculty who knew a transformation of engineering education was called for but had not yet begun to get their minds around what that might entail in a large research university. More than two hundred people showed up for the workshop.

The program consisted of talks from each of two keynote speakers, William Wulf, an Illinois alumnus and then the outgoing president of the National Academy of Engineering (NAE), and Sherra Kerns, then Olin College's vice president for innovation and research, followed by a panel discussion among Illinois engineering faculty members.

As president of the NAE, Bill Wulf had supported the writing of two major reports on change in engineering and engineering education, the Engineer of 2020 and Educating the Engineer of 2020. Sherra had just come off stints as president of the American Society for Engineering Education and was a member of the committee that wrote the NAE report Educating the Engineer of 2020. Both keynoters spoke credibly and with authority to the need for change in engineering education, and the panel discussion related the topic to the many challenges and possibilities at Illinois.

During her visit to campus, Kerns met with the expanded iFoundry team. Although she was skeptical about the effort at first, the presence of students at the table, the enthusiasm of the group, and the innovative plan for an incubator were all compelling. After awhile, she stopped in her tracks and said, "This incubator idea is different . . . and it might just work." Given her standing in the engineering education community, her experience with the Olin start-up, and her own time as a faculty member and ECE department head at Vanderbilt, a major research university, these words were comforting support to the nascent iFoundry effort and its leaders. Moreover, that evening over dinner with Bill Wulf, then Illinois Provost Linda Katehi (now chancellor at University of California, Davis), then dean of engineering Ilesanmi Adesida (now provost at Illinois), and faculty members Michael Loui and Dave Goldberg, Kerns repeated her support for the idea.

"I had seen so many bad practices," said Loui, a professor of electrical and computer engineering, who now serves as editor of the *Journal of Engineering Education*. "What did we want? Nothing less than to revolutionize engineering education."

The stars were aligning for the effort, but, more importantly, the event and the visit were the beginning of a growing relationship between Illinois and Olin, a relationship that was soon to take another step.

Birth of a partnership

The Engineer of the Future workshop helped establish iFoundry as a local change initiative and brand, and shortly thereafter in January 2008, two faculty members, Bruce Litchfield (a University of Illinois agricultural engineering professor and assistant dean) and Goldberg, started a class called Designing the Engineering Curriculum of the Future. Although Litchfield and Goldberg, among others, had been involved in forms of "creativity instruction" for many years, they recognized that this incubator was something different, with a greater possibility of a transformational impact. The initial idea was to get students involved in the accelerated planning now taking place. Eighteen students, including six graduate students, signed up for the class.

One of their class requirements was to visit other schools and benchmark the educational initiatives at those schools. One busload of students visited nearby Purdue University in Indiana, and another busload visited Rose-Hulman Institute of Technology. Because of the distance, a smaller contingent, two grad students, Jennifer Mott Peuker and Nell Keith, and Goldberg visited Olin.

During the Olin visit, the Illinois team met with students and faculty. They received a tour of the Academic Center, the many classrooms set up for hands-on studio and design work, and the fully equipped student-accessible machine shop available nearly 24 hours a day. They were told about the freshman class Design Nature, where students build nature-inspired projects individually and in teams. They were introduced to Olin's required sophomore class in entrepreneurship, Foundations of Business and Entrepreneurship (FBE), in which, among other things, students run a small business for a time and donate the profits to charity, and to another course, User Oriented Collaborative Design (UOCD), in which students study a select group of people (for example, bicycle messengers, firefighters, flight instructors, soup-kitchen workers) and work from human needs to a conceptual design for technology that might help the select group. All those things made an impression on the Illinois visitors (and later Illinois piloted FBE and UOCD with assistance from Olin), but the surprise of the visit was about to show up without fanfare, unannounced, in a manner that almost passed the team by.

It arrived during the afternoon when the team visited a second-semester freshman class on engineering systems modeling. This particular course was the second of a two-course sequence. In the first semester, students studied timekeeping devices such as clocks and electronic timers, using sophisticated computer software to simulate and help design devices the students then built and tested. In this course, the idea was similar, but instead of designing discrete systems such as clocks and timers, the students designed *distributed* systems—systems with spatial extent—again with the aid of sophisticated computer simulation software. That day the instructors in the course were testing heat sinks, devices used to carry heat away safely from electronic components so the components operate in normal temperature ranges, safely, and with long life. The class was a bit noisy as the students took their devices to the front of the room to see how well their designs had worked.

One unusual aspect about this particular two-course sequence was the degree to which students were expected to design systems for which they didn't possess the mathematical and scientific background that would usually be prerequisite to courses like these. In the traditional curriculum, students take two years of math and science and another year or so of engineering science—what are sometimes called "the basics" or "the fundamentals"—before being allowed to design much of anything. Here students were using sophisticated software without a full understanding of the math and science built into it, thereby enabling them to design earlier in their careers than would normally be possible.

Traditional faculty members might complain about this arrangement, because in their view, the students don't have "the basics" needed to use and understand the software, but in another sense, the Olin curriculum is motivationally more compelling, because students see the consequences of mastering "the basics" and are thereby more motivated to learn them after they understand their importance and value. At one level, this was very important learning for the Illinois team, but it wasn't the most surprising or interesting thing that happened that afternoon.

Back in the classroom, one by one the students were taking their heat sinks for testing, with each sink requiring a few minutes. There was anticipation of the results, and the room had almost a carnival atmosphere. Given that there were still many more heat sinks to be tested, one of the instructors told the students about the visitors from Illinois standing off to the side up toward the front of the class and suggested that students feel free to interact with the team. They quickly did so, with a number of class members coming down to the area where the Illinois team was huddled.

The Illinois team started asking questions. "What did you like most about your freshman experience? What was your biggest adjustment in coming to Olin? What was going on in this class and in the previous?"

The Olin students asked questions, too. "Why are you visiting? What have you learned? What is engineering education like at Illinois?" The exchange went on for some time, with both groups learning about the other.

David Goldberg: "The Olin effect"

I remember portions of the 2008 visit to Olin like it was yesterday, and in thinking about the episode above, I am left with a couple of impressions. First, the Olin kids were smart, articulate, and confident, and none of that was the least bit surprising. They were proud of their school and their experiences in their first year, and that, too, wasn't surprising. The part that caught me up a bit short was how they talked about their course work and their colleagues.

When asked about this course and its predecessor last semester, they started to talk about the escapement (mechanical clockwork) that one of their colleagues had made and how technically cool and elegant it was. They went on for some time, lauding their colleague and admiring his tech prowess. Some other students talked about how some of the things they made in Design Nature really showed some technological chops. I felt a shiver as though I was talking to engineers of twenty years' experience, but I was brought back to reality and remembered that these were just second-semester freshmen. I thought to myself, "Wow, this is interesting. These kids might not yet be full-fledged engineers technically, but they really *get it*."

In a very real sense, I experienced the Olin first-year students as being emotionally and in identity card-carrying engineers, and I thought longingly to the day when our first-year students at Illinois might have that same sense of emotion and identification with the spirit of engineering.

Later on, we labeled this early sense of engineering identity and emotional affiliation the Olin effect, but even though we didn't call it as such that day, I remember feeling how special it was to speak with these young people who already showed up and believed in themselves as real engineers.

The class ended, and the Illinois team moved on to their next meeting. They gathered their things and started to cross the quad to the building housing faculty and administrative offices.

Over in Milas Hall, a man with a goatee and mustache and a friendly manner awaited the arrival of the Illinois team. Michael Moody was trained as a mathematician, and his specialty involved the mathematics of biology and genetics. Prior to coming to Olin as a visiting professor in 2001, Moody had served at another four-year college with a well-regarded undergraduate engineering program, Harvey Mudd College in Claremont, California. At Harvey Mudd, Moody was known as the "pied piper of mathematics." Following his visiting year at Olin, in 2002 he joined the faculty permanently and was named founding dean of faculty at Olin and then later vice president for academic affairs in 2007. Moody was among the primary architects of Olin's pioneering curriculum. Although he was a mathematician, he believed that engineering students benefit from exposure to the liberal arts, the sciences, and business. He was an infectious teacher and an inspirational leader.

> *What if Olin and Illinois partnered and work together to transform engineering education?*
>
> **—David Goldberg**

The team walked into a conference room on the second floor of Milas Hall in the administrative offices wing and began a meeting with surprising consequences.

David Goldberg: "What if we partnered?"

The meeting with Michael Moody seemed like a pretty conventional delegation-to-delegation affair. He told us about Olin and how cool it was, and we told him about how cool iFoundry was shaping up to be and how cool we hoped it would be, and this went on in a very cordial and polite way for a fairly long time.

I can't remember what I was thinking or even what possessed me to do it. I hadn't intended on doing it, and I had no plans to do it, but pretty soon I had one of those "out of body" experiences where you notice yourself saying or doing something somewhat separately from your saying or doing it. Moody had started into another story, and I interrupted him and asked, "What if Olin and Illinois partnered and work together to transform engineering education?" I surprised myself by asking it, and I looked him in the eyes.

Moody continued on his previous train of thought as if my comment hadn't registered, and he got to the end of his sentence and paused. I repeated my question again, "What if Olin and Illinois partnered and work together to transform engineering education?"

This time Moody stopped in his tracks, looked me in the eye, and said slowly, "That's very interesting." He paused and looked out as he reflected inward. "You know it *is* in Olin's mission to serve as a *beacon* to engineering education."

There was no agreement that afternoon, but the topic was broached and out on the table as something of interest possibly to both sides. For Illinois, it would be a good deal to work with arguably the top innovator in engineering education on the planet, an institution with the right emotional and cultural stuff under the hood. For Olin, it would be a good deal to have the affirmation and the attention of one of the top engineering programs on the planet and the cooperation of an innovative incubator that had never been tried before. No one that day had any idea what such a partnership would entail, but the idea was born.

Over the summer, as plans continued for an official launch of iFoundry in the fall, Sherra Kerns from Olin and I began to formulate a memo of understanding for a partnership between Olin College and the University of Illinois. Sherra enlisted Mark Somerville, then an associate professor of electrical engineering and physics, to work as part of the collaboration. By fall, the memo of understanding was ready for signing, and iFoundry was ready to become an official College of Engineering activity.

In August 2008, iFoundry was declared an official Illinois activity. It was renamed the Illinois Foundry for Innovation in Engineering Education. It was given a modest budget, and it was instructed by Dean Ilesanmi Adesida to do "something interesting" in the first year.

On September 4, 2008, an Olin delegation consisting of Rick Miller, Sherra Kerns, and Mark Somerville came to Illinois. Rick Miller signed the memorandum of understanding to bring the Olin-Illinois Partnership (OIP) to fruition with Illinois's dean and chancellor, and a series of meetings were held to talk about how Olin's ideas and experience might be relevant to our setting and for the Olin team to better understand the iFoundry idea. It was an engaging conversation. Although the issue of scalability had been obvious from the outset of iFoundry, the conversation that day underlined its importance; the University of Illinois could not simply replicate Olin.

The Olin delegation had definite ideas about how to do things. For example, Sherra Kerns suggested that we imitate the Olin signature four-hour freshman design course Design Nature. I didn't want to be pessimistic, but I said that I would be lucky to get agreement from the departments to do a one-hour freshman pilot the following fall.

Rick Miller said, "First, you get a dormitory and put the kids together so they form a community." I wished we could as he spoke, but I had to bring them back to *my* reality. "What do you think I've got?" I asked. "I'm one faculty member in the middle of a small new initiative. If I start trying to negotiate with the Office of Student Life about creating new dormitories, it will take years. It's not a realistic starting point for us." But the emphasis on *community* and relationships did get us to wondering whether there was a less costly and more immediate way of achieving it.

Imagining the iCommunity

At about the same time that fall, Bruce Litchfield introduced a new faculty member in the College of Education to the iFoundry team. Russ Korte had just come to Illinois, and he might hold claim to being one of the oldest tenure-track assistant professors to ever be involved with the College of Engineering. Korte had worked in industry in consulting and advertising and later in life had decided to get his PhD in education. His dissertation work at the University of Minnesota, supervised by engineering education guru Karl Smith, began as a study of learning, but took an unexpected path when he uncovered the importance of connectedness and relationships in successful transitions from school to the engineering workplace. His main result showed that the single most important factor in predicting onboarding success is high-quality interpersonal *connectedness*.

Early iFoundry meetings with Korte were promising, and he said that he was interested in expanding his study to see whether the same idea held up for transitions from home to the university. The conversation quickly turned to Rick Miller's suggestion regarding the importance of community and ways to promote a kind of virtual community among students without them living together in dorms. The idea of iCommunity was born, and Korte signed on to work with iFoundry to help build a new kind of freshman community, utilizing electronic technology, that would provide support and sharing. All iFoundry students would be part of iCommunity.

Sticky clear language and the missing basics

From the initial founding of iFoundry as a bootstrap operation in 2007 until the official college launch of fall 2008, iFoundry was in a gestational period of softening up a resistant culture using YouTube, SlideShare, blogs, and other social media. The video piece was an important early win, and a number of professors chosen as iFoundry fellows prepared short informal YouTube videos on a variety of topics. (Most of these can still be viewed at www.youtube.com/illinoisfoundry.) There were, for example, professors from engineering, art and design, history, and women and gender studies, with topics ranging from engineering and hip-hop, to women in design, to some of the soft skills engineers need in the workplace. One professor, Bill Hammack, had previously run a successful NPR radio show as the "engineer guy." Hammack used his iFoundry fellowship to launch an extremely successful video series (www.engineerguy.com).

Other professors used the iFoundry channel to speak to students and faculty about topics missing in the engineering curriculum. One of these is Ray Price, the iFoundry director, who has researched and written about serial innovators and innovative organizations. Price holds a unique faculty position as the Severns Chair of Human Behavior in the College of Engineering, which allows him to focus on skills that are valuable in the workplace and in life—interpersonal skills, teamwork, leadership, and emotional intelligence. Commenting for this book, Price said, "There is an overemphasis on STEM studies and technical learning in engineering education. Emotional capabilities often make the difference in career success, yet we focus on making students technically competent. The iFoundry curriculum incubator is a big idea—teaching so-called soft skills, making student engagement a priority, and reinforcing the idea that you can really trust the students, and they usually come through."

Additionally, during this early time period, many face-to-face meetings, town hall meetings, talks to departments, and talks to assemblies of administrators were held, and many of the persuasive materials prepared are still available and archived on the web.

Critical to this effort was the use of pungent and memorable terms to both criticize the status quo and to gesture at an alternative and hopefully better future. For example, early in these persuasive outreach efforts, the term "math-science death march" was coined to describe and implicitly criticize the status quo practice of weeding out the "unfit" in a series of difficult courses with tough curves and minimal care or support. In iFoundry talks to students and educators, the team talked about the three joys: the joy of engineering, the joy of learning, and the joy of community.

In the old days, a professor would take pride in standing at the front of a class the first day and saying, "Look to your left and look to your right: two of the three of you won't be here next year." iFoundry reframed the old left-right story with the following version: "Look to your left and look to your right; those are the two people who will help you make it through a challenging educational experience."

An interesting thing about this storytelling and reframing was how quickly it changed behavior and action. Time and time again, the telling of a different story resulted *immediately* in a different behavior from students and faculty. By telling the collaborative version of the left-right story, iFoundry students immediately saw their role differently and acted accordingly. A year or two after the iFoundry launch, a number of the 2009 cohort talked about how powerful that language was and how it got them to work together with one another almost immediately.

This would be a mystery if it were not for current results in change management. A particularly influential resource in the early days of iFoundry was the Heath brothers' book, *Made to Stick*. The book makes the points that language is important in change processes and that sticky language is more conducive to change. For the Heath brothers, language is sticky when it follows the "SUCCES" model. That is, sticky language is Simple, Unexpected, Concrete, Credible, Emotional, and a Story.

David Goldberg: "The missing basics"

After iFoundry was going, there was a lecture on campus by Dan Heath, coauthor of *Made to Stick*. I had a chance to go to the lecture and meet him afterward, and I was taken by both the power of his talk and the predictive power of the SUCCES model. I realized that some of the ways in which we were using language in iFoundry to both shake up and use culture were powerful partially because they were sticky and that we could use the model to design even stickier language.

One example of this was the coinage of the *missing basics*. I had given talks about the seven things that were missing in engineering education and had labeled them with famous personages in intellectual history. The items that were missing were (1) questioning, (2) labeling, (3) modeling, (4) decomposing, (5) experimenting, (6) creating, and (7) communicating. Each is, respectively, a failure of (1) Socrates 101, (2) Aristotle 101, (3) Hume 101, (4) Descartes 101, (5) Locke 101, (6) da Vinci 101, and (7) Newman 101 (item 7 refers to Paul Newman and the famous line in *Cool Hand Luke*, "What we have here is a failure to communicate").

I realized that the overall structure passed the SUCCES model, but it needed a better name. As I reflected about the common objection that faculty raise to reform, "But wouldn't that dilute *the basics*?" I understood that a sticky name for these missing items in engineering education could simply be a counterpoint to the objection.

Thus, I coined the term "missing basics of engineering," and the coinage, the paper, and the TEDxUIUC talk remain popular ways to talk about the need for the missing critical and creative thinking skills of engineering.

Examples like these later encouraged Mark Somerville and me to highlight conceptual clarity and sticky language in courses that we offer on personal and organizational change for engineering education.

The issue of conceptual clarity has also been very important to these efforts, and the founding of iFoundry was tied to the founding of an independent series of workshops on philosophy and engineering. The Forum on Philosophy, Engineering, and Technology continues to this day (www.fpet2014.org).

The coinage of the missing basics was an important turning point in using sticky language with intention to help change culture. It was also a key element in designing the early iFoundry freshman experience.

Connecting the dots of a freshman experience

As fall 2009 approached, the iFoundry team was working toward the launch of a freshman experience, and the effort had several pieces, as depicted in the figure.

1. The iCommunity freshman community
2. A course, Introduction to the Missing Basics of Engineering (ENG 100++).
3. A particular sequence of special events
4. The use of particular aspirational language with iFoundry freshmen and faculty

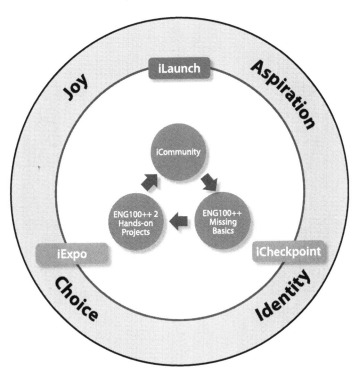

The evolution of the iCommunity freshman community has already been discussed. Here it is depicted in the figure as one of the three inner circles. It was envisioned as a "required" extracurricular effort for students joining the iFoundry cohort and as a companion to the course.

The course Introduction to the Missing Basics of Engineering, or ENG100++, took the missing basics described above and created a one-credit course with two parts: (1) missing basics discussion section and (2) projects course. Each part met for one hour a week. This course was designed to replace the existing required freshman course ENG100, a zero-credit introduction to campus and the College of Engineering.

The time sequence of special events started with a welcoming event called iLaunch to help incoming students understand iFoundry and to build community. The second event on the schedule occurred around midterm and was called iCheckpoint; it involved iTeams in iCommunity sharing their plans and progress through two short presentations per team. The final event iExpo was modeled after Olin's year-end expo as a celebration of student learning and accomplishment.

Finally, in speaking to iFoundry students, language was used so that engineering education was reframed as a more student-centered process: "We approach this iFoundry with the joy of engineering, learning, and community. We respect your aspirations, we respect your choices, and we are here to witness and support the formation of your identity as a person and as an engineer."

Faced with the need to consult and get buy-in from each of the member departments, this seemed like about the best that could be done, but how could the start-up actually start, and how could it get students to sign up for an untested program?

Managing change

Karen Hyman, a lifelong educator and administrator who had raised four children, felt a special dedication to issues of educational reform. She avidly read books and papers about the state of American education, saying that she "was a bit of a bag lady," carrying her satchels of reading material with her wherever she went. Hyman, who had a position as director of public engagement in the computer sciences department at the University of Illinois, was relatively new to the college. She had arrived when her husband was recruited for a job, and the move had initially made her nervous. "I came under a dark cloud," she admitted. "I didn't know where in the world I was going to find a home for myself." Her job in the computer sciences department turned out to be fully involving, but she was still itching to do more. Often, she felt frustrated, wondering how they could really give students more than technical knowledge—how they could help create whole, creative human beings.

One day, as Hyman was walking through the quad, lugging her bag of books, a colleague joined her and they started talking. She found herself telling him about her concerns for the students.

"Oh, are you into that?" he asked, smiling. "You have to go talk to David Goldberg. He's cooking up something amazing."

Hyman dashed off an email and was delighted to learn that iFoundry was looking for an associate director to help manage the program and the admissions process. She was immediately interested, and she had the admissions experience to seal the deal. She signed on to become, as she joked, "iFoundry's chief cook and bottle washer."

Simultaneously, the partnership with Olin College was formalized. The two institutions pledged to work together to transform engineering education through exchanges, programs, and other forms of institutional cooperation—particularly programs that demonstrated scalable innovation and reform. They also committed to trying to create a movement that would expand beyond their institutions.

The first event of the partnership was the Summit on the Engineer of the Future at Olin College in March 2009. The event had the flavor of a rally, and some of those present found themselves thinking, "This is the precursor to a movement."

How to recruit?

Meanwhile, as the framework for the iFoundry experience was being established, the recruitment for the first freshman class was well under way. Recalling the process, Hyman observed, "The University of Illinois was one of a number of schools that required students to select a specialization at age seventeen or eighteen. It's a slightly perverse system—narrowing choices at a time when they should be broader. I wanted to create a system to open up the chance for students to tell us what they were passionate about."

A letter went out to all newly admitted engineering students asking them to consider signing up for a unique opportunity. "Our approach was also designed to appeal to parents," Hyman explained. "They were sending their young kids to a large research university, and we were offering them a supportive community within that big, anonymous place." The students were asked to write two essays about their aspirations and interests. They were encouraged to write about their passions as well and name what courses would interest them outside of the standard engineering offerings. (For example, one student wrote of being passionate about the history of roller coasters; he wanted to build them someday.)

The responses revealed three types of primary interests, which Hyman charted:

- **Technology entrepreneurs.** One group was represented by a student who said that he aspired to be "the next Max Levchin," cofounder of PayPal and a graduate of the University of Illinois. In other words, this kind of student wanted to be the next great Illinois tech entrepreneur.
- **Social entrepreneurs/activists.** The second group wanted to save the world—taking direct action with their engineering skills to help people. In other words, they wanted to be social

entrepreneurs by working in the developing world for Engineers without Borders or other organizations.

- **Cool technologists.** The third group just wanted to work on and be a part of creating innovative technology.

In speaking to students about these aspirations, iFoundry leaders repeatedly expressed their curiosity for and their respect toward student aspirations as a key to the iFoundry program.

At a meeting of the iFoundry Council composed of faculty from each of the member departments, Hyman shared the responses of the students, highlighting what their interests were. Those in attendance recalled that they could hear a pin drop. It was a question that had never been asked before: *Why do you want to be an engineer?* The faculty members perked up, interested. They were unaccustomed to asking students why they wanted to be engineers or hearing concrete, heartfelt answers to the question.

Planning for the fall continued. A handbook for the iCommunity was drafted that spelled out the rules of what might be called an epistemic game. Epistemic, or sometimes serious, games are those designed explicitly with the intent of promoting learning and increase in knowledge and know-how. After analyzing the application results, plans were made to respect the aspirations of the students and populate the iCommunity with four iTeams—entrepreneurship and innovation, engineering in service to society, services and systems engineering, and art and engineering design. Each team had at least one faculty advisor (an iFA), a student advisor (an iSA), and a corporate organizational adviser (iCOA) drawn from companies such as HP, IBM, Motorola, Skidmore, Owens & Merrill, and State Farm.

In August 2009, iFoundry admitted its first group of seventy-three freshmen. It was a funny animal. It wasn't a department or a unit. It was something of a start-up but not exactly. Initially, iFoundry relied on an intrinsic desire on the part of various faculty, along with the students, to build something new.

Working with the willing

One of the principles of iFoundry was that participation was strictly voluntary. The founders wanted to work with people who were interested in the concept and program, and they didn't want to persuade the uninterested or fight with those who opposed the effort. The idea was to engage with the willing and then embrace the once unwilling as soon as they became open to change.

> *The founders wanted to work with people who were interested in the concept and program, and they didn't want to persuade the uninterested or fight with those who opposed the effort. The idea was to engage with the willing and then embrace the once unwilling as soon as they became open to change.*

In the same way, iFoundry leadership wanted to bring on board those departments that were willing to try it. Enlisting support and buy-in was a process. With student recruitment under way in the spring of 2009, each department was asked to sign a memorandum of understanding, which was essentially a social contract between iFoundry and the department. It allowed iFoundry to work with the pilot students from the particular department in specific ways, making certain substitutions for an iFoundry class. The particular agreements varied slightly from department to department, depending on each unit's appetite for change. The memorandums of understanding assumed that the dean's signature authority could be used to override curriculum requirements for the iFoundry student participants so these pilot experiments could go ahead and students could receive credit for them.

When it was all done, twelve of thirteen departments had signed up. To the organizers' surprise, an early supporter of iFoundry, materials science and engineering (MatSE), was not among them. Behind the scenes, iFoundry organizers understood that the MatSE decision was more about academic politics than about iFoundry, and it seemed like it might make a good test case for iFoundry's opt-in policy. After all, part of the use of an opt-in policy is the belief that individual units will make choices aligned with their stakeholders' interests, if only those interests are expressed and heard.

The following year, MatSE *would* join iFoundry, and how this happened is an interesting piece of the story. When students that year received the associate dean's letter inviting them to join the iFoundry freshman experience, MatSE students tried to sign up and were told that their department was not part of the program. Almost immediately, the department received requests from students or their parents seeking admission to iFoundry. MatSE quickly reversed itself and joined the effort. In short, when stakeholder interests were revealed, the *un*willing became the *willing*.

At one level, this was a lesson about the power of student engagement and choice. At another level, this episode was a lesson in the power of a dot-connecting incubator to achieve coordinated results without centralized coordination. MatSE ended up making a decision to join the reform but without coercion or control from above. Their decision to choose reform was enabled by the architecture of iFoundry as well as the forces of competition and student choice.

"Do something cool"

When classes started, one thing iFoundry did was fly in a kid named Cory Levy to give a talk to the iFoundry freshmen. iFoundry leadership had heard about Cory from ShareThis CEO Tim Schigel. Although only a high school senior, Levy was a marvel—and already a successful young entrepreneur who had an amazing ability to connect. His virtual Rolodex was stuffed with the names of some of the great innovators of the times. Levy would go on to spend a year at the University of Illinois before raising $1 million for his start-up, One.

The event took place in the NCSA Auditorium, and to the assembled students, iFoundry team, and faculty friends, the setup was a bit weird. Usually engineering departments bring in gray-haired alumni who tell war stories from long careers that are only remotely of interest to the assembled eighteen- and nineteen-year-olds, who have difficulty relating to the difference in age and life experience of the speaker. Put another way, the old guys just don't seem very relevant today.

This event was upside down and backward. Here a high school student was talking to freshmen, and he had a message that was empowering in a way that no old-timer could ever replicate.

Levy started, and he was on fire—pure inspiration. He told the story of being an enterprising ball boy for professional tennis tournaments in Houston, Texas, and piling up a ton of autographs on balls, which he began to sell on eBay. When he ran out, he approached famous entrepreneur and Dallas Mavericks owner Mark Cuban, and, remarkably, Cuban took an interest in Cory and helped him set up a sports memorabilia arbitrage system. Levy told another story of seeking an internship with a venture capital firm in Silicon Valley, failing to get an internship with his preferred firm the first year—he got an internship with a different VC firm—and succeeding the next.

The iFoundry freshmen were wide-eyed and all ears as Levy relayed story after story, tales of initiative, networking, failure, and success. The iFoundry freshmen were thinking, "If a high school kid can do this, so can I." The effect of Levy's stories would have been enough, but Cory saved his best for last.

Toward the end, he said, "Pull out a sheet of paper." The students in the audience did so. Then he said, "I want you to make a *failure résumé*. Write down all the times in your life when you failed and what you learned from them." Everyone looked a little surprised at the request, and Levy continued, "If you're not failing enough, you're not taking chances, and you're not learning." The audience members still seemed a bit stunned, but then they started scribbling madly. After a while, Levy checked in with the students and sampled some of their failures, saying encouraging words

> *Do something cool—and do it now. If you fail, that's good. Do something else.*
>
> **—Cory Levy**

about the biggest and boldest of them, but the effect was stunning. Cory had just given a group of seventy-three freshmen permission to network, permission to fail, and permission to take initiative. In essence he told them, "Do something cool—and do it now. If you fail, that's good. Do something else." And they did.

Talks like Cory's were influential and inspirational, but in the beginning of iFoundry, it wasn't clear whether any of this was working. The effort itself was a small pilot—it was only one credit hour in a sixteen- to eighteen-hour class load for the freshmen. How could such a small "peashooter" of an effort do anything interesting? But something was percolating, and the little pilot was in the process of changing educational hearts, minds, and culture in a disproportionate way. An incident a few weeks into the first semester demonstrated this vividly.

"We weren't sure you were serious"

At the beginning of the first semester, the iCommunity had been organized into iTeams with four charges: (1) perform service or projects, (2) support each other academically, (3) explore the world of work, and (4) have a social life and a team identity. The iCommunity was essentially a zero-credit activity, so there were no requirements, and early in the semester, things went well, the students elected officers, they met with their student and faculty advisors, and all seemed fine.

As part of the ENG100++ course, students were required to blog. Early on, they expressed happiness with the launch event, but as time went on, they became increasingly dissatisfied with the lack of structure in the iFoundry experience, and many of their complaints are still available online. "These iFoundry guys don't know what they're doing. Why don't they tell us what they want these iTeams to do?" The students didn't understand that the approach was intentional and the responses to their complaints were tailored to their aspirations.

Recalling the three types of students—entrepreneurs, those who wish to help others, and those who wish to build innovative technology—the iFoundry answer was clear and direct: "You're an entrepreneur. Start a business! You want to save the world. Start saving! You want to work on cool technology. Build something!"

At the time of these interactions, it wasn't clear whether any of this was working, but iFoundry leaders continued to trust the process, and as midterm rolled around, it was time for iCheckpoint. iCheckpoint was held at night in the Coordinated Science Laboratory building. The group had box meals before the session, and then each team was divided in two and made two presentations in two different rooms.

The iTeam presentations were well constructed and presented. Some teams had made more progress in the four challenge areas than others. Some presentations were better prepared and delivered, and part of the value of the session was the soft competition of comparing one team to another. No one wanted his or her iTeam to look bad or be behind.

At the end of the evening, the iCommunity came together in one auditorium for a wrap-up *kaizen* session. *Kaizen* is the Japanese word for continual improvement, and Karen Hyman started the ball rolling by saying, "iFoundry values improvement. What worked, and what should we do differently next time?"

Many suggestions were obtained. Some of them were small. Some of them were quite involved and extensive. Generally, the suggestions were helpful, and they were all recorded for future reflection and possible execution. But in the middle, one comment rocked iFoundry's (and, ultimately, Olin's) world in ways that are still difficult to fully grasp.

Jaime Kelleher, a material sciences and engineering student, raised her hand, and Karen Hyman called on her. "This isn't an improvement," Kelleher said. "I'd just like to make a comment."

Karen Hyman asked, "Jaime, what's your comment?"

And then Kelleher said the following words, which are etched in iFoundry memory:

"We weren't sure you were serious about us doing what
we wanted to do, and then we realized that you were,
and it was really cool."

Kelleher's simple observation sent shivers through Karen Hyman's body, and she looked at Dave Goldberg, and he smiled back, and both looks suggested that something special had just happened, but how special it was didn't become clear until a short time thereafter.

"What just happened?"

In the days following the iCheckpoint, iFoundry life returned to normal with missing basics course discussion sections and projects sessions, iCommunity meetings, and a general buzz of positive energy and activity, but something seemed different. Reports started coming in of students going places and doing things. Two of the teams got together and organized an iSkate social event. The art and engineering iTeam got on a bus and went to visit their iCOA at Skidmore, Owings, and Merrill headquarters in Chicago. Three entrepreneurship and innovation team members got on a plane and went to a Silicon Valley entrepreneurship conference after securing funding from their departments. The blog posts by students were more upbeat with less complaining. Something was different, and something was happening.

Earlier in the semester, iFoundry leadership had contracted with faculty members in the College of Education to do formal program assessment of the iFoundry effort, but the view at the beginning of the semester was that the assessment effort was longer term and that a semester-by-semester view would be sufficient. The recent uptick in student reports of initiative suggested that perhaps it was important to measure what was going on right now, and an emergency assessment program was put into place.

In spite of it being a peashooter program, the reviews were astonishingly positive. While there had been some confusion and frustration early on, by the end of the first semester, eighty percent of students were reporting that they understood the goals of iFoundry and felt those goals in their own work and lives.

Clearly, there was a strong shift from early in the semester to now. The intuition that something happened around iCheckpoint is supported by the data, but what happened is better represented by reviewing a smattering of student qualitative responses.

One student responded, "Sure I made the right career choice." Another said, "Making me more confident in my decision to be an engineer." And another, "I'm definitely more entrepreneurial." One more, "I think I feel more comfortable being an engineer." These responses speak clearly to vocation and identity, but one student said it in a way that speaks volumes about what iFoundry originally hoped would occur:

"Just an overall all-rounded engineer, not just a technician. A human, not just a problem solver."

One more student added, "The future looks brighter thanks to iFoundry."

A number of students in the original cohort were later interviewed for this book to reflect on their experiences. Kelleher told us what the entire experience meant to her. "I was originally attracted to the concept of iFoundry because I was excited to have hands-on experience right off the bat," she said, but she admitted that "it felt weird at first that we were left to do so much on our own and make our own decisions with our projects." In the end, however, Kelleher believed "it really gave us a clearer view of what it is like to be an engineer in the real world. I was also motivated by the enthusiasm of the other students in my iTeam."

Kelleher cited her most memorable iFoundry experience as being able to travel to Indonesia over winter break of her freshman year. "Through iFoundry, I was connected with a professor from the National University of Singapore who was helping to organize a service trip for students in their civil engineering club and had reserved extra room for a University of Illinois student," she said. "After arranging with my professors to take my final exams two weeks early, I found myself flying halfway around the world. I spent three weeks in Indonesia with twenty students from the National University of Singapore building a geotextile footpath at a boarding school. This experience really threw me out of my comfort zone and taught me a lot about working in a diverse team in an unfamiliar situation. I believe that the experience is reflected in many of my later decisions to pursue opportunities I might not have otherwise considered."

When the invitation from NUS came in for iFoundry students to join the trip to Indonesia, iFoundry leaders realized that it was right on top of Illinois final exams and assumed that no one would be able to do it. That Jaime wanted to go to Indonesia was in some sense less surprising than her daring as a freshman to miss final exams her first semester on campus and her chutzpah and initiative in arranging with faculty members to do so.

As Aman Kapur, then a general engineering student from Jaipur, Rajasthan, India, put it, "Engineers aren't robots just following orders; they are critical thinkers who can not only analyze complexities with ease but also apply themselves in areas unthinkable to anyone. They are not just people who fix problems but people who visualize a better world."

Karen Lamb, a senior who was in the second iFoundry class, said that early in her freshman year she was considering changing her major to business because the engineering classes were so theoretical. That changed when she took the one-credit iFoundry class. "I wasn't sure that engineering was right for me because I wasn't super passionate about any of my classes," she said. "I had started taking upper-level calculus and was failing because I wasn't working with any other students. I was trying to do all the work by myself, which was a huge mistake that a

Engineers aren't robots just following orders; they are critical thinkers who can not only analyze complexities with ease but also apply themselves in areas unthinkable to anyone.

—Aman Kapur

lot of freshmen make at Illinois. The iFoundry class was really small. You'd work on a project with, like, four other students. It wasn't technically super challenging, but it was a lot of fun. I found that I really liked working on a practical engineering problem where you had to build something and work with a team of students. I realized that that was really the core of what engineering is and that I should try to stick it out through some of those more theoretical classes."

That was exactly the point, and it was hitting home. Matthew Johnson, a computer engineering major from Illinois, shared, "One thing that concerned me about becoming an engineer was that there was this image of a typical engineer being some intelligent yet antisocial person who would just be sitting at a desk crunching numbers and solving physics problems all day. But I knew engineering had to be more than just cold, hard math and science. Engineering involves people; it's more social than most would think. Engineering involves creative and innovative design, drawing upon artistic concepts, and catering to the needs and hopes and aspirations of others. I think iFoundry has that same stance. iFoundry seeks to create a better engineer, not one who can just do the technical work but one who can also interact with and understand people, be creative, and make something totally unique that meets the deepest needs and desires of others. I joined iFoundry because that is the type of engineer I aspire to be."

David Goldberg: "The Olin effect at Illinois?"

As the students started to just take initiative and do stuff without permission—we called these *aspirationally assertive acts*—and as the assessment data started to come in, I was both excited by what was happening and puzzled by it. On the one hand, when earlier I had visited Olin in 2008, I had hoped for the day when Illinois freshmen would express strong identity as engineers and take initiative on their own—I longed for the day when we would have the Olin effect at Illinois, **and here it was**. I remember calling Mark and Sherra and sharing the news, and it was similarly exciting and disorienting to them.

Mark said, "Yes, that sounds like the Olin effect." The confidence. The initiative. The emotionally strong identity as engineers.

But how? How did such a small effort achieve the good stuff? The iFoundry freshman experience was a one-hour course with a zero-credit extracurricular activity in the iCommunity. It had a budget one-twentieth to one-tenth size of other Big 10 freshman programs. It lived in the middle of a traditional curriculum and a conservative culture that was focused mainly on research. How could something so modest achieve the student enthusiasm, drive, identity, and initiative of an Olin?

And the truth of it at the time was that we couldn't answer the question. By all rights, the Illinois program had not done enough. In September 2009, I was thinking about a bigger budget for 2010, more hours in the curriculum, more faculty, more students, a bigger effort. The midterm surprise of 2009 was inexplicable. In conversations with Mark and Sherra, we started to talk about intrinsic motivation as an explanation. All of us had just read Dan Pink's book *Drive*, and it seemed like even the language of intrinsic motivation wasn't enough.

In a certain sense, the results of the iFoundry 2009 pilot were a fundamental anomaly for both Olin and iFoundry. In starting Olin, it was assumed that you had to build studio-friendly facilities, redesign the whole curriculum, redesign all the courses, hire educationally committed faculty, shift the culture away from research as primary, fundamentally change the pedagogy, build cool dormitories, and construct a residential experience for maximum community and cultural effect, among many other things. And iFoundry leaders, and almost all other engineering educational specialists, believed the same things. But here in flesh and blood was a real-world example built opportunistically with scraps and duct tape, and it achieved authentic and strong student engagement and affect.

Now the result is made possible, in part, because the recognition in 2008 of the Olin effect as something to be imitated shifts the measurement away from what traditional educational assessors like to assess. If you're looking for emotional affect and not course changes and pedagogical changes, your view of change will be different.

But even still, the results were unsettling. In everyone's mind, the 2009 peashooter of an effort hadn't done enough, but it had in actuality done quite a lot. Everyone knew that this needed to be explained: the iFoundry and Olin partners both understood that in that puzzle were important clues about how to get engineering education transformation to happen broadly, inexpensively, and well. We will return to that puzzle in subsequent chapters, and later events will help us offer solutions that both solve the puzzle and show practical ways to transform engineering education.

3

The Spirit of Invention
Recapturing the Inspiration
of Engineering Education

*The engineer requires the imagination to visualize the needs
of society and to appreciate what is possible as well as the
technological and broad social age understanding to bring
his vision to reality.*

—Sir Eric Ashby

The year was 1891. At the Saturday Afternoon Club, an informal gathering of architects and engineers meeting in a Chicago chophouse, the featured guest rose to speak. He was a portly man of wide reputation, already acknowledged as one of the great architects of the era. Daniel H. Burnham had been appointed to be the chief architect of the Chicago World's Fair, known as the World's Columbian Expedition in honor of the four-hundredth anniversary of Christopher Columbus's landing in America, which would open in Chicago two years hence. His words to the gathering were by way of a complaint and a challenge. His complaint was that the engineering community had yet to come up with a towering, dramatic feat that would rival the 984-foot Eiffel Tower that had stunned the world at the Paris Exposition in 1889. He called on the engineers in the room to rise to the occasion and create something "original, daring, and unique."

There may have been some grumbling in the room, as Burnham made a point of saying that *his* people, the architects, were carrying the weight of innovation and the engineers hadn't held up their end of the bargain. But one man was listening closely, and he was not grumbling, because he thought he had the idea in his hip pocket.

George Washington Gale Ferris, a handsome young man with deep-set blue eyes and a thick mustache, had been practicing civil engineering for only a decade, but he thought he had the answer. Later, Ferris would say that the notion had been in the back of his mind since he was a boy. Now, captured by the possibility, he began to sketch out the details for a marvelous concept—a giant spinning wheel, like a grand circle in the sky, higher than any structure in Chicago, which would carry more than two thousand human riders in gently rocking wooden cars above the fair.

Soon after, Ferris presented the fair's ways and means committee with his plans and was immediately deemed crazy. He was laughed out of the building and referred to as "the man with the wheels in his head." Burnham himself scoffed at the idea that such a structure could withstand the heavy winds off Lake Michigan. The consensus was that Ferris's scheme was dramatic but utterly impossible.

Ferris was not deterred. Cheerful, optimistic, and possessing an easygoing charisma and great powers of persuasion, he went about enlisting the support of a group of prominent engineers and architects—and, perhaps more important, the financial support of investors, to the tune of $400,000. When he returned to the ways and means committee, the skeptics remained, but the opposition was softening. Unfortunately, the plan wasn't authorized until the end of November 1892, with scant months in the dead of a Chicago winter remaining for construction.

The creation of Ferris's wheel involved the labor of hundreds of engineers, architects, steelworkers, masons, steamfitters, and other skilled laborers. At times they were forced to work in drifts of snow as high as three feet. Construction ran late and wasn't completed until a month and a half after the opening of the fair. But on June 16, 1893, there it stood, a giant wheel, supported by two 140-foot towers, connected by a huge axle, gleaming above the fair in the waning light of an early summer evening.

For the wheel's maiden run, Ferris and his wife, Margaret, stepped into the first car, and it jolted upward. The mayor and other dignitaries and special guests entered other cars, their courage bolstered by a case of champagne. When the Ferrises reached the peak, Margaret stood to her feet in the swaying car, with the fair and Chicago in her sights, and raised a glass of champagne to toast her husband.

In the end, Ferris's invention became a physical symbol of engineering promise—a million and a half people would get on board during the fair. George Ferris had, in effect, reinvented the wheel.

The 1893 World's Fair was in every respect an ode to engineering innovation. While Ferris's achievement was the most visually dramatic, the engineering feat of electricity was the most dazzling. The fairgrounds were illuminated by a vast alternating current system, introduced by Westinghouse. On the opening evening of the fair, when President Grover Cleveland pressed a button, more than one hundred thousand lights burst into power, accompanied by gasps and cheers from a crowd of more than seven hundred thousand people.

In his bestselling book, *Devil in the White City*, Erik Larson describes the wonder: "The lamps that laced every building and walkway produced the most elaborate demonstration of electric illumination ever attempted and the first large-scale test of alternating current. The fair alone consumed three times as much electricity as the entire city of Chicago. These were important engineering milestones, but what visitors adored was the sheer beauty of seeing so many lights ignited in one place, at one time . . . it was like getting a sudden vision of Heaven."

Engineering rock stars

The Society for the Promotion of Engineering Education grew out of the 1893 World's Fair, and it was widely acknowledged that to study engineering was to be on the cutting edge of social and technological change. In the coming decades, engineering would herald a new era with the automobile, the airplane, continental railroads and highways, the telephone, the radio, and bridges that spanned vast waterways. Between 1850 and 1920, the number of working engineers would grow from two thousand to 136,000. At the American Society of Engineers, one speaker proclaimed, "We are the priests of material development, of the work which enables other men to enjoy the fruits of the great sources of power in Nature, and of the power of mind over matter. We are priests of the new epoch, without superstitions."

Many electrical and civil engineers during this era were like rock stars. They were the heroes and the leaders of a modern business model that featured large-scale development and world-changing inventions. Far from being mere practitioners of applied science, they practiced in a social laboratory, producing breakthroughs that had never been imagined before. In this setting,

Engineers were the innovators. They didn't just work for business; they created business models. They made things that inspired and delighted and mattered.

engineers were the innovators. They didn't just work for business; they created business models. They made things that inspired and delighted and mattered.

This romantic view of engineering began to fray in the post–World War I years as engineers became socially captive to the establishment. As David Noble put it in *America by Design*, they went from being social change makers to becoming a "domesticated breed"—and this consciousness pervaded engineering schools.

World War II shook loose the cobwebs, but this was both good news and bad news for America's future engineers.

The elevation of science

Vannevar Bush, an electrical engineer who had been dean of engineering at MIT, was appointed by President Franklin D. Roosevelt to direct the Office of Scientific Research and Development. The office was top secret, and Bush reported solely to the president. During the course of the war, the greatest scientific and technical minds of the times would work to develop the most advanced weapon systems under the aegis of Bush's office—with the grand finale being the Manhattan Project to build the atomic bomb.

In his interface with military leaders, Bush was always painfully aware of the bias against engineers in favor of "true" scientists. Among the military, engineers were unfairly and unflatteringly designated as the servants of scientific mastery. (This bias didn't end with the war, and Bush was always a bit bitter about the failure to give engineers their due. Of the 1969 moon landing he said, "The press hailed it as a great scientific achievement. Of course, it was nothing of the sort. It was a marvelously skillful engineering job.")

Despite many of the engineering feats of World War II, the word "engineer" was rarely used. Under Bush's leadership, they were all "scientists." And by 1944, Roosevelt was already thinking about how to put these *scientists* to work for the good of the nation in peacetime. He wrote Bush a letter asking him to consider the proposition: "The information, the techniques, and the research experience developed by the Office of Scientific Research and Development and by the thousands of scientists in the universities and in private industry, should be used in the days of peace ahead for the improvement of the national health, the creation of new enterprises bringing new jobs, and the betterment of the national standard of living."

Roosevelt asked Bush to make recommendations about how to achieve this, but the president did not live to see them. In 1945 Bush submitted his report, "Science—The Endless Frontier," to President Harry Truman. Front and center was the call for a new National Research Foundation to keep America on the cutting edge. It would become the National Science Foundation in 1950. The funding stream unleashed by this decision was, in large part, responsible for the increasing emphasis on obtaining research funding and the research mission, generally shifting from government labs to universities. Another effect of the war research and development effort and Bush's report to the president was in the area of engineering curriculum.

When the American Society for Engineering Education (formerly the Society for the Promotion of Engineering Education) commissioned a study on how to improve engineering education, the resulting 1955 Report on Evaluation of Engineering Education was heavy on science and physics. It was called the Grinter Report after its chief author, Professor L. E. Grinter. The original draft of the report recommended the "bifurcation" of engineering education into two tracks—one with a heavy basic science/engineering science emphasis aimed at preparing students for graduate study, and the other with a strong emphasis on engineering analysis and design to prepare graduates for professional practice. This was not received well by the deans of engineering, though, so the final report attempted to combine the two, resulting in the first track overshadowing the second. In the end, there was a de-emphasis on design and practical engineering. Perhaps with one eye toward the boom in research funding available to research universities and another toward the perceived increased status of scientific research, the report also recommended an elevation of the organization of engineering education to favor graduate programs and PhD instructors—as PhDs were needed to win NSF funding.

The Grinter proposal wasn't wholeheartedly accepted in the beginning. But then Sputnik burst into the competitive consciousness, and science won the day. Since the 1960s, this approach—heavy on science, light on design and practicality, and highly regimented—has been the standard in U.S. engineering schools. Given the United States' standing after the war, the U.S. model has also been widely studied and imitated around the world. In certain respects the move toward more science made sense for the times.

For one thing, the technologies of the twentieth century—from the radar to the airplane to mass production—relied increasingly on scientific understanding. The knowledge required to contribute to these technologies outstripped the knowledge, for example, that Ferris exploited in creating his wheel.

On the other hand, misgivings about the removal of practical and design subjects were expressed almost as soon as the Grinter changes were made. In the early 1960s, for example, a number of schools, including MIT, Carnegie Mellon, Syracuse, UCLA, Berkeley, RPI, and the University of Illinois, received grants to explore the reinjection of design into the engineering curriculum, and in 1962 a conference was held at UCLA to report on the progress of the grant-holding schools. The invention and diffusion of the now reasonably widespread practice of industrial-sponsored capstone senior design courses date back to this early reaction to the Grinter changes.

Despite these activities, the Grinter curriculum has remained largely entrenched. More needs to be said about more recent efforts to reform the engineering curriculum, but it is useful at this juncture to take a longer view of the whole notion of the university, the role of the professor, and the fate of the student in what we shall call an *assembly of experts*.

The university as an assembly of experts

Engineers moved from a place of leadership, initiative, and general stewardship of enterprise in the nineteenth century to a place of social captivity, obedience, and narrowly defined technical expertise just after World War II. In a moment, we will sweep forward to understand what has happened since the war and its relevance to engineers and engineering education, but to better understand the historical sweep and the forces at work on the university, let's turn back the clock to the eleventh century.

The year is 1088, and the location is Bologna, Italy. In that year, a sixth-century codification of Roman law discovered at Pisa started to be taught in Bologna, and students from many lands came and entered in contract to gain this knowledge. The Latin name *universitas* originally translates to a group of people forming a society, guild, corporation, or community. In the early days students were organized into groupings by country or land, and they hired scholars to teach them. This early form of student-centered education disappeared over time, and the professors formed faculties and the university became the assembly of self-governing experts we recognize today.

Sweeping forward to more modern times, universities start publishing journals in the eighteenth century, the German model of the university in the nineteenth century introduces the importance of research seminars and laboratories, and the ensuing rise of specialization continues. These organizational innovations spread, but the university in many ways remains the assembly of experts it became shortly after the founding of the university in the eleventh century.

Take 1: Information, organizations, and work

The story of the university is one of knowledge and information, and the institution that began as an assembly of experts back in Bologna came forward past World War II intact—actually strengthened—with growing stature, increased funding for scholarly activities, and greater specialization in ways that were well aligned with the cost of knowledge and information, the notion of an organization, and the practice of work in those times.

Just after World War II, knowledge and information were expensive, hard to get, and, as result, hard to synthesize. Thus, as an economist might say, returns to expertise were high. The university as an assembly of experts was in ascendance. In eleventh-century Bologna, students flocked to what was simply an archeological find of some old documents followed by the teaching of what was perceived to students as valuable knowledge: Roman law.

Fast-forward to the 1940s and 1950s and students were doing essentially the same thing, except the treasure trove of knowledge was larger, broader, and more valuable. Those who flocked to the feet of the keepers of knowledge did so with the implicit promise that the received knowledge would unlock the doors to rewarding careers. Combine these historical circumstances with veterans, in many nations, returning home from the war and these were heady times for higher education.

Simultaneously, the war effort had mobilized corporations to churn out machines and material at unprecedented scale. Many of the organizations of the time were large, hierarchically structured, and compartmentalized into functional specialties. Employees were valued for their expertise or skill, compartment by compartment.

For example, a 1947 postcard of the Ford River Rouge plant in Dearborn, Michigan, shows the huge industrial site, flanked by an ore freighter! In those days, Henry Ford made his own steel. This was not an era where consultants intoned, "Stick to your core competence." This was a time when enormous organizations integrated vertically and horizontally as it suited their owners and helped their profits. This was a time when technologies concentrated power in the hands of a few and a time when economies of scale ruled commerce like an iron law.

The notion of work then was also quite different from that of our times. Photographs show massive assembly plants with large rooms of workers dutifully toiling at station after station of almost endless assembly lines or in sterile offices with row after row of desks, neatly aligned all the same, with the workers trained the same, even dressed the same. The conformity of the times was so widespread

For workers of the time, including engineers, the way to advance was clear: learn the stuff that needed to be learned and then fit in, become an organizational cog.

that it inspired a famous indictment in William Whyte's 1956 book, *The Organization Man.* Whyte described the organization man this way: "The ones I am talking about . . . have left home, spiritually as well as physically, to take the vows of organization life, and it is they who are the mind and soul of our great self-perpetuating institutions"—such as the engineering student who graduated into "the huge drafting room of Lockheed." For workers, including engineers, the way to advance was clear: learn the stuff that needed to be learned and then fit in, become an organizational cog.

Individual initiative of the kind practiced by the Ferrises of old was frowned upon.

So, just after the war, knowledge and information were dear; experts were highly valued; organizations were large, hierarchical, vertically and horizontally integrated, and specialized; and workers were obedient and valued largely for conforming to the expectations of the organization.

The university and higher education of the time were well aligned with these phenomena. Universities themselves were large, hierarchical, and specialized, and students were expected to be and were, for the most part, obedient. The consensus of what the university was—going back to Bologna—worked for those times. That stability and alignment were soon to be shattered, the result of three missed revolutions.

Three missed revolutions

We live in a different world today. Tom Friedman tells us "the world is flat." Richard Florida tells us about "the rise of the creative class." Dan Pink says workers today need "a whole new [creative] mind." Against the backdrop of the story of the postwar world, these words sound strange. We do live in a different world. How could things be so different? What happened?

In short, between World War II and now, we've had three *missed revolutions.* We use the term "missed" in the sense that private industry was rocked by them and they barely touched the university at all. Universities do teach content related to the three missed revolutions, but it is fair to say that they don't practice their lessons in the way private enterprise does.

The three missed revolutions are:

1. The entrepreneurial revolution
2. The quality revolution
3. The information technology (IT) revolution

We touch on each one very briefly.

The entrepreneurial revolution started after World War II, and the story of Silicon Valley is familiar around the globe. Upstart entrepreneurs, household names today, started now-famous companies in Silicon Valley garages. The founders and the spirit of entrepreneurship were important, but the networking, formation of new institutions around venture capital, and establishment of a culture that valued risk taking—and accepted failure—were in many ways just as important as the founders and the businesses they created.

The quality revolution had its roots in statistical quality methods developed before the war, but after the war, the quality teaching of individuals such as W. Edwards Deming and Joseph Juran traveled over to war-ravaged Japan. Embracing both the qualitative and quantitative teachings, Japanese manufacturers eventually leapfrogged those in the West, electronics and automobiles being among the most notable examples. Today, around the globe, quality manufacturing techniques (lean, six-sigma, just-in-time production) are embraced by almost all companies, if they wish to be competitive.

The invention of the transistor happened just after the war in 1948. Over the ensuing decades, this led to the integrated circuit, the microprocessor, the personal computer, the Internet, and the graphical web browser. Taken together, this series of inventions unleashed a kind of interaction and interconnection that was unprecedented. Yes, the invention of telegraph, telephone, and radio in the nineteenth century opened the door to the wired and wireless world we now live in, but the kind of information flow made possible by the Internet allows a qualitatively different experience through the interchange of data, images, sounds, and video never before possible. The inventions individually were remarkable, their combination powerful, but how did they end up turning our world on its head? Two new laws of economics help us understand.

Two new laws of economics

In reviewing the landscape after World War II, we observed that the law of economics crucial to understanding those times was the law of increasing returns to scale. That is, in the early twentieth century up to and just after World War II, bigger was better. Large companies invested great sums in design, manufacture, and distribution, and these investments became profitable with large national enterprises selling to a growing and increasingly affluent mass market.

To understand how the three missed revolutions took place or how the world might be so different in the twenty-first century from the middle of the twentieth century, we turn to two other laws of economics. The first of these is called the *law of transaction costs*, and one version of the law says that as the costs of transacting business in the marketplace reduce, organizations become smaller and outsource more of their functions. This law was proposed by Ronald Coase, a British economist who served much of his academic career at the University of Chicago and recently passed away at age 102. His thinking about transaction costs and their effect on companies and other institutions resulted in his receiving a Nobel Prize in economics in 1991.

Transaction cost economics asks the question, "What are the consequences for organizations and the economy when using the free market is more or less expensive?" Buying, selling, contracting, and enforcing deals are not free, but many of the changes brought by the three missed revolutions have greatly reduced these so-called transaction costs. Transaction cost economics predicts that when costs of using the market increase, organizations will themselves be larger and integrate vertically and horizontally to optimize their profits. When costs of using the market decrease, companies can "stick to their core competence" and still make a good return. Seen in this way, Coase's law of transaction costs helps us understand why large vertically and horizontally integrated firms are no longer the norm. Companies more easily outsource more of their functions to contractors at home and abroad—globalization is most easily understood as a transaction cost phenomenon—and thus there is a premium to right sizing organizations.

Seen in this way, a big shift from World War II to now is the way in which the three missed revolutions have encouraged downsizing of companies. "Getting lean," "sticking to your core competence," and so forth are words of the nineties and the new millennium, not words of the postwar era. Reduction in transaction costs also has implications for the formation of institutions, and the institutions of entrepreneurial company formation and venture capital also can be understood through the lens of transaction cost thinking.

The ease with which smaller organizations can be set up and can interface with other organizations also makes employees less captive to a single employer. This leads to an increased democratization of the workplace, where strict hierarchies are more fluid, in which employees are expected to take initiative and deliver results.

But one thing is puzzling in this story. Yes, many companies are now leaner, many do outsource more of their work to independent contractors or other firms, and many companies are less rigid and more democratic. But we also notice certain kinds of companies getting bigger and bigger— Microsoft, Google, Facebook, and other Internet companies, for example. How can these growing companies be understood in economic terms, against the backdrop of transaction cost economics?

Fortunately, a second, and relatively new, law of economics helps us understand this seeming paradox. The so-called law of *increasing returns to network goods* developed by Irish-born electrical engineer and economist W. Brian Arthur suggests that there are certain kinds of goods that become more valuable as more people use them. For example, if you are the only person in the world using Microsoft Word, it is useful to you as a word processor but not as useful as it would be if more people used it and you were able to share and exchange documents with them. In general, the more people who use a network good that others know and use, the more valuable that good is. Many products and services in an Internet world have these positive returns to network scale.

Thus, because of Coase and Arthur we can now understand better why we increasingly live in a world of "core competence Davids" and "network return Goliaths," and this can also help us understand the ways in which technology and economics are working to change higher education.

Take 2: Information, organizations, and work

Earlier we took note that information right after World War II was expensive, hard to find and difficult to integrate. Organizations were big and relatively all encompassing, and workers obedient. What about now?

Today, information is cheap or free, easy to find, and easy to integrate. This is a remarkable change in a short time. The asymmetry between information "haves" and "have-nots" used to be immense. Now anyone with a laptop and an Internet connection is a "have" at the push of a button.

As the economics analysis of the last section points out, many companies today are leaner and stick to the things they are good at. For example, there are no ore freighters parked outside of the Rouge plant today, and Ford Motor is no longer making its own steel. Today, many industrial firms outsource things they routinely made in the past, things that are not directly tied to their competitive advantage.

Where once information was expensive, hard to find, and difficult to integrate, it is now cheap or free, easy to find, and easy to integrate.

We also note that many companies are *network big*, as they should be, according to W. Brian Arthur's theories. For example, Google's search engine is, in many ways, a loss leader for a vast advertising business, and the more people who use the search engine and are exposed to the advertising, the more valuable it is. Moreover, once you are signed into Google for search, it is useful, on transaction cost grounds, to offer you other sorts of services: e-mail, news, documents, and file storage, etc. So Google and companies like it get bigger, and traditional industrial firms stick to their core competence.

Finally, work isn't what it used to be. Where once companies demanded passive obedience, conformity, and the following of policy manuals and procedures, today many companies demand creativity, depend on initiative, and celebrate difference. Visitors to the Googleplex in Mountain View, California, are struck by the openness of the campus, the myriad and nicely appointed spaces and places for collaboration, and the food and personal services provided to employees to make their lives easier. Google and other more recently established companies know that their companies' futures depend on the creativity and initiative of their workers, and many of them have remade the workplace physically, culturally, and emotionally in alignment with those very different assumptions about work.

The industrial organization of today has undergone wrenching changes since the war, but, remarkably, the university of today is not so different in organization, process, or culture from times past. As noted earlier, the large, centralized, specialized organizations of the postwar era were well aligned with the universities of those times, but the university of today seems out of step. The mismatch is substantial in the domains of both teaching and research.

Challenging teaching expertise

Universities are currently abuzz about MOOCs—massive open online courses. MOOCs grew out of earlier initiatives such as MIT's open courseware initiative in which recorded lectures were put online free of charge. Viewers around the world could take advantage of renowned professors' lectures that previously could be experienced only through admission and tuition paid to MIT.

Now, companies such as Udacity, edX, and Coursera are collecting online lectures and materials from member educational institutions at an increasing pace, with member institutions signing up from around the world and individual students signing up to take the courses. Many challenges remain for MOOCs, including how to give credit for them, how to vet student performance, and how to build a business model around the whole enterprise, but the challenge to faculty expertise in the classroom is clear. Why pay salaries for faculty members to stand up and lecture, when cheap, well-produced, even, arguably, more knowledgeable and better-known professors can be watched online?

In thinking about MOOCs, the focus is often on the courseware, but the phenomenon of MOOCs is a transaction cost phenomenon. In the same way that Ford Motor Company no longer produces its own steel, some universities are experimenting with outsourcing their lectures. MOOCs are coming about because the technology of the web and Ronald Coase's law of transaction costs are encouraging it. Universities resist, but the economic forces are real, they will continue, and change will occur. Moreover, MOOC companies and institutions are network goods producers. The more people who use Khan Academy or Udacity, the more valuable those goods become. Educational institutions that reinvent themselves along network lines have the opportunity to remain large or grow. Those who view themselves in traditional terms will most likely be forced to narrow their focus to specialized core competence.

These changes will not come easily, but the laws of economics will be obeyed, and those organizations that adapt to the new reality can thrive and prosper; others may wither or die.

Challenging research expertise

Faculty members at research-intensive universities are sometimes unfazed by challenges to their expertise in the classroom. Research is the name of that game, and the entrenched status quo of the funded research can give the appearance that the forces shaking up the teaching part of higher education are unrelated to anything happening on the research side of the ledger. Unfortunately for this view, the same forces shaking up the classroom anew are undermining stability in the laboratory as well.

Recently, we received a Tweet from a young man named Jack Andraka. He had read some of our tweets about changing engineering education, and he tweeted back, "I want to change education, too." The tweet also contained an embedded link to a video that told his story.

A family friend was dying of pancreatic cancer, and Jack Andraka's work in ninth-grade biology class and online research led him to the idea of creating a cancer detection device using carbon nanotube technology. He was relatively certain the idea was viable, and he wrote to two hundred professors trying to get lab access; 199 turned him down flat, but one said maybe, and he was able to get access to the lab.

Andraka spent the next seven months at the lab, ultimately inventing a dipstick probe that successfully identified the cancer precursor mesothelin in lab rats with pancreatic cancer.

Andraka's invention won him first place at the 2012 Intel International Science and Engineering Fair, and the patenting process is ongoing. The movie attached to the link Andraka sent frames him as a modern-day Einstein, and he is an exceptional young man, but there have always been exceptional young people. A key aspect of this story is that Andraka was able to access the same papers as cancer experts, and this was a major factor in enabling him to create his invention. It is hard to imagine Andraka's counterpart in 1947 doing anything remotely similar, if only for the access problem.

Another interesting aspect of the story is what Andraka *didn't* need from the professor or the university. He didn't need their expertise. Andraka needed access to the lab and equipment, but he came to the lab and in a relatively short time did research work that in times past might have resulted in the granting of a PhD.

Andraka's story is not isolated. Increasingly, young people are taking more initiative earlier in their lives. Examples of young prowess in science and technology research continue to grow, and Mark Zuckerberg is perhaps the most notable of a growing list of successful young entrepreneurs who seem to be getting younger every week.

The larger challenge for higher education is also clear. In a world where researchers have low-cost access to research publications and materials, the university's role as a special producer of research is under attack. In many ways, the same economic and technological forces that are realigning commercial organizations are calling into question the core teaching and research missions of the university.

Shaking up a ten-century-old consensus

This discussion began at the founding of the university nearly ten centuries ago. Since then, the university has been a fairly stable assembly of experts, and there was a consensus about how learning occurred and how new knowledge was generated. Expert professors spoke, and students listened. Expert professors researched, and they apprenticed novice experts to sit at their feet. MOOCs and the Jack Andrakas of the world fundamentally shake this ten-century consensus at its core, and when we reflect about it more deeply, a different, even more unsettling, picture emerges. In a very real sense, *the whole notion of expertise is being challenged.*

The whole notion of expertise is being challenged.

In a world of open access, returns on expertise are generally diminished. This does not mean that expertise becomes valueless, but it does call into question professions that rely on narrow expertise to produce value and institutions that are overly dependent on expertise for their survival.

This is a double whammy, and good portions of the remainder of this book share reflections that are relevant to the remaking of an engineer appropriate to our times and transforming the institution of engineering education so that is sustainable in a new world of open access.

Singapore as canary in an Asian coal mine

For some time, students in Western countries have sought to become lawyers, medical doctors, and other professionals, almost anything but engineers. Although engineering was once considered a bootstrap into the middle class, it has largely lost its luster. Newspaper articles talk about the annual production of millions of engineers in China, India, and elsewhere in Asia, and if Western countries can't keep up, sometimes the argument is made that the world can make up the difference from a surplus in Asia or elsewhere. However, the dean of engineering at the

National University of Singapore, Chan Eng Soon, has been reading his enrollment figures, and he sees a trend that could be alarming to us all.

For many years in Singapore, engineering was the royal road to a good job and a high-paying salary, in much the way it was in the West, and mandated slots in engineering were filled with students seeking engineering as their first choice. But engineering as a career path is losing its luster in Singapore as it previously has in the West. While enrollment in engineering programs remains high, the field does not always attract the top tier of students. Just as elsewhere, many high-achieving Singaporean students are opting into medicine, law, and business in Singapore, and, increasingly, engineering is not considered attractive by students themselves.

Many reasons are given for this phenomenon. One reason is the differences in prestige; as students climb the socioeconomic ladder through a bootstrap profession such as engineering, they have higher hopes for their sons and daughters who pursue more autonomous, prestigious professions. Also, students are very sensitive to the marketplace, and the mismatches between engineering, engineering education, and the new world of work discussed earlier in this chapter are apparent to them and scare them off. Also, students are sensitive to the culture of different degree programs and aware of the competitive, sometimes hostile culture of engineering education; hence they opt to go into cultures that are more caring and collaborative.

To overcome these difficulties at NUS, Dean Chan has instituted the Design-Centric Programme as a platform to transform engineering education—to draw out the potential of the students, to empower them to think differently, deal with complexity, take big steps, innovate, collaborate and develop the habit of probing deeper. The ultimate goal is to attract young Singaporeans to a creative, design-oriented, and entrepreneurial kind of engineering. The program offers multiyear projects where engineering students from the different engineering disciplines can work together to develop new technologies or to solve problems that have societal impact. The culture of the educational environment encourages personal ownership of project direction, multidisciplinary teamwork, and innovations in design. The emphasis is on finding holistic solutions.

Singapore's Ministry of Education also understands the urgency of reinvigorating engineering education and making it attractive to young people in Singapore. It is spending large sums in starting a third university with an engineering program, Singapore University of Technology and Design, and many of the innovations of Olin and elsewhere have been studied and are being implemented as part of this new program.

The change in attitude of young Singaporeans toward engineering is an interesting phenomenon, one worthy of attention elsewhere. If the pattern holds up, the millions of engineers turned out in China and India might be temporary. Perhaps when those countries become sufficiently affluent, their kids won't want to be engineers, either. All the more reason to advocate for changes in engineering education that will make it relevant and highly valued in all societies.

Why can't we change?

As long as there has been formal engineering education, there has been engineering education reform. The Grinter Report and Educating the Engineer of 2020 are just two in a long line of reports advocating change over many decades. Engineers and engineering educators have always taken the mission of their profession and the education of young engineers seriously, and education reform has often been seen as a key to improvement. Over the years, reform (like Grinter) has taken place, but, more recently, the stresses of the three missed revolutions have made it difficult to reform quickly or boldly enough.

In the 1990s, the effects of the information age were being felt, and the National Science Foundation mounted a large funding program to form engineering education coalitions, in which groups of engineering schools were organized around large grants to bring about bold change. The coalitions were formed and reforms were made, but almost as soon as the money stopped, many of the changes reverted to original form. Few reforms diffused to schools not participating in a coalition, and looking back, a number of reports suggest that the reforms were not as bold or in alignment with the perceived need, even back then.

Following the perceived shortcomings of the coalitions, a number of reports and change efforts have been suggested or undertaken, and many of these contain useful reflections and suggestions. Often, the reports contain a list of recommended curricular, content, and pedagogical changes. Just as often, process concerns and implementation are left as an exercise to the readers of the report. There are two problems with this punch-list approach to education reform.

First, as long as the culture of engineering education was aligned with the world of work, modest reforms in course content, curriculum, and pedagogy were sufficient to stay abreast of the times. This chapter has suggested that the three missed revolutions leave us in a place where the culture of engineering education is fundamentally misaligned with the times, that the ten-century consensus of what a university is has broken down, and that major cultural change—not minor shifts to content, curriculum, and pedagogy—is necessary.

Second, these reports assume that the normal bureaucracy of the engineering school is capable of implementing the necessary changes. Everything in our recent empirical experience suggests otherwise. Established bureaucracies, at their best, are capable of small tweaks to existing routine, but if a major overhaul is needed, universities and schools of engineering do not have the organizational or leadership development chops to reform themselves effectively.

By contrast, private industry during the period of the missed revolutions has undergone wrenching changes, and many of these firms now regularly maintain staffs of coaches and organizational development specialists to help their executives develop and manage the complexities of our times and to help the organizations change by using a variety of change management techniques. The stability of the university and the engineering school has not previously needed these approaches, but the difficulty of the changes ahead suggests a more considered approach to the process of transforming engineering education.

Three lessons of history for engineering education

This chapter has covered a lot of territory historically to better understand the ways in which both the university and engineering have evolved to bring us to the present day. As we move ahead in the book and address what it means to be a Whole New Engineer in the environment of a whole new engineering education, we will keep in mind three challenges learned from history about this transformation.

First, the changes brought about by economics and technology in the world of work and the practice of engineering are large and cannot be addressed effectively with small tweaks to the existing curriculum, content, or pedagogical methods.

Second, students are sensitive to their world of work and to the culture of the educational system, and they reject, avoid, or leave engineering education for cause.

Third, the change management and leadership development approaches used to this point to bring about transformational change have not been sufficiently powerful to get the job done, broadly or well.

These are difficult challenges, and the remainder of the book will strive to provide sound, practical approaches that draw on our experience, good theory, and practices that are well developed elsewhere, even if not used in the academy.

The tantalizing success of efforts like those at Olin and iFoundry, together with this historical imperative, helps illuminate a path to a whole new engineer and a whole new engineering education. We start by considering how the technical mind of the twentieth-century engineer needs to be augmented with a broader view of how engineers think, feel, and show up in the world.

The Whole New Engineer
Engaging the Six Minds

The future belongs to ... creators and empathizers,
pattern recognizers and meaning-makers. These people ...
will now reap society's richest rewards and share its greatest joys.

—Daniel H. Pink

Howard Gardner grew up in the small mining town of Scranton, Pennsylvania, the son of German immigrants who had arrived in 1938, five years before he was born. They were Jewish in a community of very few Jews, who had escaped from the Holocaust, where many family members had perished. They never shared with him the story of their death-defying escape from Germany or the fact that they arrived in the United States on the very day that Kristallnacht exploded across Germany, decimating the close-knit Jewish community in their hometown of Nuremberg.

Many years later, finally hearing his family's story, Gardner would describe how "learning" about the Holocaust occurred as an emotional discovery more than a rational one. This experience would help shape the central idea of his career and research—that people come to know and understand their lives and their world in more ways than just intellectually.

He credits his tutelage at Harvard College under psychoanalyst Erik Erikson, sociologist David Riesman, and cognitive psychologist Jerome Bruner as setting him on a lifetime investigation of how humans think, know, learn, and act.

Today, Gardner is widely known for his work on multiple intelligences, which grew out of this question: *How do people come to know and understand things?* He had been taught that intelligence was a one-dimensional, fixed entity and that learning occurred in the cognitive realm. But his own life and his research showed him something else—that there were different kinds of intelligences, different entry points to learning. His understanding of the Holocaust was an example. He always found it hard to stomach a study of the Holocaust—a result of the trauma being so deeply embedded in his family's history. But he discovered that although one could "learn" about the Holocaust through history books, one could also experience and come to "know" the Holocaust through other media. He points to Robin Lakes's 1990 performance piece, *Dissonance*, which conveyed the raw torment of the concentration camps in dance. The audience viewed the dance through a barbed wire fence that had been constructed on the stage, and the dancers exquisitely and painfully re-created in movement the horrors of families being torn apart, tortured, and killed. In Gardner's view, dance was an entry point to learning about the Holocaust that was every bit as valid as a scholarly book on the subject.

As Gardner writes in *Intelligence Reframed*, "The human mind is better thought of as a series of relatively separate faculties, with only loose and nonpredictable relations with one another, than as a single, all-purpose machine that performs steadily at a certain horsepower, independent of content and context." Gardner originally proposed seven different intelligences:

- Musical
- Linguistic
- Spatial
- Bodily-kinesthetic
- Logical-mathematical
- Interpersonal
- Intrapersonal

He has subsequently proposed additional candidates for intelligences, such as naturalistic, spiritual, and existential. But regardless of the actual number of intelligences, Gardner's key claim is simple: we are able to understand, solve problems, and create things not just logically but also in myriad other ways, and success in life relies on a mixture of these intelligences.

The human mind is better thought of as a series of relatively separate faculties, with only loose and nonpredictable relations with one another, than as a single, all-purpose machine that performs steadily at a certain horsepower, independent of content and context.

—Howard Gardner

Gardner's work has not been universally accepted by psychologists, for a variety of reasons. There are not good psychometric tests for each of the intelligences, and some question whether, in defining intelligence so broadly, Gardner has undermined the usefulness of the concept. On the other hand, the theory of multiple intelligences has been widely acknowledged and adopted in much of education, particularly as teachers think about how to address different types of students and different learning styles. It's even becoming part of the vocabulary of school kids. Nowdays your fourth grader might come home from school and announce that he or she is "linguistically smart."

An opportunity to grow

Gardner's work challenges the idea that intelligence is a one-dimensional trait, summarized by IQ. Carol Dweck, a professor of psychology at Stanford, argues that as important as intelligence is, one's *beliefs* about one's own intelligence matter just as much. She traces her interest in the subject back to her sixth-grade class, where the teacher seated the students around the room according to IQ. Kids with high IQ were given all the perks and recognition in the class. Dweck noticed an interesting and perhaps unexpected result. The higher-IQ kids, afraid to lose their privileged status, were more fearful and less adventuresome. They also hated taking tests that might knock them off their pedestal.

Motivated by this early experience, Dweck has spent more than thirty years investigating the extent to which our own conceptions of intelligence color our ability to grow and perform. Her work identifies two alternative views, or mind-sets, that individuals hold about their own capacity: a "fixed" mind-set and a "growth" mind-set.

"Some students have a fixed mind-set," she says. "They believe their basic intelligence is just a fixed trait. They have a certain amount, and that's that. It makes them very concerned with how much they have. Before they do a task, they think, 'Am I going to look smart; am I not going to look smart?'—and they base their activities on whether their intelligence will be shown to advantage. Other students think that's wrong—that intelligence is something they can develop for their whole lives." These students have a growth mind-set.

Dweck and her colleagues decided to conduct an experiment to determine whether the growth mind-set could be taught. They developed an eight-session workshop on study skills and divided struggling students into two groups. One group got the study skills plus growth mind-set learning. For example, they were taught that the brain is like a muscle that grows stronger with use and were shown how they could increase their intellectual skills. The second group received the study skills without the growth mind-set learning. The result? The study skills–only group showed no improvement; their grades continued to decline. The group that learned the growth mind-set showed significant improvement by the end of the semester. The bottom line, according to Dweck: "People to a large extent are in charge of their own intelligence." When people believe that they can increase their intelligence, they can.

Twentieth-century engineering

While Dweck's and Gardner's work has had significant influence in education broadly, to date these ideas have made little impact on engineering education. "Smart" in an engineering context frequently means only one thing: good at math and science. High school career counselors encourage students with special math and science abilities— high logical-mathematical intelligence—to consider engineering and technical schools. Those with artistic talent are directed toward a liberal arts education. And, once students are studying engineering, there is a heavy emphasis on development of logical and mathematical capacities, to the exclusion of the other intelligences. Too often this is reflected in students' attitudes: "I don't need to learn to write—I'm an engineer!" This single-minded focus in engineering is in part due to the emphasis on depth in engineering education. There's a sense that because there's so much technical stuff to learn, we can't afford to spend time developing students' other intelligences.

Not only does engineering education tend to emphasize logical/mathematical intelligence to the exclusion of other ways of knowing but also it operates with a fixed mind-set. For example, most institutions have "weed-out" classes, first- or second-semester courses that are explicitly designed to eliminate students who can't cut it; there's the assumption that either you're good enough or you're not.

But as we outlined in chapter 3, the world has changed, and we face substantial challenges, with respect to both the need for a new kind of engineer and the need to attract more, and more diverse, students to engineering.

Making engineering more appealing to students with different intelligences offers the hope of increasing the pool of potential new engineers. Creating an environment that supports a growth mind-set, instead of a fixed mind-set, offers the potential of keeping those students around. And supporting those students' development across the different intelligences offers us hope of developing the Whole New Engineer—the kind of flexible, creative, socially-oriented engineer that today's world demands.

The title of this book pays homage to Dan Pink and his book, *A Whole New Mind*. In that book Pink argues that we live in a *conceptual era* in which creativity and innovation will rule. Somewhat later in the chapter we consider Pink's argument in greater detail, but other writers have also considered the present era as a special one and considered what this means for engineering, technology, and innovation.

We talk a lot about creating innovators—those who can break the mold and have an impact on the future. Bruce Vojak, an associate dean and adjunct professor in the College of Engineering at the University of Illinois, has made a study of innovators, coauthoring a book with Abbie Griffin and Ray Price called *Serial innovators: How Individuals Create and Deliver Breakthrough Innovation in Mature Firms*. Vojak spoke to us about how we encourage these breakthrough innovators. "How do innovators come to know what to do today to have an impact on the future?" he asked. The answer, he suggested, transcends traditional notions of how people *know* things. "Rather than being reductionistic, breakthrough innovators are holistic," he said. "Rather than being detached, they are intimate. Rather than being linear, they are non-linear." In other words, *knowing* for an engineer is not just the technical work, but exists in a broader universe of relationships.

Domenico Grasso is provost of the University of Delaware. Formerly the founding director of the Picker Engineering program at Smith College and dean of engineering at the University of Vermont, Grasso has long advocated a more holistic approach to educating engineers:

"Educating engineers more broadly will not only make them better designers but will also give them the tools to work productively alongside the other problem solvers they will be increasingly required to collaborate with: lawyers who resolve conflicts, economists who find the incentives and disincentives that promote positive change, historians who elucidate the present through knowledge of the past, artists who have an appreciation for form and function, and politicians who reach compromise. The ability to model and incorporate elements of economics, sociology, psychology, and business to identify possible solutions to pressing problems will be a major part of the future of engineering. "

Grasso recently edited a volume entitled, *Holistic Engineering Education: Beyond Technology*, in which this broader kind of engineering education is explored.

Peter Denning, Distinguished Professor at the Naval Postgraduate School and a regular columnist for the *Communications of the ACM*, has long advocated a different kind of education for engineers and computer scientists. In 1992, he opened a manifesto entitled "Educating a New Engineer" with the following words:

"University education is experiencing an enormous breakdown. An increasing number of students, employers, faculty, business executives, specialists, public officials, and taxpayers have declared their dissatisfaction with the education and research that is available in most of our universities. Commentators say we do not know how to educate graduates who know how to succeed in the new kinds of organizations and shifting worldwide markets that are emerging."

In speaking to us for this book, Denning suggested that the mismatch between education and the needs of effective practice have widened since the publication of that early manifesto and have become even more urgent. "Education today needs to be more about coping with and loving change," he said. It needs to prepare young people to be "better observers," and to learn how "to bring out their own talents"— not just how "to do engineering, but to be an engineer." Denning's book, (with Robert Dunham), called *The Innovator's Way*, describes eight practices that successful innovators utilize in their work. Interestingly, only two of these practices emphasize creating knowledge and ideas—the traditional focus of engineering education—and the other six emphasize the practices that lead to adoption of ideas. As engineers move from socially captive problem solvers and technicians to organizationally integrated innovators, Denning suggests, the shift to a broader array of competencies becomes increasingly important.

Making engineering more appealing to students with different intelligences offers the hope of increasing the pool of potential new engineers.

The six minds of the Whole New Engineer

Inspired by the work of these thinkers, we have spent time considering the capacities that engineers require in this new world. We propose that the Whole New Engineer needs to develop, and be able to bring to bear, *multiple minds* in his or her work. We emphasize *multiple*, because as Gardner argues, there are many ways to understand, to solve problems, to create. We choose the word *mind* to reflect two ideas: first, that these capacities extend beyond cognition and, second, that these are not fixed abilities but rather areas in which an individual can grow and develop. Specifically, we call out six minds of the Whole New Engineer as follows:

1. Analytical mind
2. Design mind

3. Linguistic mind
4. People mind
5. Body mind
6. Mindful mind

First is the *analytical mind*. Without question, engineering is a rigorous field that demands logical thought and careful application of scientific and mathematical principles. At the same time, engineers must balance analysis with a *design mind*—a willingness and capacity to imagine what does not exist, to think generatively, and to make unexpected connections. Engineers must also work with their *linguistic minds*. Communicating ideas is as important as generating them. Using a *people mind* is critical as well; engineering is a social profession and requires emotional intelligence and people skills. Engineering also requires leadership presence and intuitive decision making; we encompass these capacities in the *body mind*. Finally, we identify the *mindful mind*—the capacities and attitudes required for being reflective, finding meaning, and being intentional about one's mindset. Let's look at these in more detail.

Analytical mind

David Middlebrook (1927–2010) spent much of his career at CalTech, where he was revered not only as a top researcher in power electronics (his work on switched mode power supplies led to one of the key breakthroughs that enables cell phones to be as small as they are) but also as a top teacher. He received the Feynman Prize for Excellence in Teaching, the institution's highest teaching honor. During his time at CalTech, he also regularly taught in-house courses in circuit design at top companies around the world. His courses were described as "technical therapy." Garrett Neaves describes how they would open:

> You can hear chuckles from those in the audience when
> they hear Dr. Middlebrook describing the scenario of an

engineer working on his/her first design project. During that first design project, the engineer discovers that the analysis methods learned in college are nearly useless for the purpose of designing a circuit. The engineer proceeds by finding some existing circuit and then modifying it by guessing (maybe an educated guess?) and then checking how the resulting circuit behavior compares to the target.

The chuckles are a kind of nervous laughter of those thinking, "Hey, I thought that was my secret. I thought the other designers had a better understanding than me!" Dr. Middlebrook would then pose the question "If most of the stuff you learned in school, taught by professors turned out to not be much use, why are you here listening to another professor talking about the same old stuff?"

The *analytical mind* encompasses mathematics, logic, and science. It is closely related to Gardner's logical-mathematical intelligence, which includes the ability to detect patterns and to organize. Within an engineering context, the analytical mind implies an ability to build and implement models and experiments and an ability to interpret and to apply the results critically.

If there's an area of engineering education that most people would claim is not broken, it would be the analytical aspect. After all, most of the courses in an engineering program are very much focused on technical content, mathematics, science, and engineering science. But the analytical mind encompasses more critical thought than we often teach students. It's not just turning the crank on a lot of similar homework problems. Gill Pratt, an Olin professor and a program manager at the Defense Advanced Research Projects Agency (DARPA), frames it as the ability to *write* as well as *solve* an appropriate homework problem for the real-world situation that you're dealing with. Middlebrook talks about it as "design-oriented analysis" or, perhaps more generally, "understanding-oriented analysis." So it's not just being able to *do* a homework problem; it's being able to recognize patterns in the real world and apply knowledge to those patterns.

Design mind

Engineering is inherently a creative enterprise. While scientists ask "Why?" engineers must ask "Why not?" Engineers are responsible for imagining what has never been and then doing whatever it takes to bring these visions to reality. In this fundamental sense, "to engineer" is "to make."

But making requires more than the analytical mind. It also requires the *design mind*. The design mind can, in some ways, be thought of as a mirror to the analytical mind—and both are necessary for doing engineering. The analytical mind emphasizes convergence, identifying the right answer. The design mind emphasizes divergence, creating possible answers. Encompassed in the design mind are visualization, generativity, connecting, integrating, and seeing the big picture.

It's tempting to associate the analytical mind/design mind distinction with the "left-brain/right-brain" distinction that has gained significant popular traction. Daniel Pink points out in his book *A Whole New Mind: Why Right-Brains Will Rule the Future*, that people who are dominated by the "left brain"—overly rational and logical—tend to lack peripheral vision and business sense. They are unable to be innovators or creative thinkers. Pink calls them "good worker bees" whose interchangeability gives them less value. "Right-brained people, on the other hand, tend to be artists and inventors," he writes. "Science pegs them as being in tune with the big picture, including business savvy skills like innovating and synthesizing, developing strategies, managing projects, and leading others. Einstein made the observation that true genius lies in creativity, and he could add to this statement that it also goes a lot farther to guarantee job security." Pink's construct, outlined in his book, highlights "high-concept, high-touch" senses, which he calls aptitudes—design, story, symphony, empathy, play and meaning. These are, he notes, fundamentally human attributes, which are essential for personal fulfillment and professional success.

It's pretty clear that it's not really an either-or choice, though. In his doctoral work at Stanford, Ozgur Eris (formerly a faculty member at Olin College and now a professor at the Technical University of Delft in the

Netherlands) investigated the roles of generative questioning (questions that encourage imagination and lead to many possible answers) and convergent questioning (questions aimed at identifying a correct answer) in design teams. He found that the most effective teams asked the most questions and the questions they asked were evenly balanced between generative questions and convergent questions. In short, good design requires both the design mind and the analytical mind.

That said, it is surprising how little emphasis is placed on imagination, creativity, and design within the standard engineering curriculum today. A cursory review of the titles of courses taught and required within most traditional engineering schools shows that a very small proportion include the word "design" and even fewer address creativity in a deliberate way. Furthermore, many of the engineering design courses include very little discussion of creativity and the thought processes that underlie it. This is remarkable given the importance of this mode of thinking to the fundamental purpose of engineering.

Linguistic mind

Analyzing and designing are two fundamental activities at the core of engineering, but a third is so commonplace that it almost goes unnoticed. In seminars and workshops, we often ask participants to get into groups of four or five and make a list of what engineers do *themselves* during a typical day. The addition of the terms *themselves* and *during a typical day* is important, because without them, there is a tendency to think about the list at too high a level of abstraction. Yes, engineers analyze, design, construct, and maintain systems and so forth. However, these activities occur around the collective work of many others, be they other engineers or members of the larger workforce. When examined at the level of what individual engineers actually do themselves during a typical day, the list of things is sometimes surprising:

- Engineers write e-mails.
- Engineers write reports.
- Engineers talk on the phone.
- Engineers go to meetings.
- Engineers prepare and make presentations.
- Engineers prepare specifications, proposals, and contracts.

In short, engineers are constantly *in language*. They do not "build" much themselves usually—construction workers or manufacturing workers usually do that heavy lifting. Engineers "design" and "build" things with their computer keyboards, pencils, pens, and their vocal chords. In short, it is engineers' speech acts that result in things being built. Engineers work on design, but whether a particular design is accepted by decision makers or is implemented by those doing construction depends largely on the quality of the speech acts that engineers commit everyday.

Moreover, the content of engineering education and its emphasis on physics and mathematical analysis is misleading in that it directs attention to rather exceptional parts of an engineer's tool kit, not the everyday hammer and screwdriver. It is tempting, as some have proposed, to say that "the language of engineering is mathematics," but our view is that the language of engineering is natural language. Yes, engineers use math, but more often they use natural language, and we believe that engineering education and practice would be better if more attention and intention were directed at skilled speech and language acts.

Thus, by calling out *linguistic mind* as important to the Whole New Engineer, we are drawing attention to the ways in which the importance of skills with reading, writing, speaking, and listening are crucial to a successful engineer's education and to successful engineering practice. We no longer believe that it is acceptable to call these *soft skills*, a term that diminishes their importance. Moreover, we believe that a level of rigor needs to be brought to engineering communication that has thus far been largely absent.

Fortunately, the practice of executive coaching acknowledges the importance of these skills, what we will sometimes call "sharp soft skills." Crucial contributions to the intellectual foundations of coaching were made in the early 1980s by Fernando Flores, and many of them have recently become available in an edited volume entitled *Conversations for Action and Collected Essays*.

Chalmers Brothers's important coaching text, *Language and the Pursuit of Happiness*, draws attention to the importance of recognizing language as central: "And finally, our fifth basic claim: We live in language; we do what we do in language. We're linguistic beings. All of us, no matter what."

Brothers also builds on Flores's work and draws attention to how easy it is to overlook language and its importance in shaping our personal and work lives:

> In the same way, we're born into language and live in language. Language all around, language everywhere. And many of us do not see this; we're blind to it . . . What I'm up to is sharing some distinctions in language, some ways of looking at language that can allow us to be more conscious designers of our language and a wide variety of our results—because our language and our results are strongly connected.

The analytical mind and design mind will always be important to engineers, but balancing them with appropriate concern for natural language in the educational process should lead to the kind of changes we seek.

People mind

The popular television comedy series *The Big Bang Theory* revolves around the lives of a group of science and engineering geeks who struggle to relate in the ordinary world of work and love. Most of the jokes occur in situations contrived to show the characters as socially awkward and baffled by common human emotions, which come to them as if from another planet. Although they long for relationships, their robotic efforts to make connections usually lead to failure. In one episode, Sheldon, the physicist star of the show, tries to address his loneliness by creating an algorithm for making friends. Hilarity ensues.

The Big Bang Theory is a broadly comic exaggeration of a common notion of engineers—that they live in a world of their own, thinking, speaking, and doing in equations. No one understands them. They can't relate. Yet engineering is intensely social; put otherwise, engineering is a team sport, performed by and for people. Engineers solve problems in complex real-world situations; they design new systems and strategies to adapt to changing times; they make structures and products more user-friendly, responding to the real needs of communities and people. At its heart, engineering is about serving people. That role is enhanced by the rapid changes on the planet, which demand a facile, flexible response. As educators consider how to prepare their students to manage the challenges of the future, it has become increasingly apparent that understanding and being able to work with people—the *people mind*—may be as important as technical knowledge and in some cases more so.

In 1995, Daniel Goleman published *Emotional Intelligence*, a book that builds on and unpacks Gardner's constructs of interpersonal and intrapersonal intelligence. Goleman argues that success relies as much on self-awareness, self-regulation, motivation, empathy, and social skill as on conventional smarts—whether in the business world or in the classroom. Indeed, in his research looking at what led to successful performance in business leaders, Goleman found that these capacities outstripped technical skills and IQ by a factor of two.

As critical as the people mind is, it has been largely overlooked in engineering education. At the Engineer of the Future 2.0 Summit in 2009, Professor Woodie Flowers of MIT gave a keynote address in which he presented the results of a recent undergraduate thesis at MIT. In this thesis, a survey of nearly seven hundred recent MIT mechanical engineering graduates was conducted and analyzed. First, the study asked respondents to list the technical skills they'd learned. Next, the study asked about so-called soft skills—working with others, managing people, and so on. The study then asked respondents to evaluate how much they used the skills they'd learned in school and how much their jobs relied on other skills. The conclusion was that many—indeed *most*—of the technical skills learned in the classroom were hardly used at all in the workplace. Many of the people skills, however, were used every day and were critical to the respondents' professional success—and had not been learned in school. What students were taught in school was simply not what they were using on the job. Real-world engineering requires an array of skills—not just technical know-how but a broader range of abilities that allow projects to be managed and completed successfully.

Not only is the people mind important for doing work on a daily basis but also it's critical for innovation. One common description for innovation proposes that innovative ideas must be feasible (the idea can't violate the laws of physics), viable (the idea can't violate the laws of economics), and desirable (the idea must be something that people actually want). Benjamin Linder, a professor at Olin and a key architect of the "design stream" in Olin's curriculum, argues that engineering requires not only "designing it right"—i.e., figuring out how to turn an idea into reality—but also "designing the right thing"—figuring out what will make people's lives better. Real innovation requires asking: "*Should* we build it?" And to answer that question, you need empathy with real people.

At the heart of the people mind is the understanding that the stuff we do has meaning. It's being able to make human connections that evolve into improvements to the planet and the community.

Body mind

In the original list of multiple intelligences, Howard Gardner called out *bodily-kinesthetic intelligence* as one of the original seven, and a common interpretation of this kind of intelligence is to think directly in terms of the athletic performance of a great basketball player or the body control of a prima ballerina, but engineers need and exercise body mind in a number of less obvious but equally important ways. Here we consider two: exercising engineering intuition and decision making and working with others through a form of embodied leadership presence.

Engineering intuition and decision making. From the perspective of engineering education and practice, professors and practitioners often tell students or newbie engineers that they should develop their "engineering intuition," but such exhortations are usually not followed with a clear explanation of what that intuition is or where it comes from. Fortunately, there is a growing body of research that what we often identify as *intuition* comes to us as a felt sense from signals in our bodies.

Gary Klein in his work on naturalistic decision making has investigated how experts really make decisions. Often we assume that experts have better ways than others of rationally thinking about their domain of expertise and better rational decision-making procedures for those domains. To understand whether this is actually the case, Klein turned to first responders and other professionals under severe time constraints—for example, police officers, firefighters, medical personnel, aircraft carrier crews, and the like. In studying firefighters, who often have to make life-or-death calls with little time to think about it, he found that fireground commanders make eighty percent of their decisions in less than one minute. More importantly, Klein found that our assumption of rational decision making (i.e., the analytical mind) as a process of first generating options and then formally weighing them did not apply; instead, a kind of intuition took over.

This intuition is most easily understood as a form of pattern recognition. People experience a situation in terms of a variety of sensory cues. These patterns are then subconsciously and, to a certain extent, consciously matched with possible modes of action drawn from experience, and a top candidate for action emerges. In studies of these naturally chosen alternatives, the first option to emerge is often the best, usually beating random choice by a wide margin.

Klein began to investigate whether this naturalistic form of decision making applied in other fields—not just those with time pressures but also a whole range of arenas, including engineering, where a form of experiential thinking was involved. He cites a study of highway engineers to conclude that intuitive design strategies were the most effective, even without extreme time pressures.

In some ways, it's not a comforting picture. The whole tradition of rational thinking since the fifth century BC in Athens values reason and the logical weighing of options above all else, and this tradition has become only more entrenched with the rise of science and scientific method since the Enlightenment. But a growing body of scientific work suggests that our assumptions about how decisions are actually made are themselves not scientific. Rather than analyze a situation and come up with a reasoned course of action, in many cases real decision makers simply "know" what to do; they often trust their gut—their body sense of what to do—and they decide without even knowing why they decided. In this way, intuition can be seen as translating experience into action. It is a tacit knowledge that cannot be found in simple cognitive learning environments.

Klein says, "I think helping people to arrive at insights isn't a question of pushing the insights on the people or trying to explain it in words as much as helping people to gain the experience so they can see the inconsistency for themselves; then, all of a sudden the mental model will shift naturally and easily, and to me that's a gift that good teachers have—to be able to help the people who they're trying to support. They're trying to enlighten their students or colleagues to gain those insights."

From the standpoint of educating engineers capable of making serious and sometimes life-or-death decisions, we think it is important to actively cultivate an understanding of how decisions are actually made and how to integrate body and other ways of knowing with more analytical ones.

Engineering leadership presence. Another sense of body mind is how others perceive us and how we show up in this human vessel we call a body. In the coaching literature, this is sometimes called *leadership presence*, or the way we connect with one another physically through eye contact; body carriage; and voice speed, pitch, and modulation. In working with people on their leadership presence, so-called *somatic coaches* borrow from traditions in the martial arts and theatre to help enhance how leaders show up with others.

To the analytical mind, this may sound a bit like black magic and voodoo, but Iris Ioffreda, an organizational development consultant and executive coach, tells a story that illustrates the phenomenon. Each year, she volunteers her time to a nonprofit organization that looks for students who are usually overlooked for top colleges—primarily urban, diverse and underprivileged. One of the early factors for consideration is leadership presence. This is judged by volunteers and paid staffers of the foundation at an event in which the candidates are invited to appear and and interact wearing numbers identifying them, similar to a dance contest or a 5K running race. The judges watch them interact with each other in a series of activities like a Lego building exercise, leading a group in a discussion of a difficult issue, and preparing a skit on a topic. They evaluate the candidates based on whether they have good, better, or best leadership presence relatively. But here's the interesting part. There are no fixed criteria for what is meant by leadership presence. Judges are told to look specifically for leadership characteristics, not extroversion, so not to overlook introverted leaders. However, leadership itself is not specifically defined. And the result each year is equally interesting. When the judges get together at the end of the evening and compare notes, there is virtually unanimous agreement and no controversy about the top three or four candidates and the bottom three or four candidates. And, remarkably, this result occurs year in and year out, with a diverse group of judges from different industries and professional backgrounds. This helps us understand how leadership (body) presence is an "it"—something real, something human, and something influential.

Part of engineering effectiveness is to work well with others, and we have already called out the awareness of ourselves and others, what is often called emotional intelligence, as part of *people mind*, and we stand by that categorization, but here we are gesturing at something related but different. Specifically, we are talking about our ability to be aware of and control our bodies in ways that enhance our connection with ourselves and others.

Mindful mind

The final distinction we make is that of a *mindful mind*. Daniel Siegel, author of *Mindsight* and executive director of the Mindsight Institute, has defined mindfulness as follows: "Mindfulness is a form of mental activity that trains the mind to become aware of awareness itself and to pay attention to one's own intention."

A more playful version takes the term "noticing" as central to our ability to change. An oft-quoted passage from psychiatrist R. D. Laing states the following: "The range of what we think and do is limited by what we fail to notice. And because we fail to notice that we fail to notice, there is little we can do to change; until we notice how failing to notice shapes our thoughts and deeds."

Although there is a bit of wordplay here, the quote captures the importance of noticing or awareness—mindfulness—to personal growth and change and to the self-reference implied of a brain (or portion of a brain) being aware of itself and its contents.

Laing lived before functional magnetic resonance imaging technology, but modern neuroscience has identified the middle prefrontal cortex as largely responsible for many of these integrative functions. In *Mindsight*, Siegel cites the case of Barbara, a patient who suffered trauma to the middle prefrontal cortex, and the loss of brain function was devastating:

The middle portion of the prefrontal area, the part damaged in Barbara, coordinates an astonishing number of essential skills, including regulating the body, attuning to others, balancing emotions, being flexible in our responses, soothing fear, and creating empathy, insight, moral awareness, and intuition. These were the skills Barbara was no longer able to recruit in her interactions with her family.

While trauma and imaging have allowed us to locate various centers of brain function, they have also helped us understand how certain ancient practices, such as meditation, build connections in the middle prefrontal cortex, thereby improving mindfulness.

And the mindfulness revolution is taking place not just in the laboratory and in clinical settings. During the writing of this book, we noticed an uptick in attention paid to mindfulness in the popular media and in organizational circles, and we don't see this as some fad that is going to go away.

Chade-Meng Tan's book *Search Inside Yourself* is an important exemplar of the rising tide of mindfulness in the workplace. Tan, an engineer at Google, was curious about whether mindfulness practices could be adapted to the workplace.

In Google, the effort to make these methods widely accessible began when we asked ourselves this question: what if people can also use contemplative practices to help them succeed in life and at work? In other words, what if contemplative practices can be made beneficial both to people's careers and to business bottom lines? Anything that is both good for people and good for business will spread widely. If we can make this work, people around the world can become more successful at achieving their goals.

Since 2007, *Search Inside Yourself* has been taught at Google, and the program is being promoted as a form of continuing education for professionals in the workplace.

Here we are calling attention to the importance of the Whole New Engineer's ability to do three things:

- Notice and be aware of thoughts, feelings, and sensations.
- Reflect and learn from experience.
- Seek deeper peace, meaning, and purpose from noticing and reflection.

Particularly important in this list is the second item. There has been much talk about the importance of lifelong learning and learning to learn in discussions of higher education reform, but given the importance of mindfulness to the ability to direct learning and to learn, it is surprising that more attention has not been directed at noticing and reflection as keystones to those practices. As the book unfolds, we will return to mindfulness again, particularly in chapter 7.

Six different minds?
How are we supposed to do THAT?

In faculty discussions taking place in engineering schools throughout the world, the question of incorporating more teamwork, teaching communication skills, and heightening the emphasis on design comes up repeatedly. And there's often a strong concern raised: "Wouldn't that dilute the basics?"

It's interesting to reflect on what is meant by "basics"—it's the math, the science, and the engineering science. But that's a funny appropriation of the word "basics," which should refer to the fundamental knowledge, skills, and attitudes that are needed to be successful throughout one's life. The real-world palette of basics is much broader and more diverse, requiring skills that go beyond technical understanding and intelligences beyond logical and mathematical.

But the importance of such a breadth doesn't answer the fundamental concern that something has to go in order to make space for developing these different minds. How can we address this?

First, it's important to recognize that there already is an emphasis on some of these ideas in the curriculum. What is missing, in some cases, is the appropriate framing. For example, Middlebrook's emphasis on design-oriented analysis is an important reframing of how we think about developing the analytical mind. It's not saying we need to spend *more* time but rather that we need to spend that time *differently*. And it's a reframing that inherently makes more sense to students, because it has a real-world purpose.

In some cases, the idea of developing these different minds is implicit in curriculum but is not articulated. Most faculty members would agree that one of the purposes of education is to develop students as reflective practitioners, but that goal is rarely articulated in syllabi or interactions, nor is it explicitly supported in the types of work

The real-world palette of basics requires skills that go beyond technical understanding and intelligences beyond logical and mathematical.

that students do. Articulating the need to develop students' capacity for reflection makes it easier to focus on it. Overall, this reflective emphasis can actually lead to educational gains in other areas, as a reflective student is often a more effective learner.

Third, to a certain extent, these different minds often reflect what we call below-the-waterline skills and thinking patterns. Below-the-waterline skills add a lot with just a little effort because they propagate through everything we do.

Each of these considerations helps to address the concern about creating space for developing the six minds. But ultimately we have to confront the reality that *something* has to go. We think the key lies in recognizing the extent to which the world now requires lifelong learning. The pace of technological and economic change is higher than ever, and the cutting-edge facts that students learn today will be old news tomorrow. Given this, we believe that helping students develop as complete human beings, with whole minds and bodies engaged in learning, who are practiced in understanding in a variety of ways, is the educational mandate of our times.

5

The Emotional Breakthrough
Five Pillars of Transformation

*One of the most satisfying experiences I know is just fully to
appreciate an individual in the same way that I appreciate a sunset.
When I look at a sunset . . . I don't find myself saying, 'Soften the
orange a little on the right hand corner, and put a bit more purple
along the base, and use a little more pink in the cloud color.' . . .
I don't try to control a sunset. I watch it with awe as it unfolds.*

—Carl Rogers

It was December 11, 1940, and a thirty-eight-year-old professor of
clinical psychology at Ohio State University had been invited to give a
lecture at the University of Minnesota on the topic of "Newer Concepts
in Psychotherapy." His name was Carl Rogers, and he had begun to make
a small name for himself for his unusual idea, which he called "client-
centered" (later redefined as person-centered) psychotherapy.

Watching the lecture with interest was E. G. Williamson, a faculty member and the head of Minnesota's highly regarded counseling program. Williamson was himself a pioneer in a new form of psychotherapy, which he described as the "trait and factor" approach, also known as the Minnesota Point of View. Williamson's premise was that people possessed fundamental traits and the job of the counselor was to follow a five-step process to unearth and improve on those traits. This process involved analysis, synthesis, diagnosis, counseling, and follow-up. Williamson's directive method, with the counselor in the driver's seat, was rational, scientific, and systematic.

He listened as Rogers challenged his life's work, speaking of a nondirective approach that was emotional, intuitive, and experiential, with an emphasis on building trusting relationships. At the beginning of his career, Rogers acknowledged that he, too, had been focused on how to treat or cure or change a person. Now he asked, "How can I provide a relationship which this person may use for his own personal growth?"

This was heretical to the thinking of the times, and Williamson was deeply disturbed. Rogers's position contradicted everything he understood about psychotherapy. He didn't approve of Professor Rogers's dangerous ideas and wanted nothing to do with them in his school. It would be a long time before many of Rogers's ideas were picked up by mainstream psychology under the rubric of *positive psychology*, but Carl Rogers not only pushed the envelope in his own field but also left an indelible mark on education.

As an educator, Rogers observed that his profession cultivated a distance between professor and student, using evaluation methods and standards that objectified students. Educators, he noted, were committed to the transmission of information—to setting students "straight." He believed educators must have an entirely different mission: "There is another attitude which stands out in those who are successful in facilitating learning," he wrote in *Freedom to Learn*. "I have observed this attitude. I have experienced it. Yet it is hard to know what term to put to it, so I will use several. I think of it as prizing the learner, prizing his feelings, his opinions, his person. It is a caring for the learner, but a non-possessive caring. It is an acceptance of this other individual as a separate person, having worth in his own right. It is a basic trust—a belief that this other person is somehow fundamentally trustworthy."

This thinking led Rogers to change his own manner of teaching, and it inspired a number of early educational pilots in which trust played a central role. Today, forty-five years after the publication of *Freedom to Learn*, these ideas remain tantalizingly attractive. They seem to work sometimes, and yet they remain difficult to carry to the classroom reliably and well. We turn to them here, because in looking back over the experiences of both Olin and iFoundry, these ideas appear to be at the core of what makes twenty-first-century educational transformation tick.

We've asked ourselves how Olin and iFoundry differed, what they had in common, and what pivotal events occurred that led to key insights. This analysis has led us to articulate five pillars of educational transformation we believe are crucial for engineering education reform—and educational reform more generally—in our times.

The odd couple of educational reform

Thinking back to chapters 1 and 2, we can see that along a number of critical dimensions, the contrast between Olin College and Illinois couldn't be more stark:

- **Size and emphasis.** Olin is a small private school, emphasizing undergraduate education and teaching. Illinois is a large public school, emphasizing research and scholarly productivity.
- **Start-up vs. established.** Olin is a young entrepreneurial start-up, dating back just about a decade. Illinois is a mature, established university, dating back over a century and a half.
- **Blank slate vs. legacy curriculum.** Olin started its effort from a blank slate with new administrators and faculty hired for

their eagerness to change. Illinois started its effort from legacy curriculum with most administrators and faculty eager to get on with the research mission.

- **New vs. existing infrastructure.** Olin built a new, state-of-the-art campus from scratch. Illinois utilized existing infrastructure designed for large lectures and standardized labs.
- **Large vs. small funding commitment.** Olin was started with a large influx of dedicated funding to bring about a new curriculum. iFoundry was started with no funding and later received small amounts of financial support—much smaller than reform efforts initiated at schools of comparable size.

Looking back, we now realize how fortunate we were that the differences were so great, because they ruled out many superficial similarities as possible explanations for the good outcomes that occurred. At the time of the formation of the Olin-Illinois Partnership, both schools had hopes that we would learn many things together, but we did not have the slightest inkling that the stark differences between the schools would be such an important factor in driving our attention and understanding.

Although there were differences between the two efforts, they started with a number of beliefs in common:

- **Something needs to be done—and urgently.** Both efforts shared the belief that substantial change was necessary and that there were undesirable consequences if the change wasn't made quickly enough.
- **Change to date was not adequate.** Both efforts believed that changes attempted to this point were not adequate to the challenges of the times.
- **Change processes were insufficient.** Both efforts believed that the change processes employed were not adequate. Olin started a new school as a result. Illinois started an incubator.

- **Content, curriculum, and pedagogy are key loci of change.**
  Initially, both programs were fairly conventional in thinking that
  the core of change was in modifying content, curriculum, and
  classroom pedagogy. Later, we would come to appreciate that this
  focus on content, curriculum, and pedagogy was misplaced.
- **The new way should be more student centered.** Both efforts
  shared the belief that education should be more student centered.
- **The professor/lecturer is the prime mover of change.** Although
  both efforts believed education should be more student centered,
  both also held the belief that the primary actor in educational
  transformation is the instructor, another item that would be
  challenged later.
- **The humanist psychologists and organizational theorists of the
  fifties and sixties were on to something.** Both efforts were influenced by the ideas of thinkers such as Carl Rogers, Abraham
  Maslow, and Douglas McGregor. The ideas were there and
  implicit in many designs and assumptions, they were not yet
  central to either effort, and neither effort highlighted these ideas
  in talking about what they were doing.

These common threads formed a set of underlying beliefs or assumptions
from which both efforts went forward.

Pivotal moments

Developing a new educational initiative is not like doing a laboratory
experiment. There is no double-blind experimental setup; there is no control
group; there is no careful formulation of hypotheses. The data are of mixed
form, often qualitative, and do not lend themselves to statistical analysis.
In many ways, a new educational initiative is like an engineering project,
but not a modern one. It is more like an engineering project in Roman

times, when the predictive capabilities of math and science would have been of limited value to determine outcomes ahead of time.

Instead, in the practical design and evolution of an educational initiative, events unfold and insight is gained through a variety of lessons learned at different times, in different ways, by different actors. These lessons are frequently illuminated in pivotal moments. And although they're different from rigorous lab experiments, they are every bit as valuable.

As events unfold, certain anomalies appear that challenge people's underlying assumptions. These anomalies stimulate reflection, and people begin to reconsider the old assumptions. It is this combination of pivotal moments, the anomalies that arise, and the reflection that takes place that leads to breakthrough insights.

In looking back at the Olin and Illinois efforts, there were a number of these pivotal moments that drove key insights:

- **Olin Partner Year moment.** Although not part of the original plans, the decision to have a partner year in reaction to construction delays was a pivotal moment in that it established students in the Olin culture in a way that a normal start-up would probably not have done.
- **Candidate Weekend moment.** The Olin Candidate Weekend experience allowed a powerful encounter with community, outside the conventional markers of a "real college"—buildings, curriculum, etc. It established that while the infrastructure might be important, people would matter more than anything else.
- **"Now I know I can" moments.** The Olin Partner Year was filled with moments of both faculty and students realizing they were capable of more than they "ought to" be able to do. These moments cemented the idea that when given the opportunity, students can rise to the challenge.
- **Bouncy castle moment.** The decision of the Olin team to admit that things weren't working led to an understanding that openness

and a willingness to change trump getting the "right" answer the
first time.

- **Olin effect moment.** The visit by the iFoundry team in early 2008
led to a different understanding of what Illinois should try to
imitate in the Olin model.

- **Olin-Illinois Partnership formation.** The decision to form the
Olin-Illinois Partnership was crucial. Although not articulated at
the time, there was intuition on both sides that the other side had
some of the "right stuff" and that there would be learning crucial
to both efforts through the partnership.

- **The community moment.** The visit by Olin President Rick
Miller, with Sherra Kerns and Mark Somerville to Illinois, in
which the Olin team highlighted dormitories as way to obtain
community, combined with Russ Korte's joining the Illinois
faculty and the formation of the virtual iCommunity, formed a
"community moment" in which extraordinary steps were taken
to obtain connectedness in community—even if the physical
infrastructure was not in place.

- **The joy moment.** With the arrival of the 2009 cohort of iFoundry
freshmen described, various presentations to students and other
stakeholders started to talk about three joys: the joy of engineering, the joy learning, and the joy of community. This reframing of
engineering from tedious drudgery to a way of life that could be
both challenging and fun was important for articulating this value,
thereby resetting the culture to one based more on positive than
negative emotion.

- **"Weren't sure you were serious" moment.** When Jaime Kelleher
made her comment about iFoundry, "We weren't sure you were
serious about us doing what we wanted to do, but when we realized you were, it was really cool," it signaled that trusting the
students and sticking to that trust was important for students to
believe they are trusted and then take initiative.

These and other "moments" were important for driving our reflection about what was important in engineering educational reform. Where once we adhered to the conventional wisdom that the keys to transformation were what the faculty member did in designing content, curriculum, and pedagogy, we were drawn by empirical results and deep reflection to two conclusions: that *culture* was the real object of change and that all the key variables of change were deeply personal, rooted in the student, and fundamentally *emotional*.

We were drawn by empirical results and deep reflection to two conclusions: that culture *was the real object of change and that all the key variables of change were deeply personal, rooted in the student, and fundamentally emotional.*

These conclusions were difficult to reach. Everything in our training as engineers commanded us to speak in rational and concrete terms, but powerful experiences and events had led us to a very different place. In a way, these reckonings gave us the courage to leave the terra firma of engineering language and concepts and focus primarily on what the humanistic psychologists and organizational theorists had talked about many years before.

Some of this transition took place during the writing of this book. The ability to use a more cultural, emotional, and personal language has been both powerful for us personally and helpful in communicating to others a way of thinking about engineering educational transformation that leads us to propose a new set of fundamentals. At first these fundamentals are difficult to talk about because they are so unfamiliar in engineering education discourse. Yet our experience has been that shifting our language to these words almost immediately changes the conversation for students and instructors in ways that more directly bring about the needed changes.

Everything in our training as engineers commanded us to speak in rational and concrete terms, but powerful experiences and events had led us to a very different place.

The pillars of educational transformation

Thus, based on our experience, reflection, and long sense-making journey, we declare that there are five pillars of engineering educational transformation in our times:

1. Joy
2. Trust
3. Courage
4. Openness
5. Connectedness, collaboration, community

We briefly consider the sense in which we use these terms in this context.

We commonly understand joy to refer to a feeling of great happiness and also the thing that causes that happiness, as well as success in having or achieving something we want. All of these senses of the term are found in the stories of both Olin and iFoundry. Some of it is the joy of engineering in designing and making, some of it is the joy in close relationships, and some of it is the joy in growth and development. Whichever the case, turning the educational environment away from a dreary excursion in survival to a celebration of human spirit seems fundamental. The shift is basically emotional, and emotions are generally labeled as positive or negative. Using the term "joy" as a pillar, we put forward the belief that positive emotions bathed in freedom are more effective in the development of bold, initiative-taking engineers than fear cloaked in coercion and rigid requirements.

Trust is a simple-enough-sounding concept, sometimes defined as "belief that someone or something is reliable, good, honest, effective, etc.," but complexity lurks beneath the surface. Trusting someone involves at least two parties—the person who trusts and the person trusted. It involves difficult assessments on the part of the trusting person of the other's sincerity, reliability, and competence. Trust can also affect the person trusted in profound ways, enabling that person to undertake difficult tasks and perform them in ways that he or she might not otherwise do. In the stories of Olin and iFoundry, time and time again the process of unleashing students to take initiative and to strive until they're successful starts with trust. By calling out trust in this way, we believe that an approach that lets go and holds the student responsible for his or her success is more powerful in the long run than an approach that controls, assesses closely, criticizes, and judges along every step of the learning journey.

As discussed already, trust can lead a student to find the courage to overcome obstacles, take initiative, iterate, reflect, and really learn. Courage is defined as the mental or moral ability to persevere even in the face of great hardship or danger, and it derives from the French term for "heart." Story after story in the Olin-iFoundry narrative is about unleashed students overcoming fear or resistance and taking initiative. We call out courage as a direct challenge to the current encouragement of acquiescence and obedience.

The term "openness" is commonly defined as the free expression of one's true feelings and opinions. Part of the Olin and iFoundry experiences involves an unusual level of free expression or candor between students and other students, between faculty members and other faculty members, and between students and faculty members.

But there's another sense of openness that is important here—that is, openness to experience and the results of experience. Much of current engineering education practice is built on predictability and certainty, but we live in a world of increasing change and uncertainty. For the Whole New Engineer, openness means taking action despite not being able to predict an outcome. This kind of openness demands that engineers pay attention to what actually happens (the effects), not what they *want* to have happen (the plan), as a way to learn and determine what to do next. Sometimes openness in this sense has been called effectuation or entrepreneurial thinking, as a counterpoint to causal or planning thinking. This spirit of openness is found both in the Olin and iFoundry educational experiences and in the approach taken to designing and iterating on those educational experiences. We call out openness as a counterpart to rigidity and strict adherence to plans.

Finally, the Olin and iFoundry experiences demonstrate the importance of connectedness and collaboration between individuals and the school as a community. A community is, simply put, a body of individuals united around a common purpose or interest. The traditional culture of engineering education has been individualistic and competitive, and we call out the cultural shift toward collaboration and connection.

We came to describe these five inner emotional values as pillars, because a pillar is a foundational structure that supports the whole. We believe that each of these pillars must be present in greater measure for the Whole New Engineer to emerge and thrive. They are not dependent on the type of institution; we've already seen how two very different schools achieved similar results when these factors were present. They are not dependent on the prestige of the faculty, or the scale of research studies, or any of the other notches that schools have in their belts that make them important. We see them organically in the hearts and minds of students who want to be happy, who long to make a difference, and who dare to be great.

Having said this, we should also be clear that we are not saying every moment of engineering school should be joyful, that everyone needs to be trusted naively or uniformly, that reckless boldness should replace caution and obedience. Nor are we saying that openness should be taken to an unseemly extreme or that connectedness, collaboration, and community should replace individual initiative of any sort. To assert these extremes not only would be unwise but also would create an engineering education that wouldn't develop engineers with sufficient rigor, discipline, or depth to do the many complex technical tasks an engineer is called upon to do.

Here we echo the messages of chapter 3 in which we observed that since the nineteenth century, engineering has gone too far, become too narrow, lost portions of what made it great. And perhaps that narrowing was appropriate to the post–World War II era, but it has become counterproductive. To restore some of that earlier greatness requires a balance of the poles we have just called forth. Aristotle talked about seeking a "golden mean." More recently, the idea of "polarity management" has been used in organizational development. No matter how we frame it, it is useful to think about the pillars and their counterparts as poles or extremes and to think about righting the ship of engineering education through a kind of balancing or management process. In short, we seek to rebalance engineering education in ways that serve our students and our times.

Let's examine the pillars in more depth.

Pillar #1: Joy

Neil Armstrong, who died in 2012 at the age of eighty-two, was an American icon, the first man to step foot on the moon. He was a humble man who lived his life in gratitude for the opportunities he was given—and he was especially proud of being an engineer. On one occasion, at a National Press Club gathering, he famously said, "I am, and ever will be, a white-socks, pocket-protector, nerdy engineer—born under the second law of thermodynamics, steeped in the steam tables, in love with free-body diagrams, transformed by Laplace, and propelled by compressible flow. As an engineer, I take a substantial amount of pride in the accomplishments of my profession." Armstrong's poetic tribute to his profession is infused with the joy of being an engineer in an age of soaring opportunities. Few people symbolize so perfectly the positive identity of an engineer. He was joyful.

Yet when we look around, "joy" seems like the last word one would use to describe engineering education. The dog-eat-dog educational process is captured concisely at arguably the most renowned of all engineering schools. Go into the bathrooms at the Massachusetts Institute of Technology (MIT) and you will see an acronym scrawled on the walls of the stalls: IHTFP. It means "I Hate This F**king Place." (IHTFP is also found in the service academies and other elite engineering programs.)

Whether this remains the true sentiment of MIT students today or merely a tradition handed down from generation to generation isn't clear, but it captures the experience of many generations of engineering students, not only at MIT. For many students, by the time they've survived four years of a grueling process, the last thing they want to be is an engineer. They've had it. By contrast, one of the great lessons of the Olin and iFoundry experiences has been the degree to which a productive atmosphere of joy, pride in engineering, and collaborative accomplishment improves retention, identity, and views of self-efficacy.

These latter empirical results are supported by a growing body of theory in positive psychology and organizational behavior. The field of positive psychology is said to have launched in the 1970s when psychologist Martin Seligman proposed the idea of flipping the traditional psychological analysis from studying disorders to studying positives to be strived for. In the coming years, it became commonplace to talk about the value of well-being, but positive psychology did not make its way into the workplace until the 1990s. Today, the idea that workplace happiness and productivity are linked is well researched and accepted—and we might infer that the same holds true for education. But productivity is not the sole measure. Happy people are also more fulfilled, creative, and motivated. In other words, joy is good for the bottom line, yet it transcends the bottom line.

In a 2013 Twitter chat, we asked participants to tell us what aspects of engineering bring them the most joy. The responses of students, teachers, and working engineers were an inspiration:

Joy in being part of history.
Joy in triumphing over complexity to make something work.
Joy in seeing theory applied to real-life experience.
Joy in learning together (not from lectures).
Joy in nostalgia (seeing how far technology has come in our lifetimes).
Joy in helping students *get* something for the first time (that gleam in their eye).

Joy in unlimited possibility (in the number of options that engineering opens up).

Joy innovating and meeting needs.

Joy in coding.

Joy in finding and fixing root causes.

Joy in helping others solve their own problems.

Joy in creativity, innovation, and internationality.

Joy in machines and the majesty of technology.

Joy in creating something that didn't exist before.

Joy in working on products that save lives.

Joy in overcoming hardship or joy in doing hard stuff with simple parts.

Joy plays an important role in setting the stage for a positive and self-sustaining engineering education. Students need to aspire to something greater, to feel that they are not just training to become "cogs in a wheel." When Erica Lee Garcia, P. Eng, founder of the web site Engineer Your Life (engineeryourlife.net), looked back on her experience in engineering school, she saw a great divide between her aspirations and the reality. "I wanted to do something that made a difference, and I saw engineering as the building blocks of everything in society," she said. However, engineering school was a rude awakening. "I felt it was equipping me to be a cog in the wheel. I lost sight of how I was going to make a difference." Lee Garcia's experience was the impetus for her work. Joy in engineering involves transcending the mechanics of engineering. On her site Lee Garcia urges students to ask the big life questions, such as: *If I had unlimited time, space, and money what would I do with myself all day? Who am I when I am not working? What really matters to me? What do I want to be remembered for? What do I still want to learn or try out? What's missing my life? How can I solve the equation of my life to optimize my own happiness?*

How do we show that we value joy in the engineering classroom? We value joy when we:

- Speak about joy and show that a balance of emotions toward the positive is supported by research and is increasingly being called out as an essential quality in a good life.
- Share our stories, both personal and disciplinary, of joy and engineering, and stop propagating the myth of the engineer as a joyless and relentlessly rational person.
- Show up in joy and positive emotion.
- Encourage students to follow their aspirations and find meaning in their studies through things that interest them.
- Encourage an understanding of intrinsic motivation—a fundamental drive that transcends grades, prestige, or money—by educators and a cultivation of it in students.
- Highlight the inspiring nature of engineering by celebrating engineering heroes and telling iconic stories connecting joy and engineering accomplishment.

With an infrastructure of the positive emotions of joy and happiness, we are ready to consider the next pillar of engineering educational transformation.

An engineer in joy

At the turn of the twentieth century, in a small village in the shadow of Mt. Fuji, Japan, a young boy watched his father with intense interest as he repaired bicycles and machines for their fellow villagers. Soichiro Honda was a passionate observer, bursting with curiosity. He loved tinkering on his own and figuring out how things worked. He was overcome with excitement the first time he saw a car—even though it sputtered and coughed and poured black smoke. When Honda completed his primary education, his father encouraged him to go to university, but Honda was interested only in cars and mechanics. At the age of fifteen, he left home to become an apprentice in an auto and motorcycle repair shop in Tokyo.

In the coming years, Honda would become skilled with his hands, but his mind and heart grew as well. He had an inventive nature and an ebullient personality. His work made him happy, and he continued to look for ways to make others happy as well. Coming out of the dark years of World War II (colorblindness made him ineligible to fight), Honda made a bold decision that would shape the rest of his life. He started a motorcycle and moped company, which would later grow into the Honda Motor Company.

Honda was always a very special company, and unprecedented growth and stability have seen it through over a half century of challenges in the global automotive markets. What is the secret of its success? One might point to high-quality product design and construction, market sensitivity, and motivated workers—and all that would be true. But one might also point to a culture of joy, which was established by the founding father.

In 1951, Soichiro Honda wrote a letter to his employees about the motto of the company, which he defined as "the three joys"—the joy of producing, the joy of selling, and the joy of buying. He implored his employees to remain faithful to this motto, in spirit and action, and vowed to devote all of his strength to the model's fulfillment. Of the three joys, Soichiro wrote:

> "The first of these, the joy of producing, is a joy known only to the engineer. Just as the Creator used an abundant will to create in making all the things that exist in the natural universe, so the engineer uses his own ideas to create products and contribute to society. This is a happiness that can hardly be compared to anything else. Furthermore, when that product is of superior quality so that society welcomes it, the engineer's joy is absolutely not to be surpassed. As an engineer myself,

I am constantly working in the hope of making this kind of product.

"The second joy belongs to the person who sells the product. Our company is a manufacturer. The products made by our company pass into the possession of the various people who have a demand for them through the cooperation and efforts of all our agents and dealers. In this situation, when the product is of high quality, its performance is superior, and its price is reasonable, then it goes without saying that the people who engage in selling it will experience joy.

"The third, the joy of the person who buys the product, is the fairest determiner of the product's value . . . There is happiness in thinking, 'Oh, I'm so glad I bought this.' This joy is the garland that is placed upon the product's value. I am quietly confident that the value of our company's products is well advertised by those products themselves. This is because I believe that they give joy to the people who buy them."

The idea of establishing a mandate for joy at a 1950s car company was such an enormous culture clash that little was heard at the time of Honda's letter to employees. Businesses were not supposed to be humanistic; indeed, car companies with their mechanized assembly lines were often considered inhumane. However, in recent years, when Honda's message was uncovered by Internet searches, the response was, "Of course!" In today's world, we are surrounded by examples of companies that have re-created workplace cultures around values such as personal fulfillment, creativity, and independence.

Pillar #2: Trust

Decades before Jaime Kelleher taught us a lesson about the power of trust at iFoundry, Carl Rogers observed that an implicit assumption in professional and graduate education is that "the student cannot be trusted to pursue his own scientific or professional education." Rogers was referring to the education of psychology graduate students and therapists, but his words apply equally well to engineering education, with its highly prescribed content and emphasis on monitoring and evaluating both students and programs. Rogers often said that without trust, the teacher-student relationship is sterile and remote. Trust creates a relationship that opens up opportunities. In Rogers's view, trust involves both parties being real and acting in acceptance of each other.

Many of the Olin and Illinois stories affirm the importance of trust.

Mark Somerville: "You deserve to be here."

First-year students arrive at college feeling vulnerable and uncertain. Often they are surrounded by people who they assume are smarter and better prepared, they don't know whether they will be able to do the work, and they're treated like unknown quantities that have to prove themselves. I've been out of school for a good while now, but I can still remember the feelings of insecurity and dread—that feeling of being an imposter—that come with being a new student. I'll bet most people can.

When I speak to students during orientation, I almost always ask them this: "Raise your hands if you feel you're not smart enough to be here." Every year a sea of hands gradually, hesitantly, goes up. One year, when I asked for comments, one of the students bravely stood up and explained, "You feel like everyone around you is so much smarter than you. You think maybe you got in by the skin of your teeth or by accident." By the nervous smiles and laughter, it seemed that he had nailed it.

"We picked all of you for a reason," I assure them. "You deserve to be here. And you have what it takes to succeed and to make a difference in the world."

I'm not naive enough to believe that this solves what is a very thorny problem—indeed, we keep returning to this theme throughout the semester, the year, and the program. Still, that first sign of trust in their abilities seems to make an impression: one student, years later, recalled the relief she felt at her orientation session: "I was amazed that you thought we were capable of making a contribution to the world," she said. "You believed in us. It meant a lot."

One model of trust that is useful here is presented from the view of the trusting person—the trustor—as presented by Chalmers Brothers in *Language and the Pursuit of Happiness*. In this view, trust is a series of three grounded assessments of the other person (the trustee):

1. Sincerity
2. Reliability
3. Competence

In other words, if the trusting person believes that the other is sufficiently sincere, reliable, and competent, these assessments are combined and we say that the person trusts the other.

On the other side of the relationship, being trusted can have a powerful effect on the person trusted. In *Building Trust: In Business, Politics, Relationship and Life*, Robert Solomon and Fernando Flores suggest that trust is not an atmosphere, nor is it a medium. They argue that it's more like an investment, similar to venture capital with human beings. When you have a young person walk in the door and you know little about him or her but offer trust, it's a leap of faith, and sometimes the bets pay off and sometimes they don't.

Andrew Bell reflected on the atmosphere of trust he experienced at iFoundry: "The beauty of the situation is that they didn't put their 'iGuinea pigs' on the hamster wheel and tell them to run in place so they could comfortably observe us. Rather, they told us to run any way we wanted to see where we could possibly end up. In a sense, we got a baptism by fire because they let us play with fire. With great power comes great responsibility, but with the quality students in the program, who are striving to be the best they can be, only good things have come from the freedom and resources they gave us."

Garrett Schwanke, a third-year mechanical engineering student at California Polytechnic State University, described a physics class where there was a tremendous amount of freedom to explore what interested him in an environment of safety without worrying about failing. "I was trusted to be a master in one area," he said. "But it was a two-way street. I also had to trust the professor. It wasn't a situation where if I failed, tough luck. When I struggled, he came through offering scaffolding and a hand up. He understood when to step aside and let me grow and when to step in. It was one of the best classroom experiences I've had."

Olin students frequently remark on the high level of trust they experience from the first year. "I was surprised that there was so much responsibility and trust in the first year," said Larissa Little, a sophomore at Olin. "My view of what trust means really changed. For me trust means that the professors are going to let you run—give you big open-ended projects and take-home exams and trust you'll come to them if you need them."

In being trusted, students also become trusting. They come to understand that the professors are interested in their success. Sebastian Dziallas described a diagnostic problem in a math and physics class at Olin that was especially difficult. He stayed up until 3:00 in the morning and still hadn't cracked it. He was frustrated and also a little scared. He didn't want to get a zero for failing to do the problem. When he went to his professor and described his difficulty, she said, "It's going to be fine. Just focus on the project. Understand it will be all right." This attitude released Sebastian to continue working.

"I saw that the teacher wasn't going to screw me because the problem wasn't solved. She was interested in my learning."

In these ways, trust is important to engineering education transformation for a number of reasons. First, it continues and sustains a spirit of positive emotion and joy, further distancing the transformed environment from the older atmosphere of fear and coercion. Second, it empowers the passive listener of times past to become an active learner and participant, shifting responsibility for teaching on the part of the instructor to a responsibility for learning on the part of the student.

How do we show that we value trust in the engineering classroom? We value trust when we:

- Speak about what trust is and its importance in professional practice and relationships.
- Respect and enhance students' autonomy.
- Don't grab the broom at the first sign of failure or difficulty.
- Demonstrate through our speech and actions that we trust ourselves.

When trust is present, it can elicit the next pillar on a regular basis.

Pillar #3: Courage

In 2010, a researcher named Brené Brown gave a talk at her local TEDx event, TEDxHouston. The subject of her talk was her extensive research work on shame, wholeheartedness, and vulnerability. How did she come to these subjects of study? "I'm interested in messy topics," Brown explained, adding that her goal as a scientist was to make them less messy. "There's a big saying, 'lean into the discomfort,'" she said. "I wanted to knock the discomfort upside the head, move it over and get all As." And that's what she was out to do with her research. She was going to solve the problem of vulnerability. Instead, she discovered that accepting one's vulnerability was essential to being courageous. In *Daring Greatly: How the Courage to Be Vulnerable Transforms the Way We Live, Love, Parent and Lead*, Dr. Brown writes about vulnerability not as a weakness but as a call to engage. She proposes that vulnerability is not a choice but engagement is. "Our willingness to own and engage with our vulnerability determines the depth of our courage and the clarity of our purpose," she writes. "Thus, courage is reimagined not as the product of strength or power, but as the will to engagement in the midst of vulnerability. Embracing our vulnerabilities is risky but not nearly as dangerous as giving up on love and belonging and joy—the experiences that make us the most vulnerable. Only when we are brave enough to explore the darkness will we discover the infinite power of our light."

The word "courage" came into the vocabulary of the Whole New Engineer during the initial stages of the writing of this book in February 2012.

David Goldberg: "How do you learn courage?"

After leaving the University of Illinois, I did a considerable amount of work at the National University of Singapore, and on one of those trips, I was asked to give a talk to students at Hwa Chong Institution, one of Singapore's top high schools and one of the top high schools in the world. The audience was mainly composed of what in the states would have been ninth- and tenth-grade students (fifteen- and sixteen-year-olds), and I spoke to them about leadership presence—being able to make better decisions through authentic connection with others and being present in the moment.

When it was time for the question-and-answer period, I started high in the auditorium, and there were a number of straightforward questions, which I answered in straightforward fashion. As I came down the auditorium steps toward the front, a young woman raised her hand, I called on her, and she said, "I have a question." I said, "Yes, what's your question?" She asked, *"How do you learn to have the courage to be present as a leader?"*

I smiled at her, and I answered the question by talking about courage and fear, by talking about how fear was useful when it helps us in survival situations and was something of an overreaction when survival isn't more directly threatened. But as I reflected on her use of the term "courage," I realized that she had named a key difference between education in the twenty-first century as compared to the past century. Today we value courageous graduates, and in the past we sought obedience and following orders as a higher value. Education now is successful to the extent that it unleashes students to pursue their interests by trusting them to take action, to make decisions, to fail, to learn, and to take action again. In this way, learning courage flows from trust.

Being trusted by others or by yourself leads to courage—the courage to overcome your fears or resistance and thereby take initiative and action. It takes continuing courage to face full or partial failure and keep going until sufficient success and learning are achieved. In this way, courage is a key ingredient in the emotional calculus of educating the Whole New Engineer.

Aman Kapur, one of the founding students from iFoundry and a transfer student to Olin, described the different approaches to failure this way: "In one environment, failure means going on academic probation. At iFoundry and later at Olin, failure was an opportunity to learn."

Lawrence Domingo, who is studying biomedical engineering at California Polytechnic State University, recalled that as a freshman, people often asked whether he found his studies intimidating because he had chosen such a difficult path. But Professor Trevor Harding, whose door was open, "helped me find the courage to ask questions." He said, "Many of my freshman peers were intimidated by the professors. They were very aware of the power differential between them and these PhDs. There was a temptation to not be yourself—to *perform* for the professor. That's the dumbest thing to do. It's much more effective to just be yourself—and Trevor reinforced that."

When it's present, courage infuses the entire climate of the classroom, including professors. Kylie Hensley, also a student at California Polytechnic State University, said that her dream was for "professors to be courageous enough to openly reject doing things because that's the way they've always been done. I want them to help us see the world as it really is and have the humility to say, 'You're going to have to learn a lot of stuff I don't know.' That takes courage."

Thus, we see in these stories the role of courage in overcoming fear or resistance to take initiative, to persevere in the face of failure, and to continue until success has been achieved.

How do we show that we value courage in the engineering classroom? We value courage when we

- Challenge students to experiment and go out on a limb.
- Distinguish between routine settings when results are predictable and uncertain settings when experimentation, failure, and learning are unavoidable.
- Reframe mistakes as opportunities to reflect and learn.
- Emphasize process, rethinking the ways we can measure student achievement beyond static grades.
- Inspire students with stories of engineers whose courageous actions changed the world.

Pillar #4: Openness

After his death in 1955, Albert Einstein's brain was removed and preserved for study. Scientists were obsessed with unlocking the secret of Einstein's phenomenal genius, and they figured that the best place to look was in his brain matter. The study is still going on, and the findings of scientists who have analyzed Einstein's brain are the subject of continuing debate. One observer compared the process to viewing a Rorschach test. People tend to see what they want to see.

A better way of studying Einstein's genius might be to think about the kind of person he was. Most people are familiar with the stories of Einstein being a mediocre student, but they fail to mention the reasons why Einstein might have earned low marks. He was not so much a poor student as a difficult one. Biographer Walter Isaacson described his "casual willingness to question authority, his sassy attitude in the face of regimentation, and his lack of reverence for received wisdom"—the kinds of qualities that would have put him in opposition to the educators of his era.

Einstein's life and work were characterized by his intense curiosity and love of experimentation. He regarded failure as a step on the process to discovery, an opportunity to learn something new. He lived in the moment, once saying, "Learning is experience. Everything else is just information."

One might say Einstein was a genius because he was open.

One way of expressing openness is described by Marilee Adams in *Change Your Questions, Change Your Life*. She writes about a key tenet of openness—the ability to listen and engage without judgment. One of the most useful distinctions she makes is between judging and learning. Human beings have a tendency to instantly judge when confronted with a new and unfamiliar piece of information. This is part of our natural protective instinct. However, Adams suggests that being in judgment this way prevents us from *learning* very much. By rejecting something as bad, we don't reflect on it sufficiently long to learn whatever lessons might be embedded in the thing that we are judging.

Another sense of openness is effectuation—how we cause something to happen. Effectuation involves openness to explore, try, fail, iterate, and learn. Saras Sarasvathy, a professor at the University of Virginia's Darden School of Business, came up with a set of effectuation principles after she studied what made entrepreneurs tick. She noted that entrepreneurs, by their nature, faced unpredictable and unprecedented situations that required a special kind of intuition and fearlessness. In essence, effectuation is self-creating success; it takes advantage of the compounding effects that the entrepreneur creates. At its basis, effectuation relies on openness.

Morgan Bakies, a chemical engineering student at the University of Illinois who has been involved in iFoundry, described a physical chemistry class that became her favorite because she was allowed "free reign" and was able to make the class her own. "If I had just listened to lectures all semester, I don't think I would have learned as much. If the professor had said, 'Here are the tangible results you're expected to produce,' I wouldn't have been open to going above and beyond what was required. My experience was very similar to Daniel Pink's book *Drive*. Instead of waving the carrot in front of someone's face and trying to get them to follow the carrot, they expected us to create something. Instead of wondering if you were worthy of the carrot, you said, 'No, I can do this and I'm going to outperform those expectations.'"

As we've seen, there was a time in our history when engineering and engineering education used to value this kind of openness, but in some sense engineering is a victim of its own success. The degree to which engineers can use highly evolved and sophisticated physical and mathematical models in many areas to make detailed predictions of outcome has spoiled the field into believing that this is always the case. There are still many domains in which physical modeling is of limited fidelity.

Moreover, the existence of a single right answer in certain domains in engineering misleads engineering students (and some educators) to believe that this is always the case. When it comes to serving human needs, differing values lead to different designs and irreducible diversity and pluralism.

We value openness when we:

- Listen deeply to understand others and what they mean.
- Suspend judgment and try to learn the value in different points of view.
- Do not fear uncertainty and experiment, reflect, learn, and iterate to ultimately succeed.

- Ask open-ended questions and teach with open-ended challenges and problems.
- Are slow to jump to conclusions and repeatedly ask "What else?" in response to the presentation of a single answer.
- Teach students to ask good questions and to listen to others.
- Give students opportunities to engage with real people and solve pressing problems in their communities.
- Encourage students to be flexible and adapt when one course of action isn't working.

Openness involves our interactions with others, which leads naturally to the fifth pillar, connectedness, collaboration, and community.

Pillar #5: Connectedness, collaboration, and community

Beth Comstock, chief marketing officer at General Electric, has been upfront about the fact that when she hires people, she is looking for collaborators. "There's something romantic about the idea of the lone genius," she writes. "The early success of GE is often attributed solely to the inspiration and perspiration of Thomas Edison. But experience and research both tell us that lasting success is built by teams that drive each other through collaboration, different skill sets and, yes, tension. It's difficult to imagine the stratospheric successes of Steve Jobs without Stephen Wozniak or Mark Zuckerberg without Sheryl Sandberg. Edison had many collaborators and competitors who drove him, including the engineering genius Charles Steinmetz. Diverse teams drive more innovation. Hiring people with different styles, backgrounds and experience increases the success of teams."

It's true that in America, we tend to glorify the rugged individual. When we consider the great inventions and achievements of the past century, we usually name individual heroes, but as Comstock points out, this is not really accurate. In "The Myth of the Sole Inventor," Mark Lemley writes,

"The canonical story of the lone genius inventor is largely a myth. Surveys of hundreds of significant new technologies show that almost all of them are invented simultaneously or nearly simultaneously by two or more teams working independently of each other. Invention appears in significant part to be a social, not an individual, phenomenon."

Georges Harik, an early and prominent employee at Google, agrees, stating that pairs working together in start-ups are twenty times more productive than individuals working alone. This observation is easily supported by looking at groundbreaking pair work in recent technology—David Packard and Bill Hewlett of HP, Steve Jobs and Steve Wozniak of Apple, and Larry Page and Sergey Brin of Google.

The Whole New Engineer has a purpose in the world as part of a community. In defining the five essentials for creating innovators, Tony Wagner highlights collaboration versus individual achievement. Noting that "conventional schooling in the United States celebrates and rewards individual achievement while offering few meaningful opportunities for genuine collaboration," Wagner emphasizes that the ability to collaborate is a critical skill.

As we described in chapter 2, University of Illinois Professor Russ Korte has devoted his research emphasis, including his PhD thesis, to the question of how engineers are socialized in the workplace. He states unequivocally, "Of all the things that new hires need to learn when starting a job, building high-quality relationships with others was found to be a primary driver of success on the

> *Conventional schooling in the United States celebrates and rewards individual achievement while offering few meaningful opportunities for genuine collaboration.*
>
> **—Tony Wagner**

job. Developing an awareness of the importance of interpersonal relations in school and work is one of the objectives of our work in the College of Engineering at the University of Illinois." Korte's bottom line: "The structure of relations in which you work can leverage your abilities and your knowledge to accomplish things far greater than you can on your own or through traditional hierarchical team environments."

For iFoundry student Morgan Bakies, the message about community really hit home when she worked at a refinery during the summer. "I worked on a distillation tower. Every product in the plant comes into a distillation tower. From there it goes on to a ton of other parts within the refinery. I personally had to talk to everyone else who takes all of my products, because if I didn't talk to those people, I could have destroyed the refinery because there were a few times when my mentor wasn't there. I had free reign over my unit, which was awesome, but also terrifying. If you're encouraging people to go try and beat other people, then how are you going to respond in the workplace? You need to be actively learning as a group. It needs to be a collaborative effort. If you're not working with other people, then you're not going to have those communication abilities that they complain that engineers don't necessarily have. You're not going to be able to talk to people. Without communication I could have destroyed all our profits within a few hours."

For decades, corporate representatives have been reporting to the National Science Foundation and others that engineers need to become more effective at communication. In Korte's research, this involves the ability to establish strong interpersonal relationships within diverse teams.

It's true that lots of people don't make it through engineering programs, for a whole variety of reasons. But the leading reason for this is the message often sent: "You are on your own, and the way to succeed is by beating your classmates." Debbie Chachra, PhD, associate professor of materials science at Olin College, recalls an experience from her undergraduate engineering school that is so vivid it remains with her years later. She was in a course involving a hands-on project working in a team. "It was," she says now, "far and away the worst course I took in engineering school." She enumerates the reasons. "We were expected to create something that was totally useless. It had no interesting social value." But that wasn't the worst part. Particularly memorable to Debbie was that working on a team became a defeating rather than an enabling process. The team wasn't working together toward a common purpose. It was composed of separate people each working on a piece of the project. "I was the only girl on the team, and I ended up being stuck doing the software, which I hated," Debbie says. "I had never done it before, and I had no idea how to do it. I tried getting help; I couldn't get help. There was no social support of being on a team because the software was seen as being 'my thing.' There was no stepping-stone to get from 'I know nothing' to 'I have to write this code.'"

Her experience was indicative of the lone struggle many students face when they are asked to solve difficult problems. Yet individuals succeed by connecting with others, by being present in their interactions. Companies succeed by celebrating collaboration, not by setting employees against each other. Engineering education needs to start valuing connection, too.

Collaboration alleviates the stress of trying to be all things to all people. It releases teachers from having to put up walls to protect themselves. And it gives students a power to create that they didn't know they had. It takes them out of the mind-set of competing for grades and places them in an environment where success depends on the engagement of the team and all its members.

An interesting experiment at Rose-Hulman Institute of Technology demonstrates the team effect. Garrett Meyer, a mechanical engineering student, described an online peer evaluation tool that was used for one of his project classes. The tool includes self-evaluation and peer evaluation in five dimensions of team member contributions. "They're really action based," he said. "They're not just, 'I felt like this person did a lot of the work.' They're focused on the actions each member of the team does or does not take. Normally it becomes a modifier applied to the group grade at the end. Who better knows how people perform in a project than the people who are doing the project? The ultimate grade is dependent on everybody collaborating well and working hard on the projects."

Collaboration can have a liberating effect on students. Olin junior Liz Threlkeld describes it as "limiting insecurity. Students are generally insecure people, but I never feel insecure. When I have a problem, if I ask there will always be people to explain. I never have to worry about people thinking I'm stupid. There's no cutthroat attitude—and what's feeding this openness is the awareness that we all have different strengths and we can help each other. In every class I've been able to identify several people who I can ask for help, and when I go to them they never say, 'No, I don't have time for you.' They say, 'Let me help you out.' It has opened my eyes to the fact that you don't have to feel like you're a genius all the time. You don't have to be super smart to do something really awesome. I wasn't a top student in high school—smart, but not extraordinary. But the process of collaboration allows extraordinary work."

Out in the world, success as an engineer depends on the ability to figure out people around us, work on teams in organizations, relate to clients' needs. Educating engineers who are comfortable with collaboration can transform the workplace.

We value connectedness, collaboration, and community when we:

- Listen deeply to others.
- Speak explicitly about the importance of connectedness, collaboration, and community in engineering practice.
- Create institutional and physical structures that support the formation of community and teamwork.
- Offer experiences across the curriculum that develop collaboration and teamwork.
- Show regard for successful student-student, faculty-student, and faculty-faculty relationships, not just successful tasks.
- Support coursework, organizational development, and training efforts to support collaboration, connectedness, and community.
- Support strong mentoring, advising, and peer mentoring/advising efforts.
- Work to reframe competition and survival of the fittest to collaboration.

- Stop diminishing communication skills by calling them "soft skills" and work to offer them in ways that accelerate and advance skill.

These pillars of our journey to envision and educate a Whole New Engineer are not abstract. Together they offer a shorthand to talk about what's missing and what's important and to formulate a road map for whole new engineering education. For educators and those concerned with the future of education, the task is to put them into practice—to infuse them organically into the culture of schools and classrooms. In the next chapters, we'll describe the ways in which the Whole New Engineer needs to show up and think differently, as well as a number of educational breakthroughs that will help us carry the pillars into practice.

6

The Whole New Learner
From Carrots and Sticks to Intrinsic Motivation

*When self-determined, people experience a sense of freedom to do
what is interesting, personally important and vitalizing.*

—Edward Deci and Richard Ryan

When Edward Deci began studying psychology at Hamilton College
in Clinton, New York, in the early 1960s, he was often reminded that the
school was the alma mater of B. F. Skinner, the behaviorist who pioneered a
theory of behavior modification involving systems of positive reinforcement.
Skinner's principle had gained purchase in psychological and educational
circles: when we reward or praise desired behavior consistently, children
will perform. Skinner suggested that if children weren't motivated, it was
because the right rewards weren't offered.

As Deci continued his graduate studies at Carnegie Mellon University
in Pittsburgh, he began to question Skinner's premise. Was there not, he
wondered, *inherent* motivation in human beings? He could see examples all

around him—the child who loved to read, who loved to paint, who loved to make things just because. Was motivation only something external that "gets done" to people, or was it also something people *do*?

One day in 1969, Deci was chatting with a fellow graduate student in his office and he noticed a puzzle called Soma, newly developed by Parker Brothers, sitting on a table. It was a complex cube puzzle, consisting of seven differently shaped blocks that could be fitted together to produce millions of different combinations. Deci had been looking for a method to test a theory about motivation for his dissertation, and he lit on the puzzle.

Deci set up an experiment using two groups. He created puzzle configurations that the students would match in three different sessions. On the first day, both groups would be unpaid. On the second day, the first group would receive a small cash reward for solving the puzzles and the second group would be unpaid. On the third day, members of the paid group would be told that there was no money left to pay them.

In each session, the students worked on the puzzles for half an hour. Then Deci told them the session was over and he had to leave the room for a few minutes to input the data. During the break they could relax, read a magazine (*Time*, *Playboy*, and *The New Yorker* were provided), or continue working on the puzzle. He left the room and observed the students through a one-way window. What did he observe?

On the first day there was little difference between the two groups; both continued playing with the puzzle for some part of the break, indicating that they were interested in solving it. On the second day, the rewarded group was much more interested in continuing to solve the puzzle during the break, suggesting that the reward was motivating. On the third day, however, after the reward had been yanked, the previously rewarded group was much less interested in playing with the puzzle during the break. As Deci observed, "It seemed that once having been paid, these subjects were only in it for the money." Deci concluded that in this case the reward actually had a diminishing effect on motivation.

The Soma experiment opened up a field of investigation for Deci that would fully engage him throughout his career—and that continues to this day. He had discovered his passion. Along with his colleague at the University of Rochester, Richard Ryan, he has explored all aspects of motivation and has elevated the notion that intrinsic motivation—that which comes from the inside, with no external reward—is a key to self-determination, creativity, and innovation.

Intrinsic motivation lights up the fundamental values of the Whole New Engineer, as we described them in the five pillars. When intrinsic motivation is enhanced, students are wholly engaged, mind and body, and their enjoyment and joy are inspired by the internal sense of pleasure they get from being interested in the subject. Intrinsically motivated students thrive in an atmosphere of trust,

When intrinsic motivation is enhanced, students are wholly engaged, mind and body, and their enjoyment and joy are inspired by the internal sense of pleasure they get from being interested in the subject.

where they are given autonomy and a chance to pursue their passions. Autonomy, in turn, elevates students' interest in the material. Students are enabled to be courageous—stepping outside the bonds of external rewards to discover the satisfaction of learning to solve problems. When learning has value related to their personal goals, students are able to be fully present to the experience and fully engaged with others in the process. The value equation is shifted to the internal drive for satisfaction; the more education engages the students' interests, the more it is perceived as having value.

The meaning of motivation

Typically, we think of *people* as being inherently motivated or unmotivated. For example, we talk about the highly motivated student or the unmotivated slacker. But on reflection, it's clear that motivation exists in the interaction between a person and the environment. That is, someone who is highly motivated in one setting can be completely amotivated in another. The student who is a slacker in math might well be passionately committed to sociology studies. So it's not so simple as labeling students as motivated or not.

People also commonly think about there being two polar opposite "types" of motivation—extrinsic ("the carrot and the stick") and intrinsic—with the idea that people exhibit one type or the other. It's not that simple. In their work on self-determination theory, Deci and Ryan describe a spectrum, with many permutations along the way, from entirely external to entirely self-driven.

Jon Stolk, a professor of materials science at Olin College, has spent a number of years immersing himself in the motivation literature, researching motivation in engineering students, and applying these ideas to faculty development. He interprets some of the key points along Deci and Ryan's spectrum with the typical things that educators often hear from students. For example, *amotivation* happens when a student has no interest or is disassociated from the setting. It's associated with a feeling of helplessness—that one's actions are disconnected from outcomes. Stolk observes that when students say things such as "It doesn't matter whether I study; I'm going to fail anyway" or "I have no idea why I am taking this class," they're exhibiting amotivation.

In Deci and Ryan's framework, *extrinsic motivation* covers a pretty broad range. It refers to any sort of motivation that does not come from the inherent characteristics of the task. But within that category, there's a big difference between the ends of the spectrum. When people commonly talk about extrinsic motivation, they are actually referring to what Deci and Ryan call external regulation—that is, when a task is uninteresting and the individual is acting solely to achieve external reward or to avoid punishment. We see this in students all the time: "Just tell me what I have to do to get an A" or "If I fail this class, my parents are going to kill me."

Other kinds of extrinsic motivation are more internal and have different characteristics. For example, when the task is uninteresting but the individual understands its importance, the individual is displaying *identified regulation*. Stolk associates identified regulation with comments such as, "Well, I don't want to do this homework set, but I can see it will help me improve" or "This project might not be fun, but it will allow me to get a summer internship."

Finally, with *intrinsic motivation* the task is fully internalized. It is interesting and inherently satisfying and enjoyable in its own right; the individual is doing it because he or she wants to do it. Every professor knows what intrinsic motivation looks like. It's observed in the student who can't wait to get back to the design studio to continue work on a project, or the student who tells his or her friends how awesome a class is.

Across this spectrum, individuals can be motivated and effective even when they don't find tasks inherently interesting, as long as they experience a greater value—in the way that, for example, a campaign worker canvassing for a candidate might dislike the activity but be passionate about his or her candidate being elected. And people often exhibit different types of motivation simultaneously. For example, a student might be really interested in and excited about the material in a class he or she is taking but could at the same time be concerned about maintaining a high GPA. In life, individuals can be motivated by both curiosity and perks, by both pleasure and reward, by both love and money. Most situations are a mixed bag.

Motivation matters

Having said that, an increasing body of research highlights the importance of intrinsic motivation. People with a high degree of intrinsic motivation seem to reap the greatest advantages, including the sense of well-being that comes from self-determination. In an educational setting, intrinsic motivation leads to deeper and more effective learning. When people are intrinsically motivated in their work, they are more likely to be effective and to make exceptional contributions. Research on creativity and innovation suggests that the key characteristic distinguishing entrepreneurs and innovators is not how well they can do what has been done before but their intrinsic motivation—their *will* to innovate.

Teresa M. Amabile, a Harvard University professor who has written and lectured extensively about creativity and innovation, explains that while extrinsic motivation, which comes from "a carrot or a stick," can be effective, it does not have the same impact on creativity as intrinsic motivation. "If the scientist's boss promises to reward her financially should the blood-clotting project succeed, or if he threatens to fire her should it fail, she will certainly be motivated to find a solution," Amabile notes. "Money doesn't necessarily stop people from being creative. But in many situations, it doesn't help either, especially when it leads people to feel that they are being bribed or controlled. More important, money by itself doesn't make employees passionate about their jobs. But passion and interest—a person's internal desire to do something—are what intrinsic motivation is all about . . . People will be most creative when they feel motivated primarily by the interest, satisfaction, and challenge of the work itself—and not by external pressures." Amabile's recent book, *The Progress Principle: Using Small Wins to Ignite Joy, Engagement, and Creativity at Work*, highlights intrinsic motivation—"the love of the work itself"—as essential. She concludes, "As inner work life goes, so goes the company."

And, it might also be said, as inner life goes, so goes the classroom.

Tony Wagner, author of *Creating Innovators: The Making of Young People Who Will Change the World*, comments, "Perhaps the most important finding of my research is that young innovators are not primarily motivated by extrinsic incentives. Even those who come from families that have struggled economically are intrinsically motivated. As a consequence, the programs that do the best job of educating young innovators focus on intrinsic motivations for learning through a combination of play, passion, and purpose: playful, discovery-based learning leads young people to find and pursue a passion, which eventually evolves into a deeper sense of purpose."

Forty years after Deci conducted his cube experiment, Dan Pink, a leading voice on the changing world of work, study, and engagement, wrote a best-selling book called *Drive: The Surprising Truth about What Motivates Us*. Pink is an interesting guy. A former speechwriter for Vice President Al Gore—what he calls his last "real job"—Pink went on to carve out a specialty writing about work, in particular, the "new world" of work, which exists on a global playing field, with competition across disciplines, and the question of motivation. Having traveled an unusual road to his expertise, Pink understands that motivation, achievement, and innovation are not compartmentalized ideas.

Speaking with us for this book, Pink elaborated on his thinking. "I refer to a system of rewards as if/then," he said. "*If* you do this, *then* you'll get that. If I offer you an if/then reward, it's an effort to control your behavior. People have only two responses to control. They can comply, or they can defy. We don't want compliant engineers. We don't want defiant engineers. We want people who are engaged, and the way people engage is getting motivated under their own steam. Ask yourself: do people do their best work under conditions of control or conditions of self-direction? I don't think it's even close. Under conditions of control, you may get good things, but you never get great things. And given the ferocity of competition around the world, the U.S. doesn't have the luxury of having average, pretty good engineers."

> *We don't want compliant engineers. We don't want defiant engineers. We want people who are engaged, and the way people engage is getting motivated under their own steam.*
>
> **—Daniel Pink**

Despite the growing body of evidence around the importance of intrinsic motivation, traditional educational settings often turn external rewards, such as grades, honors, prizes, and being allowed to skip levels and opt out of requirements, to motivate students. By default, the "learning" that occurs in these settings usually has to do with meeting objective standards that can be measured by tests—memorizing information, correctly solving equations, and being able to accurately reiterate course material. Too often, students focus on *passing* rather than *learning*. And educators reinforce this tendency (with the best of intentions): "You'd better master this material, because it's going to be on the exam." Students are conditioned throughout their educational lives to seek proof of ability and potential through grades and test scores. They're taught that it's all about the high GPA, the perfect SAT. Simultaneously, we are increasingly emphasizing test performance as a measure of teaching effectiveness. When we talk about high-achieving and low-achieving schools, we point to grades and test scores as the evidence. And so, like their students, educators find their status reflected on the balance sheet of grades. Rather than supporting intrinsic motivation in students and in educators—a key to both learning and creativity—we too often extinguish it in our educational system.

Intrinsic engineering

Today's engineering graduates must be comfortable in the skin of engineering, be personally engaged in the science and culture of innovation, and become thought leaders on the most important issues of the day, such as sustainability, people-oriented design, and the human aspects of technology. All of these require passionate engagement, which comes from being intrinsically motivated.

There is evidence that intrinsic motivation is the guiding light that draws students to study engineering in the first place. According to the Academic Pathways for People Learning Engineering Survey (APPLES), the strongest motivators to enter engineering are intrinsic, both psychological ("I enjoy engineering") and behavioral ("I like to fix things"). Motivation is positively correlated with persistence and the intention to complete the engineering degree. Yet despite the importance of intrinsic motivation in learning, it has seldom served as a focal point of change in engineering education. Culturally, it is difficult for educational institutions to take the leap away from the certain measures of grades and scores for students and tenure for faculty to the uncertainty of building intrinsic motivation models. Students throughout the world are put into the Skinner box called "university," wherein they learn to respond to the extrinsic reward and punishment of grades. Thereafter, as their teachers and professors, we puzzle over why these same individuals go into the workforce lacking the skills to be creative, show initiative, or exhibit the curiosity and desire to be lifelong learners.

Entrepreneurs and innovators are highly self-motivated, are willing to take initiative and assume appropriate risks, and display high levels of self-confidence that they can complete tasks. Thus, preparing graduates to be innovators and entrepreneurs requires not only developing their knowledge and skills toward this end but also helping them to become self-directed, confident, intrinsically motivated individuals. So how can you do that?

How to increase intrinsic motivation

An example of an intentional setting of intrinsic motivation is a course at Olin College called the Stuff of History, which blends materials science with culture, cotaught by Jon Stolk and Rob Martello. If you were to wander in on any given day, you would find a high level of energy and autonomy. Teams of students sit around work tables or move about the laboratory, some chatting, some conducting experiments, some examining the results of metals testing, some clicking results into their laptops. The mood is informal—serious but playful. The classroom is constructed like a laboratory; high-end equipment fills the back end, with the tables jammed together in the remaining space. There is a productive messiness, and there are no podiums. Stolk and Martello—who refer to themselves in the course materials as "your personal trainers"—wander from table to table, listening, observing, and offering occasional suggestions. At times they are deliberately silent, allowing students to reach their own conclusions, even if they aren't likely to be successful. A popular section of the course is devoted to the study of Paul Revere, the well-known patriot and metallurgist. Martello happens to be an expert on Revere; his PhD dissertation at MIT was "Paul Revere's Metallurgical Ride," and he later published a book called *Midnight Ride, Industrial Dawn*, which is part of the course reading. Stolk brings materials science expertise to the course, and the two operate with an amazingly comfortable, turf war–free teamwork that you rarely see in college classrooms. In the class, students use their growing knowledge of material properties and analytical techniques to reproduce some of Revere's silver, bronze, or copper work; analyze the effectiveness and efficiency of his processes; and examine the social context of one of his metallurgical endeavors. Field trips to nearby Boston bring the lessons to life. For example, the class visits historical sites, such as the nearby Saugus Ironworks, and takes a yearly trip to the Museum of Fine Arts so students can give a "gallery talk" about ancient material technologies while surrounded by historical artifacts. They then study the materials Revere used and try to re-create them with current materials.

The pairing of materials science with history and culture brings to light a central tenet of intrinsic motivation—that artifacts have meaning. Classroom practices themselves promote intrinsic motivation by fostering autonomy, giving teams choices in project topics, experimental approaches and the manner of reporting findings—such as the creation of a Wikipedia page or educational video. And the class structure itself promotes feelings of community, connections to broader society and increasing competence.

Deci and Ryan identify *autonomy*, *relatedness* (the feeling of being connected to others, part of a community—either those around you or in a broader context), and *competence* (the feeling of being able to do the task at hand) as the three fundamental psychological needs that, when met, improve intrinsic motivation.

Dan Pink frames the same needs somewhat differently, listing autonomy, mastery, and purpose as the key ingredients for intrinsic motivation: people are intrinsically motivated when they have a sense of *personal volition*, a sense that they are *getting better* at what they are doing, and a sense that what they are doing *matters*. (While Deci and Ryan don't call out purpose in the same way, it is incorporated into their description of relatedness—that is, making a difference for others.)

Let's examine these factors:

1. Autonomy: Making meaningful choices is a cornerstone of intrinsic motivation.

When students are given the power to control elements of their education, they are incentivized to do well in a way that doesn't occur when they're told what to do. Autonomy is self-determination—that is, the free will to pursue one's own course in life, in work, and in study. Autonomy does not imply that one's actions might not be influenced by others—only that the choices feel right and are in keeping with an inner sense of self.

Based on their research into intrinsic motivation, Deci and Ryan developed what they called autonomy-supportive pedagogies, involving both instructor attitudes and classroom structures. Autonomy-supportive instructors, they proposed, spend more time listening, give fewer directives, ask more questions about what students want, verbalize fewer solutions to problems, make more empathetic statements, and offer greater support for students' internalization of learning goals. It is interesting to note that when K–12 teachers are led to focus on meeting testing standards, as has been the case with

Autonomy does not imply that one's actions might not be influenced by others— only that the choices feel right and are in keeping with an inner sense of self.

No Child Left Behind, they use fewer autonomy-supportive actions. It stands to reason that autonomy is anathema in a system that is based on extrinsic rewards.

Students respond to trust—to the message that they can do what they want to do and succeed in the process. Andrew Bell, a senior at the University of Illinois who was in the first iFoundry class, says, "Looking back, I really didn't know what I was getting myself into at first. As more of a generalist, I was attracted to the idea of combining engineering with other fields. Once on campus, it took my classmates and me about half a semester to realize that our professors really meant it when they said we could do whatever we wanted. No one in school had ever told us that. I also liked the fact that we had two hands-on projects as freshmen, the steam car and a computer microcontroller. That is a rarity in engineering, where there aren't usually class-sponsored projects until junior or senior year. The final thing that kept me was the people who stuck around for that first year, the ones that were curious to see what would happen in an intrinsically motivated environment where we had nearly as clear of an idea where the program would go as the staff did. I still keep in touch with the select group that stuck around. They are doing some amazing things." Through iFoundry, Bell was instilled with a sense of curiosity, purpose, and motivation. iFoundry planted the seed that he was competent and creative. It became part of his identity and will never leave him.

From the outset, students are motivated when they are given ownership of their work. When the control belongs totally to the teacher, so does the ownership. Autonomy is enhanced when educators take advantage of students' innate talents and interests to offer choices in such arenas as topics, learning methodologies, and products.

David Goldberg: **Exceptional autonomy**

For me, one of the most inspiring stories of independent (autonomous) student engagement has happened serendipitously through the Universidade Federal de Minas Gerais in Brazil. Alessandro Moreira, vice director (associate dean) of engineering, had toured iFoundry and Olin College, and he and I had many conversations. He was committed to bringing change to undergraduate education at UFMG. But where to start? He decided to launch with an exuberant welcome similar to the iFoundry iLaunch and began making plans for a program *Engenharia Recebe*, or "Engineering Welcomes You." With only a few weeks before the start of the semester, he struggled finding the staff and resources to pull off the program. Then he had an idea: he contacted members of the UFMG Junior Enterprise for assistance.

In the United States, most people are unfamiliar with Junior Enterprise, although it's been around for a while. Junior Enterprise was started in 1967 in France, and it has chapters in many countries. Its purpose is to allow students to work independently in entrepreneurial ventures outside the classroom, starting and consulting for local companies. In effect, Junior Enterprise students are at work in the world, even as they are learning in the classroom. Brazilian universities have taken Junior Enterprise to heart, and at UFMG, most of the engineering disciplines have a Junior Enterprise chapter or enterprise, and each enterprise organizes to do consulting projects for local businesses. The students engage around functional specialties—marketing, technical, administrative, etc.—and take pride in teaching each other professional skills such as PowerPoint presentations and project management. It is not unusual for there to be five to ten projects running at one time with groups of twenty-five to fifty students. Enterprises have faculty advisors, but they are largely hands-off. In fact, not all faculty fully embrace the enterprises; many teachers would prefer that students concentrate all of their efforts on their class studies.

When Alessandro called on Junior Enterprise students to help launch his program, they responded enthusiastically. A team consisting of Andre Drumond, Guilherme Lage, Jorge Raso, Paloma Assis, and others put together an outstanding launch program in a very short time with professional social media, handouts, activities, and prizes. Overall, the program was well received by students and faculty alike, and it helped kick off engineering education for first-year students at UFMG in a very positive way. The program is continuing at UFMG, and now Alessandro has brought students into his planning team for curricular change at UFMG. One possibility is the idea of having an educational transformation Junior Enterprise team to contract projects for social media, training, new course design, and other educational activities using student power and ideas to drive the enterprise.

I was blessed to be able to visit UFMG and do training workshops with both students and faculty, and after these experiences, I shifted from calling for *student-centered education* and more and more started using the term *student-led learning* instead. One might say that most education is student centered, but it's an entirely different matter to see student-led programs. It all comes back to trust and a kind of education that really unleashes students as confident lifelong learners who have the courage to take initiative. This depends, in part, on the ability of faculty members who can relinquish control and really trust students with a central role—a leadership role—in their own educations. Increasingly, I believe we will see students as the power and light of engineering education reform.

Junior Enterprise has taken root at iFoundry under the aegis of CUBE (Champaign Urbana Business and Engineering Consulting). Karen Lamb, now a senior, was the first president, and she immediately recognized that the key to success was the autonomy of this student-run program. "Junior Enterprise gives so much power to the students to create," she says. "It isn't like a top-down kind of structure. Consulting is a great opportunity to do that, and engineering consulting is a hot commodity."

Current CUBE President Morgan Bakies adds that student ownership is a breakthrough idea that is gaining momentum. "If you look at any other consulting group on campus at the University of Illinois, everyone else is being led by some sort of faculty. Yes, we have a partnership with iFoundry, which is how we get a little bit of our money. We have about $500 a year from them. But it's completely student led, which adds a totally different dynamic. We have students who used to be in a consulting class who joined CUBE solely because they knew they would have more opportunity to properly interface with the clients. The returns from CUBE have been amazing and gone high above my expectations. I think it's because you have the student atmosphere that shows this is what we accomplish as ourselves as students, even though we are taking classes. The reason that we decided to do this is because we want students to have more opportunities to work on practical engineering projects early on."

2. Purpose/Relatedness: Doing things that matter to your peers, and to the world at large, increases intrinsic motivation.

Deci and Ryan describe relatedness as "feeling connected to others, to caring for and being cared for by those others, to having a sense of 'belongingness' both with other individuals and with one's communities."

The idea that community drives motivation is gaining purchase in education and practice. Pam Rogalski, co-founder of the Engineering Leadership Council, has seen how important this can be for engineering students. She observes "a supportive community is central to harnessing the motivation that naturally exists in engineering students and maintaining that motivation over the course of their careers."

Community leads naturally to another value, which is having a sense of purpose. The recent trend toward service learning in engineering education makes enormous sense in this regard. When a student designs a product that will help less fortunate people in his or her own community or travels halfway around the world to work on a engineering project in a developing country, he or she is satisfying a need for both purpose and relatedness.

Educating students to be problem solvers in the world is a trend across the university system. One example is the Global Engineering curriculum devised by Engineers Without Borders Canada. According to Portfolio Manager Sal Alajek, the curriculum, which has been adopted in many schools, is part of a social change incubator that employs a network of stakeholders in the engineering education system, including students, instructors, professional associations, and private companies. The mission is to create systemic innovations in Canada and Africa that have the potential to radically disrupt the systems that allow poverty to persist. For Alajek and his colleagues, engineering itself is an instrument of global change. But that message doesn't always get through to young people. "Why are young people not resonating with the engineering message?" he asked. "It's not because the perception of engineering is stodgy and unhip. It's because we usually talk about linking science to the real world and that turns young people off. But when we talk about engineering in the context of problem solving and creativity—of health, happiness and safety—students are interested."

But it's not just about purpose in that bigger "making a difference in the world" sense. It's also about purpose with respect to the people immediately around you. Martello has discovered a very interesting phenomenon. He says, "I don't think that everything you're doing actually has to be your passion individually. But the community aspect creates intrinsic fun. When we've asked students, 'What was driving you in this particular project?' some of them said, 'I'm just intrinsically interested in this idea.' But many others came up with something we hadn't expected. They said, 'This isn't my thing, but my team was just so amazing that I couldn't help but be excited about what we were working on.' So even though they didn't have intrinsic curiosity about the topic, the fact that they were in the community environment, which offered many choices, made them excited. Sometimes that's enough."

This is a powerful insight about training for the workplace. In every job there are projects that are less interesting than others. Motivation has to come from something besides constant fascination with the stuff of work. Not every engineering experience is cool or groundbreaking. But it is possible to be intrinsically motivated by the environment.

3. Mastery: Being effective increases intrinsic motivation.

Mastery involves experiencing an internal sense of effectiveness—not just being able to do something but also knowing you have the ability to learn to do it. When students expect to do well, rather than expect to fail, they are more likely to succeed.

Mastery is experienced in an environment where creativity is encouraged, where trying things is seen as an opportunity to get better—even if something doesn't work the first time. When teachers encourage students to reflect on the experience of learning, to ask questions such as "What was done well?" and "What can be improved?" students focus on mastery, not just getting the right answer the first time out. Such an approach inspires a deeper experience of learning that doesn't end

Fear of failure cuts off the opportunity to learn from mistakes and to become creative problem solvers.

when the external goal is met. In this kind of secure environment, ambiguity and frustration can be used to a learning advantage. When students see that not every question has a single right answer, they can be motivated in the face of uncertainty.

In contrast, we approach many topics—particularly in engineering—as a rigid system of right and wrong answers. Here failure is a looming possibility every step of the way, and students focus solely on regurgitating knowledge presented by the instructor. In such a context, students feel powerless and uninspired. Fear of failure cuts off the opportunity to learn from mistakes and to become creative problem solvers.

Stolk points out that self-evaluation is intrinsic to self-motivation. Students can be encouraged to reflect on their learning experiences and say for themselves what they felt worked and didn't work—as opposed to relying solely on the instructor's evaluation. The ability to honestly evaluate one's own performance is not only highly motivating in the classroom but also essential in the working environment. And what of the perfectionists—of which there are arguably many in engineering schools? "Perfectionism goes beyond trying to do one's best," he cautions. "Perfectionism is hung up on being perfect. Students need to take pride in their work, but perfectionists allow their fear of making a mistake to inhibit progress." He advises that students need to learn that attempting is more important than succeeding and failure is an opportunity to learn. "Students need to see us making mistakes occasionally. We need to model and demonstrate the process of learning and recovering from our mistakes."

These ingredients together create an environment that enables students to engage, in an authentic and open way, with their education. Martello reflected on the experience of teaching at a school that fosters intrinsic motivation. "One thing you notice is that at Olin, the faculty and students alike are having a lot of fun. When I was in graduate school, there were individuals in the faculty who were having fun; it was entertaining to be in the room with them, just clowning around, but it was on the side. Or you'd see students having too much fun, and you'd worry about them or think they were nerds—say, 'That guy is having a little too much fun with quantum physics over there; what's up with him?' And you'd think, 'He's not going to be here next year.' Apart from these side trips into fun, the larger sense was one of work: we've got serious things to do here. At Olin, you worry if people aren't having fun, and I don't mean that in a frivolous way. Students and teachers who have identified their passions and goals and are achieving them are having fun. They're doing things that matter to them, and they're having a great time. And that's what goes on here. Fun is not something you experience only when you go to a football game after class. It's something you expect, even when the work is challenging. It's fun to feel enthusiasm and passion in your work. A lot of education is fear based, and students who complete courses say, 'Whew, I survived.' Here, there is a sense of victory: 'Just look at what I accomplished. That was awesome!'"

> *Fun is not something you experience only when you go to a football game after class. It's something you expect, even when the work is challenging. It's fun to feel enthusiasm and passion in your work.*
>
> **—Rob Martello**

Making intrinsic motivation the norm

If you were to poll any group of educators in the country about the value of intrinsic motivation in their classrooms, you'd get a near-unanimous agreement that it is very important. The frustration for many educators is that intrinsic motivation is too often relegated to the realm of extracurricular activities. At Rose-Hulman Institute of Technology in Terre Haute, Indiana, students clamor to work on the championship human-powered vehicle team, which regularly wins American Society of Mechanical Engineers competitions. The competitions are fun for the students, and they also appeal to a growing interest in sustainability—building vehicles that make a difference. Michael Moorhead, the faculty advisor of Rose-Hulman's team, delights in the level of student engagement he sees on the teams. "The students working on the teams want to be successful. They want to win," he says. "In some respects, they learn more than they do inside the classroom, where the focus is pretty strictly math, science, and engineering. I've seen a first-year student master ideas in fluid dynamics better than many juniors— because he needed to figure it out to do the design."

Moorhead admits that the intrinsic motivation—the drive to succeed—the students experience in cocurricular activities should be in the classroom as well. It's something he is personally committed to. "Students who come here know it's a challenging field," he says. "We need to get over the motivational hump of 'It's too hard.' I'm not just talking about students having fun in a project. When students become motivated, they take things more seriously. They care about what they're learning."

Educators such as Moorhead know that intrinsic motivation is crucial, and they find opportunities where they can. The problem is that too often the culture of higher education is purely extrinsic and the "fun" projects are typically outside the normal curriculum.

Having said that, the human-powered vehicle team experience at Rose-Hulman has a lot more learning and motivational depth than it might appear at first glance. Materials engineering student Garrett Meyer spoke of how the experience not only is about having fun and experiencing teamwork but also is purpose driven. "What really impressed me about the human-powered vehicle was that I could clearly see this project benefiting people," he said. "Even though you're a student, you can really change the face of transportation for maybe millions of people, ultimately. That's cool."

As Ryan and Deci have noted, intrinsic motivation is the norm rather than the exception in human nature. Self-motivation, curiosity, and mastery are positive and prevalent, even as there are examples of people being lackluster and unmotivated—the image of millions of people staring blankly at TVs comes to mind. Ryan and Deci became interested in how to support the positive life experiences while limiting the factors that diminish the human spirit.

In a paper on classroom motivation, Ana T. Torres-Ayala, University of South Florida, and Geoffrey L. Herman, University of Illinois, argue that intrinsic motivation is the most natural thing in the world. They write, "From birth onward, humans, in their healthiest states, are active, inquisitive, curious, and playful creatures, displaying a ubiquitous readiness to learn and explore, and they do not require extraneous incentives to do so. This natural motivational tendency is a critical element in cognitive, social, and physical development because it is through acting on one's inherent interests that one grows in knowledge and skills. The inclinations to take interest in novelty, to actively assimilate, and to creatively apply our skills is not limited to childhood, but is a significant feature of human nature that affects performance, persistence, and well-being across life's epochs."

An example of purely expressed intrinsic motivation is play. Play is fun; no carrot or stick is required. From infancy, we simply want to do it. But it has a purpose. In his study of innovators, Tony Wagner describes a developmental arc from play to passion to purpose. He notes that the founders of Google, Amazon, and Wikipedia, as well as Julia Child, all had one thing in common: they attended Montessori schools, where learning through play is practiced. In his review of Olin College, Wagner sees "ample evidence in every class of more serious forms of adult play, as well, the sense of play that comes from being so deeply engrossed in a project that you lose all sense of time; the sense of play that is an integral element in any creative endeavor."

From its inception, Olin College highlighted the importance of fun and encouraged students to do at least one thing each semester that was fun. In fact, engagement in so-called passionate pursuits was structured into Olin's life through a formal Passionate Pursuits program. Students are encouraged to pursue their personal artistic, humanistic, philanthropic, and technical interests, with the support and guidance of faculty members and, in many cases, funding from the college. Participating students complete a final project at the end of each semester and receive nondegree credit for their efforts. Examples of Passionate Pursuits projects include classical vocal technique, aerial silks, penny pressing, rock climbing, design and construction of a 3D printer, chocolate making, scuba diving, building a telescope, and Indian culinary traditions.

A similar program is under way at iFoundry, with a Passionate Pursuits lecture series, where students share their outside passions with their peers. Students advertise on a dedicated Facebook page. An example: "This week: Kevin Wolz with *Saving the World: My Philosophy, My Story, and My Summer. Free pizza and pop!*" These engagements help create well-rounded human beings and inspire creative thinking. They do not distract from study—"the real business at hand." They enhance performance in the classroom, create community, and build the underlying feelings of self-worth and pleasure.

However, these programs, too, are outside the curriculum. The real innovation is happening inside. From the outset, Olin College and iFoundry were designed to change the culture of motivation, beginning with the application process. Students who signed up for a new college or a curricular incubator were clearly motivated by something other than external factors such as prestige. They were largely motivated by the excitement and adventure of being part of something new—and many of the early students specifically mentioned being drawn to a learning experience that would release them to do the things that interested them—intrinsically.

In a visit to Olin College, which he described in his book, Tony Wagner named intrinsic motivation as one of the key elements that makes Olin radically different from most other schools. "Conventional academic classes rely on extrinsic incentives as motivators for learning," he writes. "You learn in order to get a good grade on the test so that you can have a good GPA. While professors may tout the value of learning for its own sake, they nevertheless make liberal use of the traditional carrots and sticks to ensure that students come to class and learn the material. One has to wonder how many students would show up for their classes if no grade was involved." Olin College, in contrast, believes that extrinsic incentives do not create innovators. "Teachers at Olin," he writes, "have an explicit goal of strengthening students' intrinsic motivations to be lifelong learners, to be the architects of their own learning, their own careers, to bring into being that which they desire."

Breaking curricular conventions

Curriculum becomes dynamic in a new era of flexible, student-driven learning. For example, companies such as Maplesoft and Autodesk are pioneering software programs that are having a growing impact on institutional learning.

"At the end of the day, learning is about joy and the pursuit of knowledge," Jim Cooper, president and CEO of Maplesoft, told us when we spoke to him for this book. Maplesoft provides a wide range of interactive products that help students learn in real-world contexts. It counts as its clients MIT and Stanford, among many others. Maplesoft is an example of the breakthroughs that are happening outside the university system. Cooper was blunt in his assessment of the status quo. "At one point in my life, I used to believe that universities were at the leading edge," Cooper told us. "That's not really true anymore. Leaders tend to be found in nimble new projects, mostly new professors who don't have decades of course notes to reference."

> Like Maplesoft, Autodesk is using software to revolutionize engineering education. The company, which began building interactive 3D software as an industry model, soon added an educational component—a virtual university. As President and CEO Carl Bass explained to us, "Typically, engineering academics structured their courses around book learning in the early years, but no one becomes an engineering student because they have a passion for book learning. They are most motivated by hands-on, experiential problem solving, but students could go to the end of engineering school and never build anything."

Overcoming institutional barriers to intrinsic motivation

We have to face facts. Engineering educational reform takes place in the real university system, where people have to think about what pays the bills. From an educational perspective, universities are not designed to support innovation: often, changing one class can require a year of political navigation through curriculum committees and administrative offices at a variety of levels. In addition, efforts at reform don't go too far because of the perception that they require expensive teacher training and time-consuming additional faculty effort.

As we reflected on this problem, we identified an interesting hypothesis: perhaps we can question that idea that reform has to be more costly in the long run. Maybe the problem is that we're not thinking radically enough about the opportunity that intrinsic motivation offers. After all, if students were actually working in self-directed, intrinsically motivated ways, couldn't that require *less* of some kinds of resources?

The figure on the next page (the so-called Goldberg-Laffer curve) expresses the idea, plotting the cost of different types of reform as a function of the level of student engagement. At the left is "no reform"— a professor walks in with well-tested and well-worn twenty-year-old course notes and gives the same lectures he or she always has given.

This is low cost and relatively low in student engagement, and, in engineering education circles, this situation is called *the sage on the stage.*

Most reform efforts start from this point and try to make incremental changes. We encourage the sage to adopt experiential, active, problem-based, or some other form of enhanced learning, and if the instructor does so, we say he or she has become *the guide on the side.* He or she does so, however, at some personal cost, as shown on the curve with some increase in student engagement. Since the faculty member is already fully involved in other activities, this personal cost comes out of his or her discretionary time at home, in the lab, or doing other things he or she already values. Reformers suggest that this investment is important for the young people in the classroom, but the individual instructor may or may not share their enthusiasm and commitment, and the cost is arguably the fundamental barrier to reform. Dedicated missionaries such as Rich Felder and Karl Smith have been teaching us all how to be more engaging in the classroom for two decades or more, and yet the classroom, especially in research universities, remains stubbornly resistant to wide-scale and sustained change.

When we think about more radical reform, our assumption is usually that the curve keeps increasing: more student engagement = more cost. But given the nature of intrinsic motivation, isn't it possible that the curve actually turns down?

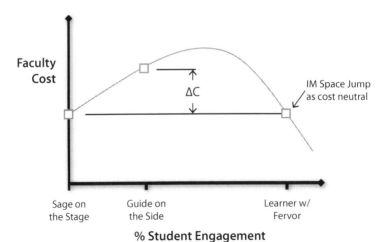

So we began to think about how to make intrinsic motivation programs pay off for schools. One such effort at the University of Illinois promises to break new ground in making intrinsic motivation the catalyst for reform. Geoffrey Herman and his collaborators decided to figure out an "intrinsic motivation course conversion" that would be both meaningful and cost effective. Herman began by looking at teaching assistants (TAs) as the best resource. Typically, TAs merely supported what the teacher was doing, but if they were given more autonomy and power, perhaps they could lead the way to intrinsic motivation (IM) conversion. In an initial IM conversion experiment, Herman and his colleagues enlisted TAs to oversee groups of students who had stated different motivations for learning. The key was to give students choices that would help them become engineers, not just book learners. They were able to pick topics and were given a variety of options. "Students can discover their intrinsic motivation only if they are given a degree of autonomy to explore the discipline on their own terms," Herman said. After making choices, the students were then formed into groups according to those options, under the guidance of the TAs.

The most dramatic results were seen with two groups in particular—one whose students were motivated by getting As and another whose students were motivated by designing cool computer architectures. "The first group flopped. They did terribly," Herman reported. "When they reflected later on their failure to get things done, the group acknowledged that learning couldn't happen if they didn't value what they were doing." And the second group demonstrated that. "Because of their passion for computer engineering, they jumped out of the gate from day one and thrived."

The IM conversion project is ongoing at the University of Illinois; Herman is working to expand it to other classes and departments. Its cost-effectiveness makes it a promising opportunity for departments concerned about the bottom line. It demonstrates that educational reform can be managed affordably.

Once we've committed ourselves to the power of intrinsic motivation in our students, the next question becomes, how do we as teachers show up to make that happen? The learning environment in which intrinsic motivation flourishes involves a shift in identity for teachers. And so we ask, who is the Whole New Professor?

The Whole New Professor
From Expert to Coach

Everybody needs a coach.

—Eric Schmidt

When Fernando Flores stands at the front of a seminar or classroom, he listens carefully, speaks infrequently, and when he does speak, his words are chosen so carefully that everyone stops to listen. But Flores, who is referred to in some circles as the intellectual father of coaching, is not interested in instructing but in engaging people in a process of deeper knowledge and transformation. And he came to his work through his own dramatic transformation.

Flores began his career as a Chilean engineer who rose up in the government at a young age to become the finance minister under President Salvador Allende in 1970. In 1973, his life changed when the military coup of General Augusto Pinochet toppled Allende's government. Flores was thrown in jail, where for three years he was subjected to torture, mock trials, and solitary confinement. He was rescued by the intervention of Amnesty International, and he and his family were relocated to California in 1976.

In prison, Fernando learned about the power of story. He knew that the story he told about his personal suffering would influence the rest of his life. "I never told a victim story about my imprisonment," he once said. "Instead, I told a transformation story about how prison changed my outlook, about how I saw that communication, truth, and trust are at the heart of power."

As an engineer immersed in technology and computer science, Flores recognized that these tools of communication and change had a deep human underpinning. He began to articulate a philosophy of technology and workplace transformation, writing a PhD thesis in 1982, "Management and Communication in the Office of the Future." His unique coaching breakthroughs brought him success and acclaim, and many companies adopted his principles. He called his philosophy the "Ontology of the Human Observer," noting that a coach was not someone who told others what to think or do but one who observed, listened, and then helped people discover things for themselves.

He described three levels of knowing. The first, "What you know you know," was a stagnant arena where experts were rigid and attached to ideas that they deemed sacrosanct. The second, "What you don't know," was an arena of failure and anxiety that people tried to avoid. It was in the third arena, "What you don't know you don't know," where transformation was possible. In that mind-set, curiosity, openness, trust, and freedom were possible.

Flores, now seventy-one, continues to captivate audiences around the world with his ideas. His style is direct, and his brilliant methods have transformed companies and individuals, and his work has given impetus to a new way of growing and learning.

Today, thanks to pioneers such as Flores, coaching has gained new respect as a vital tool of learning and competence. Even Google Executive Chairman Eric Schmidt can be seen on a YouTube video encouraging executives to hire a coach. He says that when the idea was first presented to him, he didn't get it. "I'm a successful CEO. Why do I need to hire a coach? Is something wrong?" But then he did it, and he found it to be one of the most valuable decisions he'd ever made. The greatest benefit? Perspective. "People are never good at seeing themselves as others see them."

Why coaches in the classroom?

In a discussion for this book, Dan Heath, coauthor with his brother Chip of *Made to Stick: Why Some Ideas Survive and Others Die* and *Switch: How To Change Things When Change is Hard*, spoke about how expertise, without attention to how the student's experience, leads to ineffective education. "The curse of knowledge is that once we know something, it's hard to imagine what it's like not to know it, and we devolve into abstraction and jargon," he said. "That's a barrier to effective education. You can't just impart knowledge from your head to their heads."

Coaching in the classroom as a natural outgrowth of the points made in earlier chapters, and the need to consider the student's experience. Clearly, there is a new global imperative to train engineers who are less socially captive, less obedient to the norms, and more courageous in taking initiative even when it is not accepted at the outset. We have pointed to the importance of student initiative taking and learning—the so-called unleashing reaction.

But getting to the unleashing reaction can be problematic for universities and professors today. For example, consider the need for professors to trust students. How do we unleash professors, who themselves were educated in nontrusting environments, to overcome their personal history and now trust students as a regular part of their teaching duties? How do we take professors trained as experts—people trained to say "I know"—and help them become people who can authentically say "I trust"?

How do we take professors trained as experts—people trained to say "I know"—and help them become people who can authentically say "I trust"?

Coaching has a role to play in addressing this challenge, but before we describe it, let's discuss what modern coaching is not. Modern coaching is not a form of advice giving, nor is it consulting or mentoring. There is no one-size-fits-all prescription for becoming effective as a leader or as a human being, and great coaches don't assume there is.

Instead—and this is one of the reasons why coaching has become so popular and effective over the past two decades in the corporate world—a coach takes a client as the whole human being he or she is. The coach listens, asks questions, and helps the client overcome obstacles and recognize and activate new possibilities. Put otherwise, modern coaching trusts the client as a resourceful, creative, and whole human being by specifically not knowing what the person should do and through a process of reflective inquiry helps the client live a fuller life, both professionally and personally.

The rise of coaching in the corporate world has been nothing short of remarkable. Flores wrote his groundbreaking dissertation in 1982, and since that time, coaching has seen a steady rise as a key element in leadership development in the corporate world around the globe.

We believe that the traditional professor as expert—a person who has trained to master a certain area of technical knowledge—can become more adaptable and face the challenges of the twenty-first-century classroom and laboratory more effectively by adding coaching skills and emotional capability. In this way, we call on professors to let go of "knowing" and trust students (and colleagues!) in much the same way a coach is trained to trust and thereby empower clients. This process of letting go and trusting students has been an important staple of the most effective experiences at both Olin and iFoundry.

Learning to let go

Lynn Andrea Stein came to Olin College as a founding faculty member and professor of computer science and engineering. An associate professor at MIT prior to joining Olin, Stein was eager to take a chance at a new way of being a teacher, which she defines as mostly involving coaching. "It's a risk," she says. "You have to give up control, and you have to be willing to trust the approach and trust the students. I had to learn to get out of my own way and give the students an opportunity to follow patterns that work for them. It's very different from my previous experiences. At MIT, I knew exactly what was going to happen every minute, every day, and in fact could show you at the beginning of class what chalk marks were going to be on the blackboard. There's something comfortable about having that kind of control—there's a satisfaction in believing that a class well done is one in which you covered the material you set out to cover. That you got through the ten pages of notes and that there weren't any hard student questions so they probably understood it. And if a student nodded and smiled while you were up there lecturing, it felt like a real slam dunk. Now, I feel like the less I do directly in a class, the better. Our students are all capable of engaging with difficult, complex material, at least in an initial sense; they can go sit in their room and read a reading that we've given to them, or work through an activity, or dig deep into some concept of problems they're trying to work on. They can all do that, but I want them to do that offline and then come into the class and use the fact that there are people sitting next to them who have dealt with or attempted the same thing. I stand back and watch the reflection happen—'Oh, I figured that out, too.' 'How did you handle x?' I don't need to do anything. I just need to think about what scaffolding, what activities, what preparations build them to that point where I can let the ball roll and just watch it go."

For Stein, the "fun" part is asking facilitating questions and seeing where they lead. "Students will grab the ball and run with it. They have ownership. It becomes their thing. They're excited to do it because they thought of it or they worked through it. It's not me saying, 'You shall do this.' I might give them an example so that they know how to find a solution through an application, but they've got to pick what they want to do. And they won't internalize it unless it's their thing."

Stein says, "I always have the coach hat on because in the end my goal is not to give students answers. It's to help unleash their abilities. On some

Students will grab the ball and run with it. They have ownership. It becomes their thing. They're excited to do it because they thought of it or they worked through it. It's not me saying, 'You shall do this.'

—Lynn Andrea Stein

level that means I don't have to be proficient. *They* have to be proficient. If you think about it, the best coaches aren't necessarily the best athletes."

Jessica Townsend, Olin's associate dean for curriculum and academic programs and an associate professor of mechanical engineering, concurs that while it's helpful in coaching to be able to do the things that you're coaching people to do, the classroom is a more open environment. "Sometimes when I walk into a classroom, I don't know what's going to happen—and I'm often surprised by what happens in my classrooms," she says.

This approach requires teachers to be fully present in the moment and to be willing to give up the treasured role of expert. "I've actually taught some classes at Olin that are outside my area of expertise or that combine multiple areas," says Townsend. "I wind up coaching students in the areas that I'm less proficient in. And I have gotten pretty good at asking students to help me understand what they're trying to accomplish and to ask questions. By the time I figure out what's going on, the students have actually solved their own problems because I can ask facilitative questions."

Both professors acknowledge that it is a dramatic shift—from teaching students what you know to being willing to not know everything. "They can do so much more than what you can do yourself," Stein says. "I've learned so much. Having experienced it, I have to say it would be boring for me to do it any other way." Her experience is relevant to educational reform. "The old assumption is that to change, the professor had to do double flips, back somersaults, change this, change that. But a lot of it is just showing up differently and talking differently. And when you do that, they're different."

In the conventional classroom environment, most of what we do telegraphs a lack of trust in students' innate abilities, and to some extent that comes from ego. Some professors may have an attitude that "I have mastered the material. I know things and you don't. So be quiet and listen."

In this way the message is sent that students are incompetent, which is disempowering. If we want our students to become lifelong learners and we want them to be innovators, we can't have four years of distrust and disempowerment and then say, "Go forth and be innovative!"

The beauty of not knowing

A key element in the move toward the professor as coach is the professor's willingness to be vulnerable in the face of what he or she doesn't know. Rob Martello likes to tell the story of a course he once taught at Olin called Environmental Enterprise. He'd taught environmental history but never this course. In the course description, he laid it on the line. "I wrote that I was going to be learning how to teach this course while I taught it. So if you want to come to the course, you'll learn some environmental history and you'll also help me figure out how to teach the course. When the students showed up, half of them said that they came because they really wanted to learn about environmental history. The other half said they didn't particularly care about the course, but they wanted to see how I'd be learning it with them. It could have been any subject."

Martello set up three groups, each with different readings and different assignments on the same topic, not knowing which was going to work the best. It was a very open-ended process. "It was spectacular," he says. "I think they learned so much because they had so much fun, and it ended up being really exciting. And the feedback at the end, the number one feedback was next time you teach this course, don't just teach the best things that we did. Keep it open-ended. That's how we learn."

In an environment of uncertainty, trust, and creativity, Martello's students thrived. They loved not being given one answer. They engaged through the discovery process. And Martello's role as a teacher was transformed from the wise expert to the colearner and coach.

One of the authors had a similar experience of the effectiveness of not knowing and trusting as part of his training as a leadership coach.

David Goldberg: Learning to not know what another should do

In 2010, I started coach training in the Georgetown University Leadership Coaching Certificate Program, and part of the training was to take on a number of pro bono clients and coach them for ten one-hour sessions each. I found three willing clients. After a while it was clear that two of the engagements were going quite well. However, the third—with an engineering administrator at a U.S. university—was pretty stuck in the mud. In particular, the administrator was having difficulty making effective requests. Although we worked on this issue directly and indirectly, nothing seemed to work. Technically, I thought I was listening well, asking good questions, and it seemed to me that the client's solution was pretty obvious. Nonetheless, seven sessions passed, then eight and then nine, and we were still stuck.

The classroom part of the course was coming to an end six months following the start, and on the last day of the last classroom segment, four student coaches met with a coach instructor to practice one-on-one coaching, with the instructor observing the sessions. The sessions were twenty minutes long, and each student coach picked a "client" randomly from one of the three remaining student coaches.

The first coach-client pair began, and it was an amazing session. The coach stayed with the client and asked great questions, and the client had an important insight.

The second pairing began, and it was even better. The coach in this case made a visualization move and listened well, and that led to great insight. Wow!

The third coach began, and this person was coaching me, and I thought I had brought a small tactical issue to the table, and my coach helped me see how the issue was tied to larger strategic issues I had been struggling with. I had a nice insight. Beautiful.

Finally, it was my turn to coach, and I should have been a bit nervous following these three amazing sessions, but I wasn't, and I listened well and asked some great questions, and my client had a nice insight to the point where we continued to work together following that morning.

After this was all over, we were emotionally spent, and the five of us knew that something special had just happened, but we had trouble describing it in the debriefing session. Coaches use words such as "center" and "present," but that morning none of the usual words was working. Finally, our instructor spoke up, and he said, "I have a word to describe what happened here this morning."

Almost in unison we asked, "What is it?"

He said, "Love." He went on, "What happened here today is that each of you showed up in unconditional love and trusted that your clients could find their own solutions."

We were all speechless. I thought to myself, "That's not a word we use in engineering very much." I wondered, "What does this mean to me at home, at work, and in my life generally?" It was a very powerful moment—so much so that the five of us celebrate the anniversary of "the Morning" by getting together on a conference call each year and reflecting on the lessons of that day.

Following that experience, I had to return to the final session with my stuck client, and I remembered the experience of "the Morning." Instead of knowing what my client should do, I showed up in our final coaching session not knowing and really trusting him. Remarkably, and almost as if on cue, the client had a breakthrough in that he was able to make an important request effectively with confidence, in a way that worked. I was dumbstruck. Once I let go of "knowing" what he should do, he was able to find his own way.

My takeaway from the episode was that really believing in another human being and trusting him or her to find his or her own way is difficult for many if not most of us. Technical skill is not enough; how a person shows up is as important, if not more important, than technical coaching skill alone.

Moving from "I know" to "I don't know" to "I trust" is both effective and quite difficult, but how does this shift land on students? In Martello's classroom story, it landed well, but how does having to take responsibility for one's own learning in the classroom affect students both short and long term?

How does this affect students?

We have discussed the experience of letting go (or not) from a professor's perspective, but how do students experience control on the one hand and trust on the other?

Kevin Wolz, a senior at the University of Illinois who has been a part of iFoundry since his freshman year, was inspired by the learning experience to follow his own dreams. That meant customizing a joint major in civil engineering and biology and arranging to make changes in his classes that favored the courses he wanted to take and avoided those he didn't. He has thrived in the atmosphere of opportunity, but some of his professors were resistant to his choices. "I literally had a professor tell me that if I didn't have my degree ABET accredited, I would fail in life and die poor," he says.

"I didn't agree. My career is not dictated by what an accreditation agency says about my degree. I don't want to work as a traditional engineer." He smiled and added, "I could have said to that professor, 'I'm going to die with more money than you are, because I'll be innovating.'"

Trusting and letting go are also great ways to inspire the next generation of professors. Julianna Stockton was one of the Olin partners and is now an assistant professor of mathematics at Sacred Heart University in Fairfield, Connecticut. When Stockton was preparing to graduate from Olin, she was drawn to the idea of teaching. "At first, I was nervous about going to education grad school," she admitted. "I had never taken an education class." But when she entered Teachers College at Columbia University, all her fears were unfounded. Her experience at Olin had already laid the groundwork for what it means to teach and learn effectively.

At Sacred Heart University, Stockton has found a home that is open to change. She was excited to be invited to serve on the university's Innovations Committee. "There is a recognition at the highest levels that the current model is unsustainable," she said. "We ask ourselves how we can be competitive, how we can revive a culture of innovation." The process of change is slow, but it is happening. Stockton and her colleagues have experimented with designing new courses, coteaching, and multidisciplinary courses.

"Change is hard," she concluded, laughing as she described her naiveté as a student. "I've gone back to apologize to the Olin faculty for not realizing how hard it is. I expected them to be superhuman. They were open to student feedback, but I confessed to them that our feedback was not always given in the best spirit." The response from one of her old teachers surprised her.

"After I made my apologies, he said he didn't agree with me. He saw it as a truly equal partnership. He told me, 'Anything you had to say was by definition what needed to be said.' That made a big impression on me. I try to model that in my own role as a professor."

Coaches versus ushers

These stories by themselves are fairly compelling, and recent research, interestingly, points in a similar direction. In particular, Yevgeniya V. Zastavker, an associate professor of physics at Olin College, set out to investigate faculty stories, recounting how they showed up in the classroom. With the participation of two undergraduates, Janaki I. Perera and Brendan T. Quinlivan, she studied the attitudes of nine faculty members—seven men and two women—in introductory-level mathematics, physics, and engineering classes. The research showed a set of seven emergent themes, including (1) discourse about students, (2) representation of one-on-one interactions with students, (3) perceived impact on students, (4) conceptions of their role in the development of student motivation and interest toward their courses, (5) overall teaching goals, (6) motivation towards teaching, and (7) beliefs about project-based learning as a pedagogical practice. Within each theme, and then overall, they identified two groups of faculty with divergent views, labeling them Personal Coaches and Group Ushers.

Those labeled Personal Coaches viewed teaching as their life calling and wanted to prepare students for the real world. They believed they could impact students and student motivation. They displayed positive affect through specific stories and valued one-on-one interactions.

Those labeled Group Ushers viewed teaching as just a job, whose goal was to prepare students for the next course. They didn't express the ability to impact students or student motivation. They displayed negative affect through broad generalizations and didn't value one-on-one interaction.

While the study is far more complex and nuanced than reported here (for links see Appendix A), the overall conclusion is meaningful: "We propose that the approach to teaching taken by personal coaches is of significant benefit to students. This proposition is grounded in literature, which suggests that many of the attitudes and behaviors that are found to be associated with the personal coaches have a positive impact on students' learning outcomes."

What skills and how to get them?

Mark Goulston, author of *Just Listen: Discovering the Secret To Getting Through to Absolutely Anyone*, spoke to us about the power of coaching in an educational setting. "You are not just there to teach students engineering," he said. "You are there to empower and embolden your students to be all they're capable of being." Acknowledging that there is sometimes confusion about what coaching is, Goulston recalls the response given by famed basketball coach Red Auerbach when he was asked what makes the best coach: "You have to love the bastards." Goulston said the same holds true in teaching. "The teacher as coach is a shepherd, a guardian who draws something out of students. The students respond by feeling, 'This person really cares.'"

Moving from professor or teacher as expert to coach can be beneficial to student learning, and we live in a time when the practical side of coaching and coach training is well developed. Professional organizations such as the International Coach Federation (www.coachfederation.org) credentials coaches and accredits coach training programs, and the body of knowledge and competencies put forward in these programs is good place to start for those interested in bringing coaching into the classroom.

Different resources will discuss these skills differently, but here we list some of the key skills and competencies of a modern coach:

1. Noticing
2. Listening
3. Questioning
4. Speech acts
5. Understanding and reframing stories

Let's briefly consider each of these.

The primary skill of an effective coach is noticing and awareness. Coaches are trained to notice language, body and the emotion of themselves and others—a dynamic we described in chapter 4. Coaching is about effective change, and effective change begins with noticing, so coaching begins with noticing.

Listening is a primary skill of coaching because much of what is learned in coaching is conveyed when the client tells a story and the coach listens. In coaching, the distinction is often made between level-one and level-two listening. In level-one listening, the listener relates what is said by the speaker to his or her own experience and interprets the story using only the listener's perspective.

In level-two listening, the listener suspends thinking about himself or herself and tries to understand the story from the perspective of the teller. The listener approaches the story with curiosity and without judgment and merely tries to understand the perspective of the teller. There are good sources in the coaching literature with exercises to help understand and practice the distinction between level-one listening and level-two listening.

Asking questions is another skill practiced by coaches. A distinction is often made between information-gathering and open-ended questions. In coaching, neutral, open-ended questions are usually the rule to help the client reflect on different possibilities without injecting the biases of the coach into the conversation unannounced. A simple rule for asking an open-ended questions is to begin with the word "what."

One of Fernando Flores's most lasting contributions to coaching was carrying the philosophy of *speech acts* into organizational life and thereby into coaching. Speech acts philosophy builds on a growing trend in the twentieth century to move from thinking of language as merely the static conveyance of well-formed thoughts to a more dynamic, rich, and creative kind of endeavor.

Five speech acts are commonly discussed in coaching circles: assertions, assessments, requests, commitments, and declarations. Although delving into these distinctions in detail is beyond the scope of this treatment, the conceptual clarity and precision that these ideas can bring to everyday communication are quite startling in their ability to help (1) reduce misunderstanding, (2) improve organization efficiency and speed, and

(3) help envision and enable more productive futures for new and old organizations alike.

When coaches listen to clients, they are told stories. Clients think of their stories as "true," and one of the jobs of coaches is to help the clients separate facts (assertions) from interpretations (assessments). Although this sounds obvious, it is harder than it seems, and one of the things clients find surprising is that, often, their stories can be reframed or be given different endings in ways that serve them better.

In chapter 6, we discussed how intrinsically motivated learning could change the student experience. In this chapter, we talked about how augmenting the professor/teacher as expert with skills and presence that bring about a professor/teacher as coach can set up the circumstances so that students can reliably be unleashed to effective learning experiences. What emerges from this mix is not just a new professor, or a new student, or a new classroom. The result is a new culture.

8

A Whole New Culture
From Classrooms and Curriculum to Culture

The thing I have learned at IBM is that culture is everything.

—Louis V. Gerstner Jr.

Early in 1966, Professor Edgar Schein of MIT's Sloan School of Management made his first visit to the Digital Equipment Corporation (DEC) in Maynard, Massachusetts. A social psychologist by training, Schein had been invited by the senior management at DEC to help them think about how they could improve their team function—particularly around communication, decision making, and interpersonal relationships.

Started by a couple of engineers from MIT Lincoln Labs in the 1950s, DEC is recognized today as a critical player in the rise of computing. When Schein visited in 1966, the company had just introduced the world's first minicomputer, the PDP-8, which initiated the rapid growth of the minicomputer industry. A few years later, DEC would introduce the PDP-11, considered one of the most important and influential computers in history. The list of innovations that came out of DEC is lengthy—from key technologies to fundamental concepts such as the now commonplace idea that computers should be interactive. Indeed, by 1966, DEC was well on track to achieving its eventual status as the second-largest maker of computers worldwide, surpassed only by IBM.

But the DEC that Schein encountered seemed to be anything but effective. Instead, he found an environment rife with conflict and confrontation. Individuals routinely were insubordinate to their superiors. Meetings were hotbeds of loud arguments and dissent. Colleagues openly disparaged each other outside of meetings—calling each other "jerks" and worse. And many employees expressed deep frustration at how long it took to make decisions and how little people seemed to understand their point of view.

With his background in social psychology, Schein saw DEC as a clearly dysfunctional environment, and he began making recommendations to the management about how they might improve the situation. Schein was disappointed with the results. Although a few of his recommendations were taken seriously and there was some incremental change in the situation, for the most part things remained as broken as ever.

But as Schein continued to work with DEC, he came to realize that what he had framed as something broken—that is, the high level of confrontation and conflict—was, in fact, a reflection of something much deeper. He observed that, despite the fact that colleagues could disagree vehemently in meetings and dismiss each other's points of view as stupid outside of meetings, they would remain friends. He saw that the company's processes did lead to cutting-edge products and a highly engaged workforce. How could something so apparently dysfunctional work so well?

The elements of culture

Today, Schein is widely respected as one of the leading thinkers on organizational culture, organizational learning, and career dynamics.

One of his major contributions has been the development of a theory of organizational culture, which he first published in the 1980s. The theory has three levels:

1. Artifacts
2. Espoused values
3. Underlying assumptions

Schein tells us that in every organization there is a culture that is manifested in visible "artifacts," promoted by espoused values, and founded in underlying assumptions, both spoken and unspoken.

Artifacts are the visible manifestations that allow people—even those who are not a part of the organization—to identify it. In the context of DEC, some of those artifacts included the behaviors employees displayed in meetings, the highly open and informal layout of the offices, the lack of visible markers of status, and the management structure of the company. In an academic setting, examples include the approaches used for teaching, the ways students and faculty interact, the ways assessment is conducted, and the physical artifacts (classrooms, buildings, textbooks, diplomas).

The second level, espoused values, is essentially the justification that people within an organization use to explain its properties. These are conscious strategies, goals, and philosophies—the answers that people give when asked, "Why do you do things this way?" or "What do you believe in?" At DEC, people in the company would point to personal responsibility, quality and elegance, and the importance of getting buy-in from others. In academic settings, you'll often hear justifications of "We need to be efficient" or "It's important that students learn the fundamentals."

Values and artifacts are in turn based on underlying assumptions, which are the taken-for-granted theories about the way the world works. Often, underlying assumptions are difficult to identify, because they are so embedded in the fabric of the organization that individuals within the group cannot conceive of an alternative. In the case of DEC, as Schein probed and reflected, he determined that the seemingly dysfunctional behaviors he was observing reflected some of the core underlying assumptions (the cultural foundation) at DEC:

- The individual is ultimately the source of ideas and entrepreneurial spirit.
- Individuals are capable of taking responsibility and doing the right thing.
- No single individual is smart enough to evaluate his or her own ideas, so others should push back and get buy-in.
- The engineer knows best.

Schein's initial recommendations to the DEC management were at odds with these underlying assumptions, and consequently, they didn't stick. For example, he initially attempted to increase the civility of meetings, which conflicted with the idea that "push back" was necessary for determining truth. The DEC culture acted like an immune system, rejecting ideas that were inconsistent with it.

When Schein recognized these assumptions and realized that his suggestions were at odds with the implicit beliefs at DEC, he modified his approach—and went on to have forty successful years of working with DEC.

The culture of engineering education

If you walk in the door of the Department of Aerospace Engineering at Delft University in the Netherlands, the first things you'll notice are the airplanes, rockets, and satellites hanging from the ceiling and displayed on the walls. The lobby area has a bit of the same feeling as the Smithsonian Air and Space Museum. If you're visiting a faculty member, a concierge (housed inside a glassed-in booth) will call your contact person and have him (the faculty is dominantly male) come down to the lobby to meet you.

As you walk the halls, representations of aerospace engineering are on full display. Both staff and faculty offices are decorated with aerospace-related paraphernalia, including photos of planes, models of satellites, etc. Across the department, people will cite their love of air- and spacecraft as a reason for their choice of career. Students also routinely carry bits of aerospace paraphernalia; for example, many students have a "remove before flight" key chain or strap attached to their backpacks. And students and faculty alike articulate a high level of pride around Delft Aerospace Engineering; all are aware that the department has long been internationally recognized and admired, with long lists of students wanting to attend.

For many years the centerpiece of the Delft Aerospace curriculum has been the Design Synthesis Exercise (DSE), a large-scale project in the final year of the bachelor's program in which about ten students work full time for a semester on an authentic aerospace design challenge—things such as the design of a small, reusable space plane for transport to the international space station. Both faculty and students would routinely point to the DSE as evidence of the quality and innovativeness of the program, and DSE projects are prominently displayed on walls throughout the facility.

But in 2006, Delft Aerospace Engineering also faced some significant challenges. The program was extremely hard, taking the average student almost seven and a half years to complete. Although applied knowledge and a hands-on approach were valued in the later years, and even in the first year there was some hands-on work, much of the curriculum consisted of more traditional lecture courses, delivered in large lecture halls.

As is the case at many institutions, performance on these traditional courses was often assessed with a single examination: a student would first take the course and then after attending the lectures, doing exercises, etc., would take a single exam that would determine whether he or she passed. If a student didn't pass the exam, he or she would have an opportunity to retake the exam the next term or the next year. For some classes, the typical student would end up taking the exam three, four, or five times before either passing it or deciding to stop trying; many classes had pass rates below seventy-five percent.

Viewed through Schein's model, we see a set of artifacts present in Delft in 2006: many displays of physical objects related to aerospace, a set of architectural decisions, a curriculum with some project-based work and a large component of lecture courses, the prominent display of student project work, and an examination-based system with low pass rates.

When asked to explain some of these artifacts, students and faculty provided a range of espoused justifications and values. Regarding the prominent displays of aerospace artifacts, many people in the department cited a deep affection for the technology: "I just love airplanes and always have."

Explanations of low pass rates were relatively consistent: "Aerospace *should* be hard. . .it is one of the most rigorous areas of engineering studies." . . . "[Topic X] is particularly difficult material." . . . "The low pass rates are a fact of life in aerospace studies.". . . "We need that class to separate the sheep from the goats."

Discussions of the structure and content of the curriculum included many concerns. Some faculty members expressed unease about the emphasis on the specifics of aerospace: "I worry that we are educating students who can build an airplane but who don't understand what they are doing." Others drew the opposite picture: "We do too much physics and not enough real engineering." But all agreed about the importance of the material that they were responsible for, and the difficulty associated with covering topics: "[The topic of the course I teach] is absolutely critical to aerospace." . . . "It's hard to cover all of the material I need to."

As Schein notes, it is much easier to identify artifacts and justifications than underlying assumptions. After all, underlying assumptions are, by definition, implicit. In addition, any observer brings his or her own biases to the conversation. With these caveats in mind, we speculate that some of the implicit beliefs at Delft include:

- Engineering is either about cool technology. . . or else it's about fundamental science.
- The instructor's responsibility is first and foremost to the material.
- Individual examinations are the right way to measure mastery and predict performance.

In chapter 9 we'll describe some of the breakthroughs that activated both curricular and cultural change at Delft — but in 2006, many of the underlying assumptions at Delft were representative of those that today still pervade not just engineering education, but technical education more generally. In *Freedom to Learn*, Carl Rogers outlines a set of implicit assumptions that he contends are broadly held by most professors and institutions:

- "The Student cannot be trusted to pursue his own scientific and professional learning."
- "Ability to pass examinations is the best criterion for student selection and for judging professional promise."
- "Presentation equals learning. What is presented in a lecture is what a student learns."
- "Knowledge is the accumulation of brick upon brick of content and information."
- "Creative scientists develop from passive learners."
- "Students are best regarded as manipulable objects, not as persons."

What's striking about the assumptions that Rogers identifies is how, in spite of being narrow, rigid, negative, and elitist, they are reflected in the language of the academy, in our curricular structures, and in the questions that we ask.

Consider, for example, the language we, as instructors, routinely use in engineering education. Faculty members ask questions such as, "How can we make sure we are producing high-quality graduates?"—a question we might equally ask about car transmissions. We express concern about limited class time, because we're worried about "making sure that material is covered," as if the instructor covering the material is interchangeable with the student learning the material. Professors will often frame particular topics as "foundational," suggesting a brick-by-brick framework for knowledge. And we often use "collaboration" in the same breath as "cheating." The culture in engineering education doesn't encode assumptions about just students and content, though. We also often hold implicit beliefs about our colleagues, our institutions, and our profession that can get in the way of helping students develop as Whole New Engineers. Think about the jokes we tell (example: Q: How can you identify outgoing engineers? A: They're the ones who look at *your* feet while they're talking to you). Or consider the ways administrators talk about managing faculty (example: "herding cats") or the ways faculty talk about their jobs (example: "teaching load" to refer to teaching responsibilities).

Consider the language we, as instructors, routinely use in engineering education. Professors will often frame particular topics as "foundational," suggesting a brick-by-brick framework for knowledge. And we often use "collaboration" in the same breath as "cheating."

In the 1990s, Michael Moody, who went on to become the founding dean of faculty at Olin, spent a year on sabbatical at the University of Vienna. He loved the city and particularly enjoyed its coffeehouse culture. Each day he would visit the same coffeehouse, sit at the same table, and pull out his mathematics to work on. Each day the same waiter would acknowledge him ("Herr Professor Doktor") and wordlessly bring him his standard order, *ein grosser brauner*. The environment, the tradition, and the quality of the coffee all made Mike very happy.

About ten years later, Mike visited Vienna on holiday and dropped by the coffeehouse for old times' sake. He sat down at his table and pulled out his journal to do some work on a problem that he'd been thinking about—and was astounded when the same waiter greeted him and placed *ein grosser brauner* before him. *Nothing had changed.* Indeed, Vienna at times feels like a city that is always looking to the past. You can sit in a wine garden and overhear people talking about the antics of the emperor's dog—a dog that died a century ago. It's quite charming. On the other hand, it can also be very frustrating if you're trying to do something new. Perhaps it's not surprising that Kafka hails from this part of the world.

The underlying assumptions about change and time that gird the culture in Vienna are, of course, what make it a lovely city to visit and to live in. Unfortunately, those same assumptions—"things used to be better" or "change is neither possible nor desirable"—are too often present in engineering education and in higher education more broadly. Tradition plays a key role at most institutions—from homecoming games to the curriculum. We consistently hear faculty members lament the state of today's students, talk about how the curriculum used to be much more rigorous, and express deep skepticism about proposed changes at any level in the university. It's no surprise, considering that universities were originally founded to protect knowledge, to ensure *against* change. But it also presents a real challenge for engineering education, because the world *is* changing.

The past is not the future: the need for culture shift

During the time Schein was working with DEC, he saw the company rise to the very top of the industry. Then, some years later, he also witnessed the company's death. The demise of DEC is, not surprisingly, a complex story. It involves the organizational challenges associated with rapid growth, as well as the technological challenges associated with a shift from the minicomputer paradigm that DEC had created to the personal computer paradigm that we associate with IBM, Compaq, Dell, Apple, and others.

But, while there are myriad explanations for the demise of DEC, Schein argues that, in many ways, these explanations have their roots in the interaction between technological change, organizational change, and a *culture* that was resistant to change. Indeed, some of DEC's underlying cultural assumptions, which had allowed the company to be so successful early on, became an Achilles' heel when the environment changed.

It's instructive to consider how DEC responded to the rise of personal computing. In 1974, well before the popularization of the PC, people within DEC proposed a personal computer system. However, as Schein wrote, the PC proposal and what it implied for the company "went against the engineering culture grain in too many ways."

A few years later, it was clear that the PC was here to stay, and at that point, DEC set out to enter the market. Again, the culture at DEC drove the decision making. The focus of the design effort was on elegance and quality—"the engineer knows best"—with the associated implicit assumption that the market would be willing to pay extra for the high-quality engineering. The design efforts also emphasized DEC's culture of product innovation; rather than creating a PC clone or an open system, they chose to create proprietary personal computers: the Rainbow, the DECMATE, and the Professional. Not one of them was remotely successful.

After these initial failures, engineers in the company proposed that DEC create a PC clone, a strategy that would a few years later be at the core of Compaq's rise to success. But again, the company's culture kept it from making a necessary change. As Schein describes it, "It was the deep assumption about product quality and DEC's role as an innovator that was being challenged by the engineering groups proposing a clone. So even though all three PC entries failed to become successful products, the assumptions about what a product should be held firm. DEC would not compromise on quality or elegance, and DEC would not be a copycat."

In short, the company's assumption that *the engineer knows best* became a weakness when the industry shifted toward personal computing. The elegant and high-quality solutions that DEC had been producing, while compelling and technologically polished, were simply too expensive and had too many features for the new customer base. Other companies were making computers that were less elegant, less advanced, less feature laden—but also simpler and cheaper—and these were the designs that won the day. The culture that had served DEC so well in an earlier environment was inappropriate for the new reality and led to the company's disappearance.

A changing environment for engineering education

If Sugata Mitra is right, the school as we know it may be obsolete— that is, if you define school as a place of learning where experts pass on a body of knowledge to students who arrive as empty vessels. Mitra, who grew up in Calcutta, one of the poorest and most disadvantaged places on earth, became a scientist, earning a PhD in solid-state physics from the Indian Institute of Technology. But the science that fascinated him most was the science of the mind and, in particular, how learning happens.

Thinking about poor children in the slums of India, Mitra wondered how they would ever have a chance to become educated and rise above their poverty. It seemed like an impossible dream. But then he began to conceptualize it differently. He realized that people think about kids going to school as if they were talking about batteries that need to be recharged. Kids without access to schools walk around like partially charged batteries because they have no place to plug in. But what if school wasn't a place? What if school was an opportunity out in the world—or, as he would later describe it, "in the cloud"?

What if school wasn't a place? What if school was an opportunity out in the world?

Mitra became famous for putting that idea to the test in his "hole in the wall" experiment. He dug a hole in a wall in a slum in New Delhi and placed a networked computer in the hole, for free use by children. Then he set up a hidden camera to watch what happened.

The children who approached Mitra's hole in the wall had never seen a computer or learned how to use one, but they played around and quickly learned how to use the computer and get connected to the Internet. Then they taught other children. This experiment, which was the inspiration for the movie *Slumdog Millionaire*, was the origin of Mitra's work on self-organized learning. He continued doing experiments and found time and again that if you left students alone to work in groups and access information on the Internet, they could learn almost anything.

"At first, I thought that the children were learning in spite of the teacher not interfering," Mitra told an interviewer. "But I changed my opinion and realized this was happening because the teacher was not interfering. At that point, I didn't become entirely popular with teachers. But I explained to them that the job has changed. You ask the right kind of question; then you stand back and let the learning happen."

Mitra agrees with the notion that the age of the expert has passed. In the introduction to his book, *Beyond the Hole in the Wall: Discover the Power of Self-Organized Learning*, Mitra wrote, "I finished this book on a rainy August 15, India's Independence Day. But there is another Independence Day I would like to talk about here. It is the day we achieve independence from an educational system that is more than 2,500 years old. It is time to begin that journey."

We see aspects of this journey reflected in the growing popularity of MOOCs. Thomas Friedman is an enthusiastic proponent of MOOCs, which he says, are here to stay, kinks and all. In "The Professor's Big Stage," a March 5, 2013, op-ed in the *New York Times*, Friedman expands on his premise: "Institutions of higher learning must move, as the historian Walter Russell Mead puts it, from a model of 'time served' to a model of 'stuff learned.' Because increasingly the world does not care what you know. Everything is on Google. The world only cares, and will only pay for, what you can do with what you know. And therefore it will not pay for a C+ in chemistry, just because your state college considers that a passing grade and was willing to give you a diploma that says so. We're moving to

> *Increasingly the world does not care what you know. Everything is on Google. The world only cares, and will only pay for, what you can do with what you know.*
>
> **—Thomas Friedman**

a more competency-based world where there will be less interest in how you acquired the competency—in an online course, at a four-year college or in a company-administered class—and more demand to prove that you mastered the competency."

Friedman's piece generated a storm of protest from defenders of traditional institutional education. There's a feeling of threat in the air. As with any new technology, the early introduction of MOOCs has often been rocky. There are things a MOOC can't provide that a traditional classroom can. Nonetheless, MOOCs stand as a crack in the fortress of linear education. And they're not going away.

Within engineering, this kind of technology is altering the transfer of skills *outside* the university. "Before the internet came along, it was fairly difficult to share technical knowledge with others from outside your workplace," noted Jeff Shelton, co-host of "The Engineering Commons," a bi-weekly podcast that covers engineering-related issues. "Apart from swapping stories at conferences or conventions, engineers didn't have much opportunity to share insights with those who worked for different employers. Now the story is vastly different. Engineers regularly share design ideas on wikis and forums, explain design decisions in blogs, and demonstrate devices and inventions on YouTube. Electrical engineer Dave Jones gets nearly a quarter-million visits from electronics enthusiasts each month on his EEVblog website, with an additional 1.5 million views of his online discussion forum. If I were a student interested in electronics, I'd be highly motivated to watch an experienced engineer like Dave explain design trade-offs while comparing output waveforms on a digital oscilloscope. Having my electronics professor throw up one more lecture slide consisting of a schematic and an equation would seem rather blasé in comparison."

In short, as we argued in chapter 3, the environment today is radically different from what it was in the Sputnik era—but the culture of engineering education has not adjusted. For example, we need to attract more, and more diverse, students to engineering. But women—more than 50 percent of the world's population—are still woefully underrepresented in the STEM fields. Meagan Pollock, an engineer, educator, researcher and consultant, has studied the reasons why. It is not that women aren't good at tech, but rather it's the cues—a limiting stereotype with no basis in reality. Pollock points out, women are not choosing STEM fields because they are conditioned to believe they can't succeed. "Females receive cues from early on that math, science, and tech are gendered—and more appropriate for males," Pollock writes. "These messages come from deeply rooted implicit biases that exist in our culture, and become stereotypes."

Cultural intransigence is a fact in educational institutions. Trevor Harding, department chair and professor of materials engineering at California Polytechnic State University, has written extensively on engineering education and classroom methods. "The problem," he told us for this book, "is a mechanistic view of education. The classroom is an educational factory. The students are products that perform well or poorly. The teacher is a manager seeking maximum performance." Harding points out that in the factory culture, being smarter, better, and faster is a high value. "What's lost in the process is the individual well-being of students and teachers. I've seen a lot of suffering at all levels." Yet even incremental changes are hard-won. Even when a culture is not working, it can take time and, yes, suffering, before people within the culture see a new path. One of the best contemporary examples of this is the American auto industry, which struggled with anachronistic production models to the point of near destruction before accepting dramatic changes such as just-in-time manufacturing, teamwork, and shared sacrifice.

Two cautionary tales

To date, change efforts have largely focused on content, curriculum, and pedagogy. It's an appealing approach. Content is what professors know best, and curriculum is the visible manifestation of this. Pedagogy is in some ways analogous to the "technology" of teaching; we talk about "state-of-the-art

Aligning education and industry

Increasingly, education and industry thought leaders are looking beyond incremental classroom changes to a bigger picture. Jim Spohrer, director of IBM's University Programs (IBM UP), spoke with us about the need to reframe university systems in alignment with industry and local communities to create a smarter planet. "Twenty years ago, knowledge was segmented," he observed. "For this century technology and systems support a multidisciplinary approach, with the goal of creating whole individuals for the good of society." Spohrer observed that the old idea of educating innovators was a winner-take-all game, geared toward individuals rising above the pack. "The winners in this game moved to places like Silicon Valley, leaving the weaker link regions and locales dry. But the big getting bigger is not a sustainable strategy." Spohrer's program involves spreading the "wealth" of innovation to every region and local community—thus utilizing brain power everywhere. "If we're serious about building a smart planet, we have to reframe the university as the key to regional economic development."

pedagogical approaches" and of using "proven best practices." But time and time again, we've seen that this focus alone doesn't lead to the kinds of results that we need for the twenty-first century.

We recall a recent visit to a school that had made a large-scale commitment to doing project-based education. The administration was excited about the change, and they reported that many faculty were using project-based approaches in their classes. But when we questioned faculty about the project-based learning emphasis, many expressed deep skepticism. More disturbing was our observation of a faculty member who *had* adopted the new approach. As we watched a student present his project work, the faculty member continually interrupted him with corrections of details and instructions about what he should have done instead. Embedded within this manifestation of "project-based education" were many of the same assumptions about education that have been in place for the past hundred years.

We also recall the seeming impossibility of spending our way to a new approach in engineering education. The National Science Foundation made enormous investments during the 1990s on change in engineering education. Coalitions of schools across the United States developed new pedagogical approaches and new curriculum. But fifteen years later, the consensus in the community is that, while there were many innovative and interesting ideas developed through the coalitions, the reality is that once the money stopped, much of the change slowed, stopped, and gradually reversed.

From curriculum to culture

In earlier chapters of this book, we've argued that we need to change our education to develop students as Whole New Engineers. We've identified a set of core principles, the pillars, that help to explain how two incredibly different institutions were able to ignite and unleash students. And we've discussed what a whole new engineering education might look like, both from a student perspective and from a faculty member perspective.

The external environment is demanding a change in the culture of engineering education. In the same way that DEC died because its culture could not adapt to a new reality, engineering education must change if it hopes to survive in a world of ubiquitous information and accelerating technological advances. Transformation is coming, whether we like it or not.

At the same time, there's an opportunity here, a pull for us to create a new culture. Ultimately, helping students develop as Whole New Engineers requires a culture that is supportive of this type of education. When Schein attempted to make change at DEC without paying attention to the culture, he was unsuccessful: culture is an immune system. Some of the underlying cultural assumptions in engineering education are antithetical to the artifacts and values that are necessary to support intrinsic motivation in students and to have instructors move from a sage-on-the-stage orientation to a coach orientation. If we're going to trust students, if students are going to have the courage to take risks and learn from failure, if we're going to move from a competitive framing of education to a collaborative one, if we are going to develop students' openness and willingness to reflect, and if we hope to make the learning of engineering joyful instead of painful, we will need to change not just the curriculum. We need to create a new culture of engineering education.

But how can we do this? What are the instruments of change that reflect both breadth and depth? How do we spark a change process that is truly a shift in culture?

Changing How We Change
From Bureaucracy to
Change Management

People change what they do less because they are given analysis that shifts their thinking than because they are shown a truth that influences their feelings.

—John Kotter

For Linda Vanasupa, the process of change in an institution is "a little like a root canal." Linda is a professor and former chair of the materials engineering department at California Polytechnic State University and has often been frustrated by the ways in which engineering education strays from its higher purpose. She cites the engineering ethics creed of the National Society of Professional Engineers, whose lofty language is meant to inspire a generation of engineers to do good in addition to doing well. In particular, it vows "to place service before profit, the honor and standing of the profession before personal advantage, and the public welfare above all other considerations." Notes Vanasupa, "This is our creed, but it isn't part of our conversation as teachers. Our conversation is how we prepare students to work at Intel. And when the university talks about the globe, the context is about striving to get a competitive edge—about economic domination, not the fact that we have a shared responsibility for progress and sustainability. The challenge isn't just to be competitive; it is to be collaborative."

Vanasupa believes that collaboration is the unique responsibility of the new engineer, yet undergraduate students are exposed to little in the way of collaboration in their intensely grade-centric educational experiences. Nor do teachers model collaboration, particularly in teaching. The norm is for them to jealously guard their fiefdoms and do little to cooperate even within their departments—much less outside their departments.

In 2009, Vanasupa and her colleagues at California Polytechnic received a grant from the National Science Foundation to launch a five-year experiment in interdepartmentally led, community-based programs focused on sustainability. The concept was so outside the box that the college contemplated giving the money back rather than going forward. When they finally proceeded, it was far from a smooth process. No one had fully appreciated just how difficult cross-departmental collaboration would be.

> *The faculty tended to be dedicated to curriculum as if it were a truth from on high—as if it were scripture. It was a challenge to listen to other voices.*
>
> **—Linda Vanasupa**

Many objected to inserting a new focus into a curriculum that was already packed with material they believed an engineer must learn. Others wondered whether the question of sustainability was really crucial to engineering education.

"We had hundreds of hours of faculty meetings to determine what was necessary and what was not," Vanasupa said. "In the zone of abstraction, the faculty had trouble seeing where classes were overlapping and might be changed. The faculty tended to be dedicated to curriculum as if it were a truth from on high—as if it were scripture. It was a challenge to listen to other voices."

Four years later, the culture has been deeply changed—suddenly, faculty and students are talking to one another on a level that had not existed before. "Mostly we talk about what we're experiencing in real time," Vanasupa said. "How we've been trapped by cultural habits. How we've had to build a relationship of trust with one another. PhDs spend their lives developing and crafting their egos. This has been a little bit like a root canal—tough on the ego."

Looking ahead to the end of the grant project, Vanasupa believes that the experience with interdisciplinary integrated learning has the potential to precipitate further changes within the institution. "Once you've changed, you can't go back."

The missing ingredients for change

Engineers have the reputation and often the self-image of being highly logical individuals, unswayed by emotional considerations in decision making. It's not surprising, then, that engineers often take on change efforts with a rational mind-set. The problem is framed as defining the right curriculum and the right pedagogical approach, with the idea that by using a careful, rigorous process, we can prototype, measure, and improve on the educational system.

It's a scenario that we've seen play out over and over again. A leader (a dean, a president, a department head, a passionate faculty member, an NSF program officer) identifies a need that is not being addressed. A committee is appointed to investigate, write a report, and propose a new curriculum. Weeks, months, and years are devoted to the work, and if it's successful, a clearly defined, new approach is proposed, voted on by the faculty, and accepted by the dean. Victory is declared. And then ... *nothing really changes*.

These kinds of experiences often lead to the conclusion that change in the academy is impossible. But as Linda Vanasupa found, change is possible; it's just not easy, and it's certainly not purely rational.

We find a number of thought leaders around organizational change to be particularly helpful in taking on the challenge of change. John Kotter has written for years about organizational change; his reframing of change from an event to an eight-step process—(1) establishing a sense of urgency, (2) creating the guiding coalition, (3) developing a change vision, (4) communicating the vision for buy-in, (5) empowering broad-based action, (6) generating short-term wins, (7) never letting up, and (8) incorporating changes—is widely recognized as a critical contribution to change management. The Heath brothers, in their book *Switch*, make a complementary argument that change requires three components—emotion, reason, and process—which they colorfully refer to as the elephant (emotion), the rider (reason), and the path (process). Schein's take on change is strongly grounded in his understanding of culture; he argues that change requires three stages: *unfreezing*, which involves both creating the motivation to change and the belief that change is possible; *learning*, which involves taking on new concepts, new standards, and new interpretations of old concepts; and *internalizing*, or *refreezing*, these new concepts and standards.

All three recognize that there are multiple ingredients to change, both rational *and* emotional, and that change takes time and attention to process. As we described in the previous chapter, Schein's attention to culture—particularly, artifacts, espoused values, and basic underlying assumptions—is a key framework for any change effort.

Stories of successful change

Despite the skepticism many express about change in the academy, we find stories of transformation, such as the effort at CalPoly, bubbling up from institutions around the world. Although we know the stories of Olin and iFoundry best, history offers many inspiring examples.

In the late 1960s, Worcester Polytechnic Institute was a school in trouble. In the words of Professor William Grogan, "WPI was dead in the water." The curriculum was stagnant and rigid, and both the faculty and students were unconvinced of the value of the educational program. Bill Shipman, a faculty member at the time, remembers his own lack of faith in the institution. "The mother of one of my [Sunday school] students asked me if I could talk to him about which colleges he might consider," he said. "I thought to myself, 'Here I am at Worcester Tech, and I can't think of a reason why I would want to go here. What does this school have to offer that I couldn't get somewhere else for less money?'"

Finally seeing a clear need for change, WPI undertook a large-scale reinvention from the ground up. They developed an amazingly student-centered and inventive approach—"the Plan"—which included substantial project work, both technical and interdisciplinary; a heavy humanities emphasis; a comprehensive competency examination; and a new grading system, a new academic calendar, and a huge increase in student flexibility. While not every element of the original Plan remains in place today, WPI's change effort had long-lasting impact on the institution, and it remains among the most innovative undergraduate engineering programs. WPI really changed.

When Babson College conducted a study in 1986 to evaluate its MBA program, it learned that the school was considered mediocre, and Babson graduates were "just so-so." In response, Babson mounted a complete rethink of its graduate program. The change effort eventually led to a similarly scaled revision of its undergraduate program, a major shift in institutional culture, and a transition from Babson being yet another business school to its current status as number one in entrepreneurship, according to *U.S. News and World Report*.

While change at Babson and WPI came at times when the institutions were under threat, Harvard Medical School's story suggests that change is possible even when survival is not at stake. In 1977, Dean Tosteson began a change process that would last nearly ten years. Different faculty would assume leadership roles, and the leadership of the school itself would change during that decade, but the end result was a rapid and radical transition from a very traditional lecture-based program to the experiential "New Pathway" approach to medical education. This approach continues to have widespread influence on how medical schools across the world think about medical education. Somehow a school that was internationally recognized as the best of the best was still able to make real, and lasting, change happen.

We've seen the same thing in engineering education. In 2006, the aerospace engineering faculty at Delft University in the Netherlands was widely admired and internationally recognized, with an academic staff of eighty, three departments, and seventeen chairs. There were long lists of students waiting to get in, and the school's graduates were in high demand. In this environment of success, the dean—sparked not by a crisis but by his strong sense that they could do better—put a change effort into motion that would, over the course of five years, lead to large-scale revisions to the undergraduate and graduate programs.

And we see many programs that are in the midst of major change today: from Iron Range Engineering, an innovative project-based program that targets community college students in northern Minnesota, to the new ATLAS program that integrates liberal arts and engineering at the University of Twente in the Netherlands, to the Design Centered Curriculum that shifts the emphasis from engineering science to hands-on engineering design at the National University of Singapore, to new efforts at Purdue University's engineering technology program, to leadership engineering at the University of Texas at El Paso—to name only a few of the change initiatives currently under way.

What lessons can we learn from these efforts?

Unmanned learning

Thanks to a combination of technology and ingenuity, modes of learning are possible now that weren't envisioned even a decade ago. You can even start your own university, designed for brand new specializations. That's what the founders of an innovative new idea, the Unmanned Vehicle University, did. When we spoke with Dr. Jerry LeMieux, President of Unmanned Vehicle University, we were intrigued by this concept, which was designed for the graduate level. We were surprised to learn how many different applications there were for unmanned vehicles—not just the more familiar military uses, but also police work, fighting fires, atmospheric research and customs and border patrol. Currently, over seventy countries are creating hundreds of different types of designs for commercial application. The U.S. has been lagging behind, but LeMieux's online Unmanned Vehicle University could change all that.

This field is tailor made for the whole new engineer. Engineers will be the key players; they're needed to design, develop, integrate, test and sustain these vehicles. To build an unmanned system curriculum, "It is important that the engineers that design these vehicles have experience in aeronautical, aerospace, mechanical, electrical and human factors engineering," explains LeMieux. "In addition, these vehicles are very complex in terms of technology and a systems engineering approach is needed to ensure the vehicles are built efficiently and safely." Not finding any established school that could fit the bill, he set out to create his own curriculum from scratch. Today, it is the only program offering advanced degrees in unmanned systems. "Our mission—to educate and train the best unmanned systems engineers from across the globe for the benefit of mankind," LeMieux says. This is yet another example of engineering education that is untethered from tradition. Schools that are bound by Cold War principles—and structures—will be left behind in this brave new world.

Lesson: Build the community, not just the curriculum.

We've seen the "appoint a committee to design the new curriculum" approach many times. Earlier we described the fatal flaws of this approach. In particular, we have been struck by the extent to which the conventional process breaks down around fundamental misunderstandings about the nature of the proposed change, as well as by a lack of buy-in in the community about the need for the change. At one school, we spent time interviewing faculty and students during just such a change process, and the comments from the community were sobering.

Interviewees provided grossly inaccurate pictures of what the proposed new curriculum was. In this particular case, the proposal (which was widely circulated) actually involved a small *increase* in the number of credits for mathematics and physics; nonetheless, many expressed concern that the new curriculum was drastically reducing mathematics and physics coverage. Similarly, many interviewees believed that the new curriculum involved a radical shift to project-based education—when, in fact, the amount of project work was staying almost the same.

Despite the belief that the new curriculum was radical, interviewees also were deeply skeptical about the likelihood that it would lead to any real change. One faculty member commented, "[The revision] will look major, but in the end, the change won't mean that much—it will be cosmetic only." Others talked about how they expected only minor changes in their own courses: "a bit of a pain, but not that big a deal, really."

Most troubling were the assessments by some long-time members of the faculty. One full professor observed, "The [Curriculum Revision Committee] is treating this like an engineering design project—deadlines, milestones, freezes. But this is more complex than an engineering project. You need to get commitment. Offer people an interesting job to do." Another faculty member put it this way: "The funny thing is you have [the committee], which cares very much, and then you have the people who say, 'I'll see what comes out.' You need all people to stand behind the project; otherwise people will be forced to do it, and this won't work."

In contrast to this approach, we've taken part in and also seen efforts in which the change agents pay serious attention not just to the change they are trying to make but also to the *people* who have to take part in the change and to the importance of creating community around the change. For example, when WPI was pursuing the Plan, a committee first identified twelve different options for how WPI might move forward. Then WPI President Harry Storke canceled classes for a day so that the entire community, from trustees to faculty to administrators to students, could meet, discuss, vent, and imagine the future. This event set in motion a lengthy period of conversation, with the intent of making sure that everyone felt his or her voice had been heard. Professor Charles Heventhal, a member of the committee, remembered this process as critical. "The community needed a way of looking at itself and at the possibilities for what it might become," he said, "and it needed to know that it had the power to bring about change."

Delft University's aerospace faculty took a similar tack. A passionate dean initiated the change process, and the initial steps were more focused on curriculum than community, but the committee soon realized that most of the community was skeptical about their work and that, ultimately, success depended not only on developing the right thing but also on having people believe in and own it.

Stepping back from its detailed curriculum blueprint, the committee reached out to the different departments to enlist the faculty's input and help. That's when the institution began to perk up. Sixteen of the seventeen chairs committed a couple of people to the effort, and, eventually, more than forty faculty members (approximately half of the staff) were involved in substantive ways. These forty faculty divided into design teams and interviewed students to get ideas for projects they cared about. They held multiple large-scale harmonization meetings, in which everyone got a chance to see what the different design teams were doing, to provide input, and to get a sense of the progress the community was making.

In the end, the committee created a visual display of the design results in a large room. It was a dramatic physical representation of what aerospace would be like for students, with posters for every experience, so that people could walk through the curriculum semester by semester and get a visual and emotional feel for how it all fit together. That poster display was an example of collective ownership, and everyone was proud. Faculty and students felt the success: "Wow, this is really coming together." "One of the best things about this is that now I actually know what is going on here." "I can't believe we actually got here."

Watching the excitement, the committee was reminded that faculty members are people, too. When you engage them emotionally, they respond. Real change is about the people. If you don't find ways to invite others into the change, to help them develop, and, ultimately, to have them own the change, you're not going to build something that lasts.

Lesson: Don't just tell me. Show me; let me experience it.

John Kotter writes, "In highly successful change efforts, people find ways to help others see the problem or solution in ways that influence emotions, not just thoughts. Feelings then alter behavior sufficiently to overcome all the many barriers to sensible large-scale change."

In his book, *Buy-In*, Kotter tells the story of someone presenting a plan to provide new computers for a local library. Describing it, he writes, "When dissenters don't listen because they don't think there is a problem with the current computers, the presenter has two options. He could use PowerPoint slides to compare the library's computers to current computer models sold in stores, showing the difference in processing power, memory capacity, and modem speed. Or he could relate the true story of a local fourth-grader from a poor family who relies on the library's computers for homework—computers that are too slow and outdated to allow her to finish her assignments, leaving her underprepared for school." It's easy to see which of these approaches might lead to change. When you engage people emotionally, they are more inclined to buy in.

This idea of "show; don't just tell" resonates with our own stories: when people are able to experience what a new culture can be like, instead of just being told, new possibilities are opened. We've seen this happen in small and large ways, at the University of Illinois, at Olin, and elsewhere.

David Goldberg: **Seeing is believing**

In September 2009, as we were launching iFoundry, some of the corporate advisors came down from Chicago to talk informally with the students. One of them was Gerry Labedz, who was an early pioneer at Motorola and a graduate of the University of Illinois. I met Gerry through the National Center for Supercomputing Applications. Gerry was now a Motorola fellow and a well-regarded senior member of the technical staff at Motorola.

It was a beautiful fall day, and Gerry was sitting outside surrounded by a team of students and was entertaining them with war stories about early cell phone technology. The students were enraptured. They were just eating it up. I was enjoying the moment when one of our iFoundry council members walked by and paused when he saw the rapt students. He's a mechanical engineering faculty member who had often complained that the students didn't have enough math courses. He wasn't wholly on board with what we were doing.

"What's going on?" he asked me. I explained that Gerry was one of our corporate advisors and he was meeting with one of the teams. I went on to describe Russ Korte's work and our conviction that social connectedness was the most important variable in making the transition from school to work, and we also believed that was true for students making the transition from high school to college.

He was half listening to me, and I could tell his real attention was on the students surrounding Gerry. Finally, he said thoughtfully, "That's really important, isn't it?"

"Yeah," I replied. "It is."

Subsequently, this professor who hadn't been fully convinced about what we were doing became much more supportive. All because of that moment on the lawn. Reflecting about it later, I realized I had learned a lesson: people don't change their minds; they change their hearts—and then their minds. The single most important thing that you can do as part of an initiative is have them witness authentic student engagement. When people witness or even are company creators of authentic student engagement, that's when they change. That's when they stop fighting and say, "Huh, this is what education is really about."

Olin's Candidate Weekend is another example of the power of seeing and experiencing. Although applicants to Olin have read promotional materials and in principle understand what Olin is about, it's only when they come to campus and experience the culture that they "get it." The emotional arc of the weekend begins at "I'm skeptical about this" and ends with "I want to be part of this!" Consistently, candidates say that before coming to the Candidate Weekend, they'd considered Olin as their third or fourth choice, but after the experience, Olin became their top choice. By taking part in the Candidate Weekend, students emotionally experience the idea that education can be different.

When people are able to experience what a new culture can be like, instead of just being told, new possibilities are opened.

As we described in chapter 2, when the iFoundry team visited Olin, it wasn't the discussions about curriculum that stuck with them. Rather, it was seeing students working together and observing that even freshmen already identified as engineers. Those things made them realize that something special was going on.

We've seen this when we've talked to people in K–12 who are trying to make a change. The Center for Advanced Professional Studies, a new high school program that is spreading in the Midwest, reframes the high school experience by connecting students, teachers, and local businesses. Students taking part in the program spend substantial amounts of their day doing project-based work on-site at local companies with industry mentors; it provides great opportunities for students, teachers, and industry participants to learn from each other. While it's an exciting program, most of the excitement is visible only if you actually go and *visit*. As a leading administrator of the program characterized it, "People don't know that they want it until they see it."

The insight that providing people with the chance to see and experience the change is critical to making the change happen strongly informs some of the successful strategies we've witnessed. Sometimes piloting is viewed as a way to safely try things out without being subjected to excessive scrutiny, but piloting is also a way to show people what the new world can be like. The choices made in the creation of iFoundry—from the early communication strategy to the "opt-in" structure—were made so that people could both see and feel that the change was possible. A similar approach was used at Harvard. Gordon Moore described the strategy this way: "You run a prototype because you intend to scale it up at some point, so a prototype has to build enthusiasm."

Lesson: Unleash students for change.

Linda Vanasupa's team launched the Center for Sustainability in Engineering at CalPoly SLO with nine faculty members overseeing teams of students in community-based projects. They recruited first-year students for the program, in part because new students were perceived as most open to thinking in different ways but also because they felt they could do the most for them. Vanasupa recalls, "They are the most at risk for not making it … We believed that what they learned here would serve them all four years."

The students responded—but not simply as recipients of the change. "We saw right away that student voice was the catalyst to faculty change," Vanasupa observed. "The students embraced it wholeheartedly, and they grew so much from meaningful community involvement. When asked to reflect on different aspects—failure and success, safety and risk—their comments were profound. They said, 'I feel I can learn anything on my own. It's my life, my learning.'"

Authentic involvement of students in reform efforts is, on the one hand, critical for implementing both of the lessons above: it's hard to build community without students, and it's hard to show what the new world can be like without actually creating that new world through a prototype or program. At the same time, unleashing students is, in itself, a critical step toward building the new culture we need. One of the words that comes up time and again when we talk to students who have been substantively involved in reform efforts is "ownership." It's an interesting word to reflect on in the context of changing the educational culture. For decades, we've framed education as purely transactional: "I pay tuition; you give me knowledge." Unleashing students is about involving students authentically, leading them to the belief that "I am in control of my own learning. I am going to make decisions that help me to improve. I am paying tuition to be in an environment and with people that support me in this quest." In other words, we need to help students move from being consumers to creators of their educations.

The children will lead us

When we talk about unleashing students and moving away from a mechanistic view of learning, we find much to be hopeful about in the exciting projects that are becoming more common in the lower grades. In changing the culture of engineering education, we see that the process is enhanced when it starts in grades K–12.

Engineering Is Elementary is a program of the Museum of Science in Boston that provides learning materials and opportunities for K–12 students across the nation. Christine M. Cunningham, founder and director, describes the mission this way: "Children are born engineers— they like to design their own creations, figure out how things work, and take things apart. Could this natural curiosity be tapped to teach engineering principles in elementary schools, alongside math and science content skills? Could we create a curriculum that interests and engages *all* students—including girls and boys, children of all races and ethnicities, children from a variety of socioeconomic backgrounds, and children who are most likely to be 'at risk'? And could we do so in a way that is readily accepted and implemented by elementary school teachers who are often uncomfortable with science and engineering topics?"

A *New York Times* feature highlighted one such effort at Clara E. Coleman Elementary School in Glen Rock, New Jersey. There, kindergartners learned engineering principles via "the Three Little Pigs"—figuring out design solutions that might thwart the Big Bad Wolf.

Project Lead the Way provides hands-on, project-based STEM curricula for middle and high school students across the country. More than five thousand schools are enrolled. Impressive independent research shows that PLTW students outperform their peers in school; are better prepared for postsecondary studies; and are more likely to consider careers as scientists, technology experts, engineers, mathematicians, healthcare providers, and researchers compared to their non-PLTW peers. Vince Bertram, President and CEO of Project Lead The Way, cites key factors for PLTW's success. "PLTW provides rigorous and relevant curriculum for students and professional development for teachers. Our teacher training encourages teachers to instruct differently—acting as facilitators of learning, rather than traditional instructors. It gives them the content knowledge and confidence they need to affect change in the classroom, and teachers often say their experience teaching PLTW courses renews their passion for teaching. From the students' perspective, PLTW's activity-, project-, and problem-based curriculum is engaging and shows students the relevancy of their learning to the world around them, inspiring their passion for STEM subjects and careers."

Another program, "Invent It, Build It," sponsored by the Society of Women Engineers, tackles the gender gap in engineering by creating a hands-on engineering experience for middle school girls, culminating in a project show at the annual Society of Women Engineers conference.

Dean Kamen, an inventor and entrepreneur, set out to help young people discover the excitement and rewards of science and technology, creating FIRST Robotics. ("FIRST" is an acronym: For Inspiration and Recognition of Science and Technology.) He envisioned a cultural transformation "where science and technology are celebrated and where young people dream of becoming science and technology leaders."

FIRST sponsors projects, challenges, and competitions for kids as young as K–3, enlisting more than 120,000 volunteers and 3,500 corporate, educational, and individual sponsors. Among its programs are a national robotics competition for grades 9–12, a tech competition for grades 7–12, a Lego League for grades 4–8, and a mini–Lego League for K–3.

An interesting feature of FIRST's philosophy goes to the heart of the below-the-waterline change we're talking about. The program is not just about doing cool stuff; it's about interacting with others in a value-driven way. MIT's Woodie Flowers, one of FIRST's advisors, coined the term that describes its ethos: "gracious professionalism."

"With gracious professionalism, fierce competition and mutual gain are not separate notions. Gracious professionals learn and compete like crazy but treat one another with respect and kindness in the process. They avoid treating anyone like losers. No chest thumping tough talk, but no sticky-sweet platitudes, either. Knowledge, competition, and empathy are comfortably blended."

Chris Rogers, a professor of mechanical engineering at Tufts University who works with its Lego Engineering Design Group, emphasizes that a key principle of teaching young kids is to evoke many different solutions. "We measure success in the diversity of answers, not just one right answer," he says. As an example, Rogers gave elementary school students a specific number of Legos and told them to build a duck. They created many different kinds of ducks. Rogers's conclusion: "There is no right duck."

Lesson: Choose your words carefully.

Both Schein and Kotter identify the need to communicate. Schein talks about disconfirmation—exposing people to the idea that some of their assumptions are incorrect—as well as the need to help people see that a change is possible. Kotter talks about the need to articulate and tirelessly communicate the vision for change.

The need to communicate is clearly a major component of a change effort. But it's not just what you say; it's also how you say it that matters. Language is often forgotten as a cultural artifact, but as we've discussed in earlier chapters, it's a powerful tool that can be leveraged in change efforts and certainly must be accounted for.

Language serves as an invisible enforcer of the existing culture, because language works not only at the level of denotation (what the formal meaning of a piece of language is) but also at the level of connotation (the implied and often subconscious meaning of the language). As we noted above, academics often refer to the educational responsibilities of instructors as their "teaching load." While "teaching load" has a clear denotation—the number of courses an instructor is expected to teach in a year—it also has a very strong connotation: *teaching is a burden*. We have yet to hear an institution or an individual refer to a "research load."

Because language operates at these two levels, it is important to query existing language, which often reinforces underlying assumptions, and to also be intentional in creating new language. This new language then leverages our existing assumptions and reinforces the new assumptions we are trying to create.

When Harvard was pursuing the New Pathways curriculum change, the committee referred to the project as "an experiment." Why? For good reason, as Professor Leon Eisenberg recalled: "How could any scientist object to an experiment?" Similarly, in creating iFoundry, Goldberg coined the term "the missing basics" to refer to a variety of competencies that are typically not addressed in engineering programs. How could any educator object to addressing the basics? At Olin, the creation of the Passionate Pursuits program involved both the creation of a cultural artifact in the form of the program and the creation of a piece of language that embeds an implicit assumption that students should be able to pursue their passions. It's tempting to think that the name of a policy or program doesn't matter, so long as you get the content right, but, in reality, naming can be a powerful lever for cultural change.

Lesson: You can't just tick a box.

We've seen what we call "tick-the-box" change happen again and again. The existing organization decides that a change is necessary and attempts to use existing hierarchical structures to implement the change. The order for change comes from the top down, e.g., from the dean's office to the departmental office to the individual faculty member.

However, existing bureaucracies, while effective at day-to-day operations and small changes, are often incapable of large-scale change. Actors at the low level in the system often recognize that the chance of success in the change is low, and as a consequence, they rationally choose to spend their energy showing how the status quo is actually already accomplishing the proposed goals. While this leads to increased energy expenditure in reporting up the chain of command, the actual change on the ground is minimal at best.

We think this is why so many successful change efforts have involved the creation of new structures, outside the day-to-day bureaucracy, that are designed to be capable of the change. Babson's change was in part enabled by President Bill Glavin's decision to create three decision-making bodies, DMBs, to pursue programmatic plans. He made no secret of the fact that the DMBs would be composed of those who were most passionate about transformational change. That's when they took a radical step, adopting a phrase common in business vernacular: "zero-based planning." That is, none of the assumptions underlying the current program was accepted as a given. *Every* element of the curriculum, whether old or new, had to be justified. They were starting from scratch, and the DMBs were empowered to make radical change. It was anything but business as usual.

WPI's change was likewise enabled by an approach that was far outside the normal way of doing business. Up until the creation of the Plan, power over the curriculum, and most other matters, was concentrated with the department heads and the senior administration. Faculty governance was nonexistent, and faculty meetings were rare formalities. President Storke found change in that environment to be almost impossible, and consequently, he created a new group, outside of the normal power structure, to pursue change. Although Storke's team still encountered the normal structure's resistance—Professor Grogan, chair of the group, recalls reporting to

the department heads as being "like running into a room full of feathers"—
the group was nonetheless able to move forward.

Through a cultural lens, part of the power of going beyond "tick the box" is the creation new artifacts that enable the change and that have new underlying assumptions associated with them. Although on one hand underlying assumptions can act as an "immune system" for new behaviors, at the same time, creating new structures that have different associated beliefs can allow for new kinds of behaviors and the creation of new social norms. Just as new language can act as a lever, new structures (and, of course, the naming thereof) can help create new culture. It's not just that old structures can't accommodate change; it's also that the creation of new structures can help make the change real.

Lesson: You don't have to know where you're going.

Earlier we spoke of the importance of effectuation, citing the work of Saras Sarasvathy, a professor at the University of Virginia's Darden School of Business. In 1997, Sarasvathy set out to discover how entrepreneurs think. Spending months traveling and interviewing entrepreneurs from a variety of industries, Sarasvathy came to a somewhat surprising conclusion. Rather than finding that the entrepreneurs were unified in their high level of risk tolerance or driven by a need for financial success, Sarasvathy instead discovered that they were unified in their approach to planning: they *effectuate* rather than simply employing causal thinking. She explains:

"Causal rationality begins with a pre-determined goal and a given set of means, and seeks to identify the optimal—fastest, cheapest, most efficient, etc.—alternative to achieve the given goal . . . [Effectual reasoning] begins with a given set of means and allows goals to emerge contingently over time from the varied imagination and diverse aspirations of the founders and the people they interact with." More prosaically, entrepreneurs might have a general compass *direction*, but they don't necessarily have a *plan*. Rather, they take advantage of what's around them and take what seem like the best steps at the time.

A second contrast between effectuation and causal reasoning lies in the attitude toward failure. "Effectuators do not seek to avoid failure; they seek to make success happen," she says. "This entails a recognition that failing is an integral part of venturing well. Through their willingness to fail, effectuators create temporal portfolios of ventures whose successes and failures they manage—learning to outlive failures by keeping them small and killing them young, and cumulating successes through continual leveraging."

> *Effectuators do not seek to avoid failure; they seek to make success happen.*
>
> **—Saras Sarasvathy**

Change often requires an effectual approach. In Olin's case, there was not a plan for a Partner Year. Rather, the environment (students were applying, but the campus and the curriculum weren't ready) required doing something different from the planned rollout. The whole experiment could have gone down in flames at that point, but by changing course Olin was able to turn what could have been a disaster into an opportunity. In the end, the Partner Year was critical to Olin's culture and success. And, while it was not planned, it was something that Olin arrived at intentionally through effectuation.

At Babson, when Dean Tom Moore was asked by the Babson board to explain how the new MBA program had come into existence, his description of the process revealed an effectuator's approach: "With 20/20 hindsight, almost anything can be made to look logical and well reasoned . . . But there were countless times when this process felt *anything but* logical and reasonable."

Our sense is that most change processes can be described this way and that change requires a willingness to accept this ambiguity and keep your eyes open to potential stepping-stones that might not have been visible when you started.

Changing our assumptions

In engineering education reform, we've too often focused our attention on the wrong object of change. While restructuring curriculum and reforming pedagogy are, without a doubt, worthy causes, making real change in engineering education requires whole new *assumptions*. It requires that we shift our underlying beliefs, along with those of our colleagues and students, by building community, by showing people the new world, by using language intentionally, by using structures intentionally, and by being open to changing course. In doing this we begin the process of shifting our culture to one that is trusting, joyful, collaborative, open, and courageous. And, thus, we begin to enable the creation of the Whole New Engineer.

Epilogue
An Invitation to Collaborative Disruption
Will Disruption Shape Us, or Will We Shape It?

*There are exciting possibilities on the horizon for education.
The reason we haven't progressed down these paths doesn't have
to do with the state of the technology. It has to do with how the
technology has been implemented. Employing a disruptive
approach presents a promising path toward at long last
realizing the vision of a transformed classroom.*

—Clayton M. Christensen and Michael B. Horn

In the end, it's difficult to find the right words to bring this book to a close. After all, it's an unusual book, as far as books in engineering education reform go. Unlike many texts before it, it wasn't commissioned by a national or royal academy or sponsored by some philanthropic foundation with a mission to aid higher education. It isn't a presentation of research findings funded by a national agency, engineering education society, or global engineering education powerhouse. It isn't a compendium of pedagogical tips or a neatly categorized list of class or curriculum features. Nor is it a presentation of learning outcomes. In writing this book we've set aside many of the conventions of academic discourse and intentionally wrote it

231

as a collection of stories, anecdotes, and snippets from research outside of our direct expertise.

Of course, when we started, we confessed that we were up to something unusual, and we promised to document an improbable journey: the unlikely story of the founding of Olin, an upstart engineering school that shouldn't have happened; the unconventional rise of iFoundry, a programmatic incubator for educational change that grew from the grassroots without official sanction; the formation of the Olin-Illinois Partnership, as unlikely a pairing since Felix and Oscar formed the Odd Couple. And we believe we've kept those promises. In a certain sense the book is a joint memoir of experiences in engineering education transformation, and we've tried to stay true to both what we believe we know objectively about the events we've described and our subjective experience of them.

The telling of the Olin, iFoundry-Illinois, and Olin-Illinois Partnership stories in chapters 1 and 2 led us to reflect on the larger arc of history in engineering and engineering education in chapter 3. Although we have attempted to be historically accurate in our telling, neither of us is a professional historian. Nonetheless, we think that citing pivotal moments in the nineteenth century, certain phenomena post–World War II, what we called the three missed revolutions, and then connecting them to certain key technological inventions and ideas in economics helps give a fresh and helpful perspective on the current moment in history and why certain technical, economic, and historical forces appear to be pushing education transformation in a particular direction.

Thereafter, in chapter 4 we reflected on Howard Gardner's theory of multiple intelligences, Carol Dweck's mind-set theory, Dan Pink's call for a whole new mind and other influences to discuss the six minds of the Whole New Engineer: analytical, design, linguistic, people, body, and mindful. This led to a reflection on the fundamental conundrum of the Olin-Illinois Partnership—that is, how could the 2009 "peashooter" experience at Illinois yield the emotional unleashing of the Olin effect, the combination of confidence and courage necessary for creativity and lifelong learning in the twenty-first century? That reflection led in chapter 5 to an articulation of the five pillars of the whole new education: joy, trust, courage, openness, and connection.

Finally, the last four chapters have connected intrinsic motivation, coaching, organizational culture, and change management to engineering education transformation. We might subtitle this section of the book "Essential tools and technologies of trust and transformation." These topics are not traditionally contained in books on engineering education reform or higher-education transformation, but our interpretation of successful transformations is that each topic is critical to successful educational change. It concerns us that, with rare exception, each of these is largely missing in both the thought and the action of most change initiatives. We believe that past failures are largely explained by their absence and that future successes depend on reframing education change in exactly these terms and away from the usual debates over content, curriculum, and pedagogy.

When viewed from within the walls of the university, our approach seems odd, perhaps, but when viewed from within the walls of business today, there is little unusual in our telling. We are surrounded by examples of companies that have re-created workplace cultures around values such as personal fulfillment, creativity, and independence. We see it in the most successful companies, where a culture of innovation is standard: companies such as Nike, where experimentation is encouraged and the model is "break the sewing machine"; companies such as Google, whose open "campus" is legendary and whose culture is commonly cited in reviews of the best places to work; companies such as SAS, the data analytics firm that encourages "creative anarchy" among employees to inspire new ideas. Even the old standard companies, such as Procter & Gamble, IBM, and General Electric, boast that they are in a process of reinvention.

Moreover, the book is well aligned with business and journalistic observers of the modern scene. When Dan Pink says you need a whole new ("creative") mind, and Richard Florida says there is a "rising creative class," and Tom Friedman says "the world is flat," the book lines up nicely with those conceptual framings and ideas and many others that have come along thereafter.

The book is also aligned with much of the educational innovation that is taking place outside of colleges and universities. For example, interesting innovations are happening in for-profit educational institutions, and they are being rewarded by increased market share. Technology-based innovators such as Khan Academy and MOOCs are changing the landscapes of established nonprofit educational institutions without their permission. Microinnovators abound, with many individual performers choosing to go into private or nonprofit practice rather than align with established university and collegiate cultures that are unable to fathom the need for, motivation for, or application of the innovators or their innovations. In the new "flat world" educational environment, we see rigid hierarchical institutions giving way to fluid, more collaborative, egalitarian programs, many of which cross the brick-and-mortar barrier into cyberspace.

These programs highlight the opportunities of our era. They also highlight the challenges.

Key takeaways

When we give seminars and workshops together, we frequently request that participants sit and reflect at the end of a day and ask what were their key takeaways. Here, we invite you to scan back through the chapters and consider your key takeaways. What was interesting or surprising to you? What did you learn? What would you like to know more about? And what inspires you to take action, and what actions would you take? We hope you'll pause now before reading further and reflect on these questions.

Having asked the questions, however, we'd like to take a moment and point out some of our own key takeaways from the experiences described in the book and from writing the book. We've intentionally kept the list short to highlight crucial points. And, of course, our list is not the "right" answer. Underlying the book is a principled pluralism, and we're not going to abandon that stance now. Nonetheless, we believe there are seven essential takeaways from the book:

- Engineering education is **misaligned** with the twenty-first century.
- The twenty-first century calls for **courageous**, not obedient, engineers.
- The cultivation of courage requires **trust**.
- Training educators to show up as coaches who trust is a deep **emotional** shift.
- Moving educational institutions formed as impersonal bureaucracies to become more democratic and caring is a deep **cultural** shift.
- New understandings of brain, social, and organizational science give us the **tools and technologies** for deeply emotional and cultural transformations.
- The necessary change is too complex and emotionally and culturally challenging to do in competitive isolation from one another and requires **collaboration**.

Let's briefly consider each of these takeaways.

Misaligned with the times. We believe that engineering education is severely misaligned with the times. Being aware of this helps us understand many of the knottiest difficulties in engineering education that are often discussed but rarely tackled successfully. For example, we believe that most pipeline problems are connected to this misalignment: young people avoiding engineering school altogether, high dropout rates and low retention, small numbers of women and underrepresented minorities in the pipeline, and dissatisfied graduates who seek employment outside the profession. We believe that these are all symptoms of the misalignment, and once we know that, we can begin to tackle the root problem.

Courage, not obedience. The essential misalignment is that times have changed, and where the 1950s demanded the production of socially captive, obedient engineers, the twenty-first century demands the unleashing of creative, ever-learning courageous engineers. This is a big shift—really a paradigm shift—and it has come about very suddenly.

Trust, not control. The reason this shift is so challenging to address is that the cultivation of courage requires positive emotion and trust, but we have educators and educational institutions that work through fear and control. We now require a completely different operating system for our educational institutions.

Change as emotional. Looking at it through educators' eyes, for centuries we have trained narrow disciplinary experts to say "I know," and now we ask them to say "I trust." The changes demanded from the standpoint of educators and students are deeply personal, and all the relevant change variables are emotional ones. We are calling on educators to manage polar opposites—expertise and trusting others—in a flexible, agile way, and this demands self-awareness, emotional intelligence, and a deep vulnerability in ways the old roles did not.

Change as cultural. The larger democratizing forces in society and the workplace calling for these personal changes are also calling on institutions of higher education to move from old-style impersonal bureaucracies to the more supportive, caring kinds of organization that are emerging in the private and nonprofit sectors elsewhere. These changes are deeply cultural. Existing forms of administration and governance are being challenged as never before.

Tools of trust and transformation available. Fortunately, we live in times where the brain, social, and organization sciences are delivering a bounty of understanding that can help us make these changes more efficiently and effectively. Positive psychology and coaching help us make the personal transformations necessary. Culture theory and change management techniques worked out in the private sector can be applied in education. The changes needed are complex, but we have a variety of tools and technologies at our disposal for tackling them.

Change requires collaboration, not competition. Yet even with this bounty of tools and technologies at our disposal, when we stand back from the extreme nature of the shifts being demanded, the change task is so large and difficult it exceeds the capacity of any single organization from tackling it without help from others. We believe this is the case, and we'd like to consider this takeaway next.

Disruptive innovation is inevitable

We began this book with the story of a journey—how two unlikely collaborators, in the midst of extraordinary circumstances, found surprising keys to the transformation of engineering education. At the time, we noted that Olin and Illinois were very different institutions and unlikely collaborators, but we are struck by the gifts we were given by the collaboration—gifts we did not anticipate, gifts that essentially handed us the key insights that made the writing of the book necessary. In short, collaboration was essential to push us far enough to grasp the underlying nature of the transformation being demanded, and it is not clear that either institution working alone would have come to that understanding.

We think the larger lesson of the Olin-Illinois Partnership for educational change right now is that in similar ways, formerly independent institutions of different sizes, shapes, and missions need to come together and become collaborators—and there isn't a moment to lose. We hope that many of the challenges going forward will be made easier given the framing of this book and the understanding achieved in the Olin-iFoundry/Illinois collaboration, but even with some of the intellectual challenges taken off the table, the emotional and cultural challenges are enormous, and only by coming together can they be solved.

Coming together won't be easy. Academic institutions are fiercely independent and competitive. Even small differences in teaching calculus or engineering mechanics are often believed to hold competitive advantage over the engineering school down the road, and so schools innovate within their own four walls and rarely come together with other schools. And perhaps this competitive viewpoint has served us well in times where small tweaks or modest changes to the larger system were sufficient to align with larger societal demands. But the changes needed now are too large and deep to move the existing system under the current competitive paradigm. Either we come together or the existing system of universities and colleges worldwide risks being *disrupted.*

Clay Christensen has written for many years about *disruptive innovation*, beginning with his groundbreaking book, *The Innovator's Dilemma.* He writes that in business, certain kinds of innovations to a product or service line can be integrated within an existing organization, thereby allowing the company to be successful in a competitive marketplace. There are, however, innovations that challenge the underlying assumptions of the current product so much so that a company and its culture are unable to adapt. As a result, with disruptive innovations, other companies arise to produce the product or service embodying the disruptive innovation. In time, the once successful and once larger company is put out of business or severely reduced in size. Interestingly, Christensen believes that higher education is undergoing exactly this kind of disruption right now and puts forth this premise in *Disrupting Class: How Disruptive Innovation Will Change the Way We Learn.*

One of the common—and dangerous—patterns in disruptive innovation is for those in the organization being disrupted to ignore the threat and move ahead confident that the status quo will continue, perhaps modified slightly but continue nonetheless. In the case of universities, the nearly ten-century stability of higher-educational institutions makes becoming aware of the real threats even more difficult.

Earlier we used the metaphor of an operating system to talk about what needed to be changed, but if we take the metaphor literally, it points to a current trend that has effectively blended competition and collaboration in practice. In particular, if we look at the open-source innovation that underlies operating systems such as Unix and Android, we see that it is possible for otherwise independent, competitive actors to come together to share both the risks and the rewards of developing new systems.

Olin, Illinois, and the Olin-Illinois Partnership

It seems like a lifetime ago, but it's been only seven years since Olin College and Illinois first came together to collaborate on engineering education transformation. Since that time, Olin, Illinois, and the Olin-Illinois Partnership have continued to work individually and together to advance the effective engineering education transformation.

iFoundry continues as an incubator for educational change, and Illinois continues as an institution committed to engineering education transformation. Following the 2009 freshman experience and a scale-up in 2010 to approximately three hundred students, the freshman experience was scaled to the whole freshman class in 2011 with the advent of the Illinois Engineering Freshman Experience. This scale-up involved modification of the original program, but many of the elements pioneered in 2009 and 2010 were carried forward. Other initiatives undertaken beneath the iFoundry banner include a new innovation certificate, an intrinsic motivation conversion initiative, and the establishment of a Junior Enterprise chapter at Illinois, the first in the United States.

Notably, many of the individuals who supported iFoundry in the early years have gone on to higher positions. Ilesanmi Adesida was dean of engineering who supported iFoundry's movement from a grassroots effort to a college activity, and he has gone on to become Illinois's provost. iFoundry reported directly to Associate Dean Chuck Tucker at the time of its official establishment (2008), and he was recently named associate provost for undergraduate education and innovation at Illinois. Andreas Cangellaris, iFoundry cofounder, became department head of electrical and computer engineering at Illinois shortly after iFoundry's official establishment; he was named dean of engineering at Illinois last year. Dean Cangellaris (in cooperation with Provost Adesida) is planning a significant upping of the ante of engineering education transformation at Illinois, in part because of the success in moving the cultural needle at Illinois during the original iFoundry push.

As Olin graduated class after class of new engineers snapped up for top positions in industry, government, and the academy, it gained confidence that the Olin effect could and should be shared with others. Each year, more and more individuals, schools, and companies would visit Olin to learn about its culture. Olin's aspiration to contribute to change in engineering education, combined with this high external interest in what was happening at Olin, led Olin to first develop the Initiative for Innovation in Engineering Education (I2E2) and, more recently, the Olin Collaboratory. Central to the Collaboratory vision is the idea that although the underlying principles (which we've referred to as the pillars here) remain the same across all institutions, each institution and culture is also different. Thus, one size does not fit all, and *collaborative* approaches and partnerships are necessary for transformation.

Through the Collaboratory, Olin now welcomes on the order of two hundred different organizations each year to campus for discussions about how to change engineering education. Every year the Collaboratory runs a variety of workshops that engage participants from around the world in thinking together about how to design for student engagement and motivation and how to effect curricular, cultural, and organizational change. And, inspired by the success of the Olin-Illinois Partnership, the Collaboratory structure is enabling Olin to actively partner with institutions ranging from the University of Texas at El Paso to INSPER in Brazil to realize meaningful cultural—and curricular—change.

The Olin-Illinois Partnership itself has continued to pay benefits to both institutions. The Olin-Illinois Exchange was set up to allow students from either organization to attend the other, in much the same way that students visit schools overseas. The first Engineer of the Future event has led to two more, and changes in leadership at both schools have led to a recalibration of activities going forward and a commitment to a deepening and continuation of the partnership. As both institutions move ahead, the forging of official collaboration with the other has been a significant strategic advantage in moving agendas at home and in the larger world.

Big Beacon and collaborative disruption

Perhaps one of the key things to come out of the early years of collaboration was the need to both enhance and institutionalize the notion of collaboration itself. Some of the pivotal events occurred in early 2011.

Mark had recently been promoted to associate dean and was in a position to think strategically about the ways Olin could share its mission with others, and Dave had recently resigned his tenure at Illinois to take training at Georgetown University as a leadership coach and to start ThreeJoy Associates Inc.; he was thinking about ways to work with clients around the world to bring about effective transformation. Together, we wondered how could we continue our work in ways that would help bring about the kinds of beautiful experiences that we had witnessed at Olin and Illinois.

As we pondered these possibilities, a vision started to emerge. Could we use open innovation and collaboration to carry these ideas to a broader coalition of the willing? The elements of such an effort seemed clear:

- Finding a coalition of willing collaborators.
- Creating a network of positive exemplars or bright spots.
- Using incubators at collaborating organizations to allow pilots to survive separate from traditional organizations.

- Generating practical alternatives on the ground that would change hearts and then minds.
- Using open innovation across organizations to create an operating system for a whole new education.
- Using cultural infection to help get authentic experiences in new outposts of change quickly and well.

This all seemed logical and reasonable enough, but the vision was large, the budget was small, and it seemed as though we needed some leverage in the marketplace to make this work.

After seeing an interesting tweet about thought leadership, we contacted its author, consultant Peter Winick, and sought his advice about carrying this impossible task to the next level. He listened to our pitch and looked at our materials and said, "Oh, you guys are trying to create a movement." That was the first time the word "movement" had been used in connection with what we were doing, but we loved the framing and immediately liked the connection to things such as the Salt March and Quit India movement in India or the civil rights movement in the United States. Peter went on: "And to create a movement, the first step is to write a manifesto, and the second step is to write a book." The two of us had both thought about a book before, but a manifesto was not on our plate; however, we liked the suggestion and started to craft a manifesto and write a book.

In thinking about a name for the movement, a good one had occurred to us earlier. As we started to make these plans back in 2011, we recalled the words of the late Michael Moody, who said, "Olin is intended to be a beacon to engineering education," and almost immediately as we were crafting our plans, we had our name. Through the power of collaboration, this movement would be the *Big Beacon*, drawing people to the light of a whole new kind of engineer and engineering education.

The choice to transform

The Big Beacon launched officially on June 4, 2012, with the online publication of the Big Beacon manifesto (available at www.bigbeacon. org). Gesturing back to the early Cluetrain manifesto, the Big Beacon manifesto starts with an aspirational preamble. It then continues in three parts—the *whole new engineer*, a *whole new engineering education*, and *educational rewire*—and finishes with an optimistic note for the future. In sharing the manifesto with others, the response has been heartening, but a recent story helps convey the sense we get from it.

Dave was recently in Toronto at the 2014 Engineers without Borders national convention. In a workshop, "The Emotional Rescue of Engineering Education," the Big Beacon manifesto was used as a way to provoke participant reflection. After the workshop, Dave was walking out of the room when a young woman, a senior engineering student, walked up and said, "I want to thank you. I really enjoyed that workshop."

Dave asked, "What was it that you enjoyed?"

She reflected for a long while and then replied, "I never thought I belonged in engineering throughout my education, but the things you shared help me understand that I do."

The more we share the manifesto and the ideas of this larger movement with others, the more we are convinced that they hold the keys to engineering and technology education becoming much bigger tents than they are now. But in order to get to that time when more young people feel they belong in engineering and technology, we need to work together to help collaboratively disrupt the status quo.

With the release of this book, we believe the movement will grow, and our main hope for the book is that it helps drive a global conversation on engineering and technology education. And as that conversation grows, some will be moved to try their hand at transforming their own engineering schools and colleges, and we intend for the Big Beacon to be there as a sender of new messages for a new culture; as a dot connector; and as a promoter of collaboration, partnership, and open innovation—as a mover and shaker for global action.

Big Beacon is organized as an Illinois not-for-profit corporation and is headquartered in Douglas, Michigan. On December 28, 2012, Big Beacon signed its first memorandum of understanding with Franklin W. Olin College of Engineering. That "Olin-Beacon Understanding," or OBU, designates Olin as the "Founding Institutional Member of Big Beacon," and since that time, Big Beacon and Olin have collaborated in offering short courses together, in the writing of this book, and in continuing to try to understand effective system-wide transformation of engineering education.

A call to action through reflective questions

- **Students.** In what ways does this book stimulate you to think differently about engineering as an education and as a career? In what ways might you help to bring about the kinds of changes in engineering education at your school?
- **Parents.** In what ways do the messages in this book resonate with your aspirations for your son or daughter? What actions can you take to help bring these ideas to the attention of their teachers?
- **Educators.** In what ways are the messages of this book heartening and disheartening, given what you know about the culture of your school? What steps can you take to act to collaboratively bring about change with your colleagues?
- **Administrators.** What are the biggest challenges and possibilities for change poised by this book? As someone in responsible charge, what practical little bets can you make to seek small wins that might lead to greater opportunity and change?

- **Vendors.** In what ways do your products and services align or not with this vision of engineering education? In what ways can you collaborate generously with those customers who seek this kind of transformation?
- **Employers.** In what ways is the vision of the Whole New Engineer aligned or misaligned with your workplace? In what ways can you collaborate to help transform your feeder schools?
- **Coaches and consultants.** In what ways are your practices aligned with this text and the manifesto? What special challenges might be involved in moving from a corporate environment to an educational environment?
- **Volunteers.** What is it that moves you about this book or the manifesto to want to volunteer to help bring about transformative change? What are you most passionate about changing?

As the wraps come off the book and the movement comes out from under the radar, the Big Beacon is looking to sign other memoranda of understanding with other educational, media, and organizational members, affiliates, and partners. We are also growing Big Beacon as a volunteer organization, and those with passion, skill, and drive are welcome to join our growing ranks.

As these events unfold, it is difficult to know exactly what will happen and how change will occur. But we believe that this kind of change comes about with leadership from all actors at all levels, whether they have official titles or not. We approach the future with the knowledge that we all have a part to play, involving making some important choices:

Will we choose deep change, understanding that we are part of a global cultural transformation in the way we live, work, and learn? Or will we choose the status quo, with incremental changes in curriculum and pedagogy?

Will we choose an intrinsically motivated, creative pursuit of lifelong learning? Or will we choose a rigid math-science focus that minimalizes the importance of design, creativity, and personal growth?

Will we choose an open learning environment, where professors collaborate and coach and students are trusted to excel through experimentation and a full engagement in their learning? Or will we choose to maintain an expert class of professors whose role is to impart knowledge to students in an authoritarian manner?

Will we choose to create a collaborative environment of openness, listening, and shared insight? Or will we choose to maintain our distance, as institutions and individuals, valuing the solitary pursuit of lone wolves?

Will we choose wholeness, valuing engineers as not just minds but also social, creative, emotion-driven human beings who live and flourish in the world? Or will we continue to view engineers in a narrow, technically composed construct, limited by the strictures of math and science?

Finally, will we choose joy in learning, doing, and being an engineer, believing that to practice engineering is to be engaged in the most exhilarating pursuit of our era?

These choices are ours to make—as educators, as students, as parents, as alumni, as taxpayers, as schools, as companies, and as a society. They are choices between the past and the future. For ourselves, we choose the future. Will you join us?

Appendix A
Notes

Introduction: An Improbably Journey

The National Academies: Committee on Prospering in the Global Economy of the 21st Century; Committee on Science, Engineering, and Public Policy; Institute of Medicine; Policy and Global Affairs; National Academy of Sciences; National Academy of Engineering; *Rising above the Gathering Storm: Energizing and Employing Americans for a Brighter Economic Future.* (Washington: The National Academies Press, 2007.)

The National Science Foundation has poured: Robert C. Serow, "Curriculum Reform and the NSF Engineering Education Coalitions: A Case Study," March, 1997; "Final Report of the Progress of the Engineering Education Coalitions," May 2000. www.nsf.gov.

The Duderstadt report: James J. Duderstadt, "Engineering for a Changing World: A Roadmap to the Future of Engineering Practice, Research, and Education." (The Millennium Project at the University of Michigan, 2001.)

the NAE Engineers of 2020 tackled: The National Academy of Engineering, *The Engineer of 2020: Visions of Engineering in the New Century.* (Washington: National Academies Press, 2004.)

1: Engineering Happiness
The Olin Experience

Opening quote: This frequently referenced remark by Thomas Edison was said to occur when M.A. Rosenoff, a new employee, joined Edison's laboratory and asked him about the lab rules.

It seemed a fantastic dream: Founding stories about the birth of Olin College of Engineering and the biography of Franklin Olin at www.olin.edu.; also Gloria Polizzotti, *From the Ground Up: The Founding and Early History of the Franklin W. Olin College of Engineering: A Bold Experiment in Engineering Education*. (Needham: The Needham Historical Society, 2009.)

Employee number one: Author interview with Rick Miller.

Babson's dean: Author interview with Charlie Nolan.

In a more conventional: Author interview with David Kerns.

"We felt a huge": Author interview with Sherra Kerns.

The Bold Goals were: S.E. Kerns, D.V. Kerns, R.K. Miller; "Designing from a Blank Slate: The Development of the Initial Olin College Curriculum." (Washington: The National Academies Press, 2004.)

Gathering under a tent: President Rick Miller's remarks to Olin partners. www.olin.edu/about_olin/docs/remarks_partnership.asp.

Polina Segalova: Author interview.

Susan Fredholm Murphy: Author interview.

The partners had: Susan Fredholm, James Krejcarkek, Stephen Krumholz, Dan Linquist, Sean Munson, Steve Schiffman, John Bourne; "Designing an Engineering Entrepreneurship Curriculum for Olin College." (Washington: The American Society of Engineering Education, 2002.)

The creation of Olin's honor code: www.olin.edu/student_life/honor_code.aspx.

In his inaugural: www.olin.edu/sites/default/gfiles/inaugural-address.pdf.

When the CDMB members: "Once Upon a College." http://www.olin.edu/sites/default/files/final_cdmb_report.pdf.

It's notable that: *The Best 376 Colleges, 2012 edition*. (Princeton: Princeton Review, 2011.)

2: The Incubator
Helping a Big Old Dog Learn New Tricks

Opening quote John Milton Gregory: from *The Seven Laws of Teaching*; citation below.

When John Milton Gregory: Maynard Brichford, "A Brief History of the University of Illinois." (University of Illinois Archives, www.archives. library.illinois.edu.)

In his remarkable book: John Milton Gregory, *The Seven Laws of Teaching*. (Grand Rapids: Baker Books, 1884.)

Responding to the demand: David E. Goldberg blog post: "Philosophy of engineering not a contradiction in terms." www.entrepreneurialengineer.blogspot.com. May 24, 2006. These ideas were formalized into a number of lectures, like that given at the Royal Institute of Engineering of the Netherlands in The Hague, April 1, 2010. The lecture was titled, "3 Reasons Why Philosophy Should Matter to Engineers." www.ifoundry.illinois.edu/ blogs/3-reasons-why-philosophy-should-matter-engineers.

A 1994 whitepaper: David E. Goldberg, "Change in Engineering Education: One Myth, Two Scenarios, and Three Foci," (ILLiGAL Report No. 94003, June 1994.)

A whitepaper: "For an Illinois Foundry for Tech Vision and Leadership (iFoundry)," July 18, 2007. ifoundry.illinois.edu/media/readings.

As president of the NAE: National Academy of Engineering, "The Engineer of 2020: Visions of Engineering in the New Century." (Washington: The National Academies Press, 2004); National Academy of Engineering, "Educating the Engineer of 2020: Adapting Engineering Education to the New Century." (Washington: The National Academies Press, 2005.)

"I had seen": Michael Loui: Author interview. Loui, the editor of the *Journal of Engineering Education*, has published extensively on engineering and ethics, including "Ethics and the development of professional identities of engineering students" (*Journal of Engineering Education*, vol. 94, no. 4, pp. 383–390, October 2005) and "Can instruction in engineering ethics change students' feelings about professional responsibility?" (with G. Hashemian. *Science and Engineering Ethics*, vol. 16., no.1, pp. 201–215, March 2010).

In August 2008: The Olin-Illinois Partnership agreement: http://ifoundry. engineering.illinois.edu/sites/default/files/pdfs/mou_olin_illinois_ partnership.pdf.

Korte had worked in: Russell Korte, "A Case Study of the Socialization of Engineers: How New Engineers Learn the Social Norms of Organizations." (Ann Arbor: ProQuest, 2007.)

The video piece: http:/ifoundry.illinois.edu/blogs/top-10-ifoundry-youtube-videos.

Price holds a unique: Abbie Griffin, Raymond L. Price, Bruce A. Vojak, *Serial Innovators: How Individuals Create and Deliver Breakthrough Innovations in Mature Firms.* (Redwood City: Stanford University Press, 2012.)

A particularly influential: Chip Heath, Dan Heath; *Made to Stick: Why Some Ideas Survive and Others Die.* (New York: Random House, 2007.)

The course: David E. Goldberg, "The Missing Basics: What Engineers Don't Learn and Why They Need to Learn It." www.missingbasics. org; www.slideshare.net/deg511/the-missing-basics-what-engineers-don't-learn-and-why-they-need-to-learn-it.

Karen Hyman: Author interview.

A handbook for: iCommunity Handbook—http://www.slideshare.net/ifoundry/icommunity-handbook.

a kid named Cory Levy: Regina Sinsky, "19-year old gets $1M to launch a social app . . . watch out, Zuckerberg," (*VentureBeat*, August 3, 2011.) Levy's web site at http://about.me/cory; http://vimeo.com'8061997.

Jaime Kelleher: Author interview.

Aman Kapur: Author interview.

Karen Lamb: Author interview.

For additional writings and background on iFoundry, visit: www.ifoundry. illinois.edu, http://asmarterplanet.com/studentsfor/blog/2011/12/changing-engineering-education-for-a-smarter-planet.html; http://www.slideshare.net/deg511; http://www.slideshare.net/ifoundry; http://www.youtube.com/ifoundry.

3: The Spirit of Invention
Recapturing the Inspiration
of Engineering Education

Opening quote by Sir Eric Ashby: from *Today in Science History*. www.todayinsci.com.

At the Saturday afternoon club: Dennis Bell, "The Man Who Invented the Wheel and Paid the Price." Freepages.genealogy.rootsweb.ancestry. com/~wanda/ferriswheel.html.

In his bestselling book: Erik Larson, *The Devil in the White City: Murder, Magic, and Madness at the Fair that Changed America*. (New York: Crown, 2003.)

The Society for the Promotion: Reference for engineering education history: Lawrence P. Grayson, *The Making of an Engineer: An Illustrated History of Engineering Education in the United States and Canada*. (New York: Wiley, 1993.)

As David Noble: David F. Noble, *America by Design: Science, Technology, and the Rise of Corporate Capitalism*. (New York: Knopf, 1977.)

In 1945, Bush: Vannevar Bush, "Science and the Endless Frontier." (Washington: United States Government Printing Office, 1945.)

The Grinter Report: Linton E. Grinter et al., "Report on Evaluation of Engineering Education." (*Journal of Engineering Education*, September 1955, pp. 25-60.) www.asec.org/papers-and-publications/publications/ The-Grinter-Report-PDF.pdf.

The year is 1088: Hanna Holburn Gray, "The University in History: 1088 and All That." (Chicago: University of Chicago Colloquim, January 17, 2001.)

For example, a 1947: www.thehenryford/rouge.

The world of engineering: William H. Whyte, *The Organization Man*. (New York: Simon and Schuster, 1956.)

We live in a different: Thomas L. Friedman, *The World Is Flat: A Brief History of the Twenty-First Century*. (New York: Farrar, Strauss and Giroux, 2007.)

Richard Florida: Richard Florida, *The Rise of the Creative Class and How It's Transforming Work, Leisure and Everyday Life*. (New York: Basic Books, 2002.)

Dan Pink: Daniel H. Pink, *A Whole New Mind: Why Right-Brainers Will Rule the Future*. (New York: Riverhead Books, 2005.)

The law of transaction cost: R. H. Coase, "The Nature of the Firm." (*Economica*, New Series, Vol. 4, No. 16 (Noe. 1937), pp. 386-405.)

The so-called law: W. Brian Arthur, *Increasing Returns to Path Dependence in the Economy (Economics, Cognition, and Society)*. (Ann Arbor: University of Michigan Press, 1994.)

Universities are currently: Global Industry Analysts estimated the growth of MOOCs. www.yourtrainingedge.com.

Now, companies: *Udacity*. www.udacity.com, *EdX*: www.edx.org,

Coursera: www.coursera.org.

The more people: Khan Academy. www.khanacademy.org.

Recently, we received: Jack Andraka's story has reveived wide media play, including this excellent feature in *Smithsonian* magazine: Abigail Tucker, "Jack Andraka, the Teen Prodigy of Pancreatic Cancer." (Washington: *Smithsonian* magazine, December 2012.)

To overcome these difficulties: More information about the NUS design-centric program can be found at www.eng.nus.edu.

4: The Whole New Engineer
Engaging the Six Minds

Opening quote by Daniel H. Pink: from *A Whole New Mind: Why Right-Brainers will Rule the Future*. (Reference below.)

Howard Gardner: Howard Gardner is the Hobbs Professor of Cognition and Education, Harvard Graduate School of Education. A selection of his past and current works is available at www.howardgardner.com.

Carol Dweck: Carol S. Dweck, *Mindset: The New Psychology of Success*. (New York: Random House, 2006.)

The title of this book: Daniel H. Pink, *A Whole New Mind: Why Right-Brainers Will Rule the Future*. (New York: Riverhead Books, 2005.)

We talk a lot: Author interview with Bruce Vojak. (Coauthor) Abbie Griffin, Raymond L. Price, Bruce A. Vojak; *Serial Innovators: How Individuals Create and Deliver Breakthrough Innovations in Mature Firms*. (Stanford: Stanford University Press, 2012.)

Domenico Grasso is provost: http://www.uvm.edu/~cems/explore/holistic.pdf.

Grasso recently edited: Domenico Grasso, Melody Brown Burkins; *Holistic Engineering Education: Beyond Technology*. (New York: Springer, 2010.)

In 1992, he opened a manifesto: http://denninginstitute.com/pjd/PUBS/EdEngr.pdf.

Denning's book: Peter J. Denning, Robert Dunham; *The Innovator's Way: Essential Practices for Successful Innovation*. (Cambridge, MA.: MIT Press, 2010.)

David Middlebrook: Author interview.

Crucial contributions: Flores, Fernando. *Conversations For Action and Collected Essays: Instilling a Creative Commitment in Working Relationships*. CreateSpace, 2013.

Gil Pratt: Author interview.

Daniel Pink points out: Daniel H. Pink, *A Whole New Mind: Why Right-Brainers Will Rule the Future*. (Riverhead Books, 2005.)

In his doctoral work: Ozgur Eris, "Effective Inquiries for Innovative Engineering Design." (Redwood City: Stanford University, Jan 31. 2004.)

Fortunately, the practice: Chalmers Brothers, *Language and the Pursuit of Happiness*. (Naples, FL: New Possibilities Press, 2004.)

In 1995: Daniel Goleman, *Emotional Intelligence: Why It Can Matter More Than IQ*. (New York: Bantam, 1996.)

At the Engineers of the Future: Woodie Flowers, "Man Who Waits for Roast Duck to Fly into Mouth Must Wait a Very Long Time." Engineer of the Future 2.0 keynote presented at the Summit for Transforming Engineering Education, Olin College. www.youtube.com/watch?v=F84LtXvLT+A.)

Gary Klein: Gary Klein, *The Power of Intuition: How to Use Your Gut Feelings to Make Better Decisions at Work*. (New York: Crown Business, 2004.)

Dan Siegel, author: Daniel J. Siegel, *Mindsight: The New Science of Personal Transformation.* (New York: Bantam, 2010.)

To the analytical: Author interview. Iris Ioffreda, MA, ACC, Ola Consulting. www.olaconsulting.com.

Chade-Men Tan's: Chade-Men Tan, *Search Inside Yourself: The Unexpected Path to Achieving Success, Happiness (and World Peace)* (New York: HarperOne, 2012.)

5: The Emotional Breakthrough
Five Pillars of Transformation

It was December: Howard Kirschenbaum, *The Life and Work of Carl Rogers.* (Ross-on-Wye, UK: PCCS Books, 2009.)

"There is another attitude": Carl R. Rogers, *Freedom to Learn: A View of What Education Might Become.* (New York: Charles Merrill, 1969.)

Neil Armstrong: Armstrong's speech to the National Press Club, www.greatachievements.org/Object.File/Master/4/254/na_speech.pdf. February 22, 2000.

Erica Lee Garcia, P. Eng.: www.engineeryourlife.net. Author interview.

At the turn: Soichiro Honda, "The Three Joys." (*Honda Monthly*, December 1, 1950.) www.world.honda.com.

One model of trust: Chalmers Brothers, *Language and the Pursuit of Happiness.* (Naples, FL: New Possibilities Press, 2004.)

In Building Trust*:* Robert Solomon, Fernando Flores; *Building Trust: In Business, Politics, Relationships and Life.* (Cambridge: Oxford University Press, 2003.)

Andrew Bell reflected: author interview.

Garrett Schwanke: Author interview.

I was surprised: Author interview with Larissa Little.

Sebastian Dziallis described: Author interview.

Brené Brown specializes: Brené Brown, *Daring Greatly: How the Courage to Be Vulnerable Transforms the Way We Live, Love, Parent and Lead*. (New York: Gotham, 2012.) Brown's TED Talk can be viewed at TED talk https://www.ted.com/talks/brene_brown_on_vulnerability.

Aman Kapur: Author interview.

Lawrence Domingo: Author interview.

Kylie Hensley: Author interview.

After his death: Melissa Healy, "Einstein's Brain: Even on the Surface, Extraordinary." (Los Angeles: *The Los Angeles Times*, November 28, 2012.)

Biographer Walter Isaccson: Walter Isaccson, *Einstein: His Life and Universe*. (New York: Simon and Schuster, 2007.)

One way of expressing: Marilee Adams, *Change Your Questions, Change Your Life: 10 Powerful Tools for Life and Work*. (San Francisco: Berrett-Koehler Publishers, 2009.)

Another sense of openness: Saras Sarasvathy, *Effectuation: Elements of Entrepreneurial Expertise*. (Northampton: Edward Elgar Publishing, 2009.)

Morgan Bakies: Author interview.

Beth Comstock: "How I Hire: There Is No Lone Genius." www.linkedin.com/today/post/article/20130923225748-how-i-hire-there-is-no-lone-genius-hire-a-team-with-these-4-types-on-the-four-types.

In: Mark A. Lemley, "The Myth of the Sole Inventor." (Redwood City: Stanford Law School, July 21, 2011.)

Georges Harik: Goldberg, D. E., "The Importance of Pairwork in Educational and Interdisciplinary Initiatives." Proceedings of the 39th ASEE/IEEE Frontiers in Education Conference. Link to citation http://dl.acm.org/citation.cfm?id=1733731. link to paper http://philsci-archive.pitt.edu/4627/1/deg-pairwork-3-20-09.pdf.

Morgan Bakies: Author interview.

As we described: Russell Korte, "A Case Study of the Socialization of Engineers: How New Engineers Learn the Social Norms of Organizations." (ProQuest, 2007.)

Debbie Chachra . . . recalls: Author interview.

Garrett Meyer: Author interview.

In defining: Tony Wagner, *Creating Innovators: The Making of Young People Who Will Change the World*. (New York: Scribner, 2012.)

Olin junior: Author interview with Liz Threlkeld.

6: The Whole New Learner
From Carrots and Sticks to Intrinsic Motivation

Opening quote by Edward Deci and Richard Ryan: www.selfdeterminationtheory.org.

When Edward Deci: Edward L. Deci, *Intrinsic Motivation Perspectives in Social Psychology*. (New York: Plenum Press, 1975); Edward L. Deci, *The Psychology of Self-Determination*. (New York: Free Press, 1984.)

Edward Deci and Richard Ryan: Edward L. Deci, Richard M. Ryan; *Intrinsic Motivation and Self-Determination in Human Behavior*. (New York: Plenum Press, 1985.)

Jon Stolk: Jonathan Stolk, "Engineering Students Conceptions of Self-Directed Learning." (Washington: American Society for Engineering Education, 2008.)

Teresa M. Amabile: Teresa M. Amabile, *The Progress Principle: Using Small Wins to Ignite Joy, Engagement and Creativity at Work*. (Cambridge, MA: Harvard Business Review Press, 2011.)

And it might also: Tony Wagner, *Creating Innovators: The Making of Young People Who Will Change the World*. (New York: Scribner, 2012.)

Forty years after: Daniel H. Pink, *Drive: The Surprising Truth about What Motivates Us*. (New York: Riverhead Books, 2011.)

Speaking with us: Author interview with Dan Pink.

According to Academic Pathways for People Learning Engineering Survey: Center for the Advancement of Engineering Education. www.eng.washington.edu.

Martello happens to be an expert: Robert Martello, *Midnight Ride, Industrial Dawn: Paul Revere and the Growth of American Enterprise*. (Baltimore: Johns Hopkins University Press, 2010.)

Students respond: Author interview with Andrew Bell.

For me: https://www.facebook.com/EngenhariaRecebe; Junior Enterprise: http://www.brasiljunior.org.br.

Junior Enterprise: Information about CUBE at www.cubeillinois.com.

Current CUBE: Author interview with Morgan Bakies.

One example is: Author interview with Sal Alajek, Engineers Without Borders Canada. www.ewb.ca.

Rob Martello: Author interview.

Jon Stolk: Author interview.

At Rose-Hulman: Author interview with Michael Moorhead, faculty advisor of Rose-Hulman's championship human-powered vehicle team.

In a paper on classroom motivation: Ana T. Torres, Geoffrey L. Herman;

"Motivating Learners: A Primer for Engineering Teaching Assistants." (Washington: American Society for Engineering Education, 2012.)

In his study of innovators: Tony Wagner, *Creating Innovators: The Making of Young People Who Will Change the World*. (New York: Scribner, 2012.)

"At the end of the day": Author interview with Jim Cooper, president and CEO of Maplesoft.

Like Maplesoft, Autodesk: Author interview with Carl Bass, president and CEO of Autodesk.

Geoffrey Herman and his cohorts: Dr. Geoffrey L. Herman, Dr. Mark H. Somerville, Dr. David E. Goldberg, Kerri Ann Green; "Creating Low-Cost Intrinsic Motivation Course Conversion in a Large Required Engineering Course." (Washington: American Society for Engineering Education, 2012.) Author interview with Geoffrey Herman.

7: The Whole New Professor
From Expert to Coach

Opening quote by Eric Schmidt: Interview with *Fortune* magazine, June 19, 2009.

When Fernando Flores: Harriet Rubin, "The Power of Words." (New York: *Fast Company*, January 1999.)

He began to articulate: Fernando Flores, "Management and Communication in the Office of the Future." (Berkeley: University of California, Berkeley, 1982.)

In a discussion: Author interview with Dan Heath.

Lynn Andrea Stein: Author interview.

Jessica Townsend: Author interview.

Rob Martello: Author interview.

I spent most of my teaching career: David E. Goldberg, "Do Universities Retard the Development of Their Faculty?" Blogpost, www.threejoy.com/2012/10/21/do-universities-retard-the-development-of-their-faculty.

Kevin Wolz: Author interview.

Julianna Stockton: Author interview.

In particular, Janaki Isabella Perera, Brendan Thomas Quinlivan, Dr. Yevgeniya V. Zastavker; "Faculty Perceptions on Undergraduate Engineering Education in First Year Engineering, Physics and Mathematics Courses." Presented at the ASEE annual conference, Atlanta, Georgia, June 2013.

Mark Goulston: Mark Goulston, M.D., *Just Listen: Discovering the Secret to Getting Through to Absolautely Anyone*. (New York: AMACOM, 2009.) Author interview.

Professional organizations: www.coach.federation.org.

Listening is a primary: Henry Kimsey-House, Karen Kimsey-House, Phillip Sandahl, Laura Whitworth; *Co-Active Coaching: Changing Business, Transforming Lives*. (Boston: Nicholas Brealey America, 2011.)

Asking questions: Marilee Adams, *Change Your Questions, Change Your Life: 10 Powerful Tools for Life and Work*. (San Francisco: Berrett-Koehler Publishers, 2009.)

Speech acts philosophy: John R. Searle, *An Essay in the Philosophy of Language*. (Cambridge: Cambridge University Press, 1969.)

8: The Whole New Culture
From Classrooms and Curriculum to Culture

Opening quote: Louis V. Gerstner, Jr., is the former CEO of IBM.

Early in 1966: Edgar H. Schein, *Organizational Culture and Leadership*. (4th edition San Francisco: Jossey-Bass, 2010; originally published 1985.)

But the DEC: Edgar H. Schein, *DEC is Dead, Long Live DEC*. (San Francisco: Berrett-Koehler Publishers, 2003.)

If you walk: For more information about Delft's Department of Aerospace Engineering: www.ae.tudelft.nl/.

In: Carl R. Rogers, *Freedom to Learn: A View of What Education Might Become* (New York: Charles Merrill, 1969.)

If Sugata Mitra: Sugata Mitra, *Beyond the Hole in the Wall: Discover the Power of Self-Organized Learning*. (New York: TED Books, 2012.)

Thomas Friedman: Thomas L. Friedman, "The Professor's Big Stage." (New York: *New York Times*, March 5, 2013.)

Meagan Pollock: www.meaganpollock.com.

"Before the internet": Author interview with Jeff Shelton. "The Engineering Commons" podcast. www.theengineeringcommnos.com.

Cultural intransigence: Interview with Trevor Harding.

Increasingly, education: Author interview with Jim Spohrer, director of IBM's University Program.

9: Changing How We Change
From Bureaucracy to Change Management

Opening quote by John P. Kotter: from *The Heart of Change* (Harvard Business Review Press, 2002).

For Linda Vanasupa: The Center for Sustainability in Engineering; author interview.

John Kotter has: John P. Kotter, *Leading Change*. (Cambridge, MA.: Harvard Business School Press, 1996.)

The Heath brothers: Chip Heath, Dan Heath. *Switch: How to Change Things When Change Is Hard.* (New York: Crown Business, 2010.)

Schein's take on change: Edgar H. Schein, *The Corporate Culture Survival Guide.* (San Francisco: Jossey Bass new and revised, 2009.)

In the late 1960s: Worcester Polytechnic Institute information at https://www.wpi.edu/academics/library/history/plan/, retrieved November 2013.

When Babson College: The story of Babson College's curriculum change effort was published by the Harvard Graduate School of Education, based on a paper by Joseph P. Zolner for the Harvard Institutes for Higher Education, 1999.

And we see many: Innovative program references include Iron Range Engineering (www.ire.mnscu.edu), the ATLAS program at the university of Twente (www.utwente.nl/en/), National University of Singapore's design centric program (www.eng.nus.edu), Purdue College of Technology (www.tech.purdue.edu), and Leadership Engineering at the University of Texas at El Paso (bsle.utep.edu).

Thanks to a combination: Author interview with Dr. Jerry LeMieux, president Unmanned Vehicle University, www.uxvuniversity.com.

In his book: John P. Kotter, *Buy-In: Saving Your Good Idea from Getting Shot Down.* (Cambridge, MA.: Harvard Business Review Press, 2010.)

The Center for Advanced Professional Studies: www.brcaps.org.

Engineering Is Elementary: www.eie.org.

A New York Times *feature*: Winnie Hu, "Studying Engineering Before They Can Spell It." (New York: *New York Times*, June 13, 2010.)

Project Lead the Way: www.pltw.org.

Another Program: "Invent It, Build It": Society of Women Engineers, www.swe.org.

Dean Kamen: FIRST Robotics: www.usfirst.org/roboticsprograms/fre.

Chris Rogers: www.tufts.edu/crogers.

When Harvard: Developing the John H. Holland Prototype, HM Case 3.98, Case Study prepared by Dr. J. Abby Hansen, as well as from personal discussions with Dr. Elizabeth Armstrong.

We've seen what: http://bigbeacon.org/tag/tick-the-box-change/

Saras Sarasvathy: Saras Sarasvathy, *Effectuation: Elements of Entrepreneurial Expertise*. (Northampton: Edward Elgar Publishing, 2009.)

Epilogue: An Invitation to Collaborative Disruption
Will Disruption Shape Us, or Will We Shape It?

Opening quote Clayton M. Christensen and Michael B. Horn: from *Disrupting Class*; citation below.

Clay Christensen: Clayton M. Christensen, *The Innovator's Dilemma: The Revolutionary Book That Will Change the Way You Do Business*. (New York: HarperBusiness, 2011); Clayton M. Christensen, Michael B. Horn; *Disrupting Class: How Disruptive Innovation Will Change the Way We Learn*. (New York: McGraw-Hill, 2008.)

Olin's aspiration: More information about the Olin Collaboratory at www.olin.edu/collaborate/collaboratory.

The Olin-Illinois Exchange: More information about the exchange at www.ifoundry.engineering.illinois.edu/student-opportunities/olin-illinois-exchange-program-OIX.

. . . David had recently: Threejoy Associates, Inc: www.threejoy.com.

Could we use: Henry William Chesbrough, *Open Innovation: The New Imperative for Creating and Profiting from Technology*. (Cambridge, MA.: Harvard Business Review Press, 2003.)

Through the power of collaboration: Information and the manifesto for The Big Beacon: A Movement to Transform Engineering Education, at www.bigbeacon.org.

After seeing: thoughtleadershipleverage.com.

Gesturing back: http://www.cluetrain.com.

In a workshop: David E. Goldberg, "The Emotional Rescue of Engineering Education." www.slideshare.net/deg511/the-emotional-rescue-of-engineering-education.

About the Authors

DAVID E. GOLDBERG is president of Big Beacon, a nonprofit organization founded as a movement for the transformation of engineering education. He is known as an author, educator, entrepreneur, and artificial intelligence researcher. Author of the widely cited bestseller *Genetic Algorithms in Search, Optimization, and Machine Learning* and co-founder of ShareThis, in 2007 he co-founded the Illinois Foundry for Innovation in Engineering Education (iFoundry). In 2010 he resigned his tenure and professorship at the University of Illinois to work full time for the transformation of engineering education. As a movement leader, leadership coach, and change management consultant, Dave now works with individuals, organizations, and networks around the world to collaboratively disrupt the status quo.

MARK SOMERVILLE is a professor of electrical engineering and physics at Olin College, where he also serves as associate dean for faculty affairs and development. He joined Olin from Vassar College in 2001. An electrical engineer and liberal arts double major, Rhodes scholar, and semiconductor researcher, Mark is passionate about active learning and student engagement. Mark has collaborated with institutions in North and South America and Europe to spread change in engineering education, particularly through the use of collaborative design in curriculum revision. Mark and Dave worked together, first on the Olin-Illinois Partnership and then as cofounders of the Big Beacon movement. Mark remains active in the classroom and works to spread effective transformation methods as part of Olin's Collaboratory outreach and training efforts.

About the Big Beacon Movement

BIG BEACON is a non-profit organization formed as a collaborative social movement, to transform engineering education and higher education more generally. A network of individuals, organizations, and institutions, The Big Beacon is a natural outgrowth of the events described in *A Whole New Engineer*. Dave and Mark invite interested individuals, organizations, students, parents, educators, employers, and other change agents to come together to disrupt the status quo. For more information about this book, for information about joining the revolution, and for useful change resources go to the website

www.bigbeacon.org